The Death of a Democracy

The Death of a Democracy
Greece and the American Conscience

by Stephen Rousseas

with the collaboration
of Herman Starobin
and Gertrud Lenzer

Grove Press, Inc. New York

To Andreas G. Papandreou

καὶ μὴν ὅπου γε δῆμος αὐθέντης χθονός,
ὑποῦσιν ἀστοῖς ἥδεται νεανίαις·
ἀνὴρ δε βασιλεὺς ἐχθρὸν ἡγεῖται τόδε,
καὶ τοὺς ἀρίστους οὕς τ' ἂν ἡγῆται φρονεῖν
κτείνει, δεδοικὼς τῆς τυραννίδος πέρι.

Again, where the people are absolute
rulers of the land, they rejoice in having
a reserve of youthful citizens, while a king
counts this a hostile element, and strives
to slay the leading men, all such as he deems
discreet, for he feareth for his power.

Euripides, *The Suppliants*
—lines 442-446

Contents

Preface

Andreas Papandreou is, at this writing, in the Averoff jail in Athens awaiting trial for conspiracy to commit high treason. He is to be tried by the military Junta which seized power on April 21, 1967. In the chapters that follow, I have frequently referred to him by his first name in order to distinguish him more easily from his father, George Papandreou, and because he is invariably referred to throughout Greece as "Andreas."

The events described in this book are much too recent for me to make any claim to historical objectivity. I confess that I am partisan to the cause of the Center Union party of Andreas Papandreou for reasons which will become obvious in the reading of this book.

Many of the incidents I have described were a part of my own personal experience while on sabbatical leave from New York University, and are based on my close association with Andreas in Athens from August 1966 to January 1967. My description of events in Greece just prior to and immediately following the coup are based on privileged information and reports which I cannot at this time make public, for obvious reasons. Copies of my files and papers have been placed for safekeeping with an American historian, and I hope to be able to make them available in due time to interested scholars in this field.

Chapter 5 was written by Herman Starobin, who also collaborated with me on Chapter 8. The analysis of the *New York Times* in Chapter 7 was written by Gertrud Lenzer. I am indebted to both for their interest and their help. I am particularly indebted to L. S. Stavrianos of Northwestern University for his time and his encouragement, and to my colleague at New York University, Robert J. Clements, who first suggested the idea for the book and who, in addition to providing its title, made the initial contact with Barney Rossett of Grove Press. Dr. Nicholas Nicolaidis, the General Secretary of the Center Union Party in Exile, was good enough to read the entire manuscript and check it for factual error. He is, of course, in no way responsible for my interpretation of events. Athanasios Mineikos and his wife, Fabienne, also provided me with valuable information and I wish to acknowledge, in addition, their gracious hospitality during my stay in Paris from August to September of 1967.

I would also like to single out Vassilis Petratos and Demosthenes Costas who were very helpful in looking up dates and other information and aiding in the general research. Special mention should go to Miss Sylvia Preston who did such an excellent job in typing the manuscript and who helped me so efficiently in the last rush to meet the deadline.

Parts of this book appeared in the *Nation* (March 27, 1967) and *Ramparts* (June 1967). Their permission to use the material here is gratefully acknowledged.

I have left for last a very special case, my fourteen-year-old nephew, Philip D. Zaneteas, who shared many of my experiences in Athens and who brought out some important information upon his hurried return in May of this year—not the least of which were lists of political prisoners, whose names he smuggled out by writing the letters in a tiny hand above the sixty-fourth-note runs in his book of Mendelssohn sonatas.

New York City   S.W.R.
September, 1967

Part I
Political Developments in Greece: 1963-67

Greek Political Parties, Governments, and Elections

Political Parties

	Presidents	*Founded*	*Political Spectrum*
Center Union (EK)	George Papandreou	1961	Center
Liberal Democratic Center (FIDIK)	Stephanos Stephanopoulos	1965	Center-Right
National Radical Union (ERE)	Panayiotis Kanellopoulos	1956	Right
Progressive Party (KP)	Spyros Markezinis	1955	Right
United Democratic Left (EDA)	Ioannis Passalidis	1951	Left

GOVERNMENTS

Prime Minister	*Party*	*Sworn In*	*Resigned*	*Vote of Confidence*
Constantine Karamanlis	ERE	October 6, 1955	June 11, 1963	Yes
Panayiotis Pipinelis	ERE	June 19, 1963	September 25, 1963	Interim Government
Stylianos Mavromihalis	—	September 28, 1963	November 8, 1963	Caretaker Government
George Papandreou	EK	November 8, 1963	December 24, 1963	Yes
Ioannis Paraskevopoulos	—	December 31, 1963	February 19, 1964	Caretaker Government
George Papandreou	EK	February 19, 1964	July 15, 1965	Yes
George Athanasiadis-Novas	EK	July 15, 1965	August 5, 1965	No (167 against, 131 for)
Elias Tsirimokos	EK	August 20, 1965	August 29, 1965	No (159 against, 135 for)
Stephanos Stephanopoulos	FIDIK	September 17, 1965	December 21, 1966	Yes (152 for, 148 against)
Ioannis Paraskevopoulos	—	December 22, 1966	March 30, 1967	Caretaker Government
Panayiotis Kanellopoulos	ERE	April 3, 1967	April 21, 1967	Caretaker Government (no vote of confidence taken)

Elections

May 11, 1958; October 29, 1961; November 3, 1963; February 16, 1964; May 28, 1967 (scheduled but never held because of the coup d'état on April 21, 1967).

Chapter 1

The "New" Politics in Greece

I

On the afternoon of April 20, 1967, in the Old Psychico section of Athens, Andreas Papandreou, a deputy in the Greek Parliament and former minister in the Center Union government of 1964–65, was entertaining a member of the the the central committee of the Danish Social-Democratic Party. Greek elections had been scheduled for May 28 and, in anticipation of a major Center Union victory, part of the discussion that afternoon concerned the implementation of an agreement for the training of Center Union politicians in Denmark. Later in the evening, Andreas Papandreou decided to sleep in his own home. It was one of the few times in several months that he had risked the chance since it was well known that the King and his American advisers were very disturbed over the prospects of a Center Union victory in the forthcoming elections and that a military coup by the King's followers was a distinct possibility.

At 2:30 A.M. on Friday, April 21, a contingent of the American-equipped Greek army surrounded Papandreou's house. A few shots were fired into the air. At the same time, the sound of broken glass could be heard as the front door was smashed in. The immediate reaction of everyone in the house was that a gang of terrorists was breaking in to assassinate Andreas. With the help of his fourteen-year-old son, Papandreou was boosted onto the roof from an outside balcony on the second floor.

Eight soldiers with machine guns, pistols, and rifles with fixed bayonets charged into the bedroom of Papandreou's twelve-year-old daughter and overturned the bed with her

3

in it. The officers and the men under their command were very unsure of themselves and in a state of extreme nervousness. They ran around wildly, pulling everyone out of bed, shouting and screaming, "Where is Andreas? We want Andreas." They seized Papandreou's security guard and began beating him in the living room, trying to force him to reveal Andreas' whereabouts. After tyrannizing everyone, breaking open closets, and scattering the clothing around at random, they jabbed Papandreou's wife, Margaret, with their pistol butts and threatened to kill Papandreou's son unless he told them where his father was. At that point Papandreou gave himself up. As he jumped down four feet from the roof to the balcony, he cut his knee severely on an outside wall light. The soldiers started beating him and then shoved him into the bedroom and forced him to dress. He was then taken away, together with his security guard, who was later brutally beaten that night and the next day for having "lied."

When they left, Margaret Papandreou drove up to Kastri, the home of her father-in-law, George Papandreou, the president of the Center Union. The streets were deserted and American Sherman tanks could be heard rumbling in the distance. At Kastri the situation was the same. The army had come for the former Prime Minister.

At six o'clock in the morning an announcement was made on the radio informing the Greek people that the army had taken over the country in order to preempt a communist takeover. The announcement went on to list the articles of the Constitution which had been suspended by authority of the King. The coup had been carefully planned and swiftly executed. It captured the leaders of most political parties and arrested several thousand additional key members of political organizations on that first day. Since then, more arrests have been made, with approximately 20,000 persons in jail or crowded on a few barren islands in the Aegean which serve as concentration camps for political prisoners.

The coup had been executed by a military triumvirate of relatively junior officers—Brigadier Stylianos Patakos, Colonel George Papadopoulos, and Colonel Nikolas Makarezos. Lieutenant General Gregorios Spandidakis was brought in at the final stages of preparation, with front-man Constantine Kollias, the chief prosecutor of the Greek Supreme Court, providing the civilian façade as Prime Minister.

The Junta, lacking any popular base of support, started to consolidate its position in a series of edicts. The army was quick to issue its orders to the civilian population.

ARMY STAFF PROCLAMATION

In view of the decree of Law DXTH of 1912 "Concerning a State of Siege" put into effect under Royal Decree No. 280 of April 21, 1967.

WE HAVE DECIDED AND
ORDER FORBIDDEN

(1) Gatherings in the open country of more than five persons.

(2) Gatherings in closed spaces, excluding public entertainments.

(3) The exercising by any means of anti-national propaganda, as well as the announcement or publication by any means, of information liable to cause anxiety or fear to the citizens and trouble public order.

(4) The carrying of arms and the possession by individuals of arms of any kind, including hunting rifles, munitions, explosives, any kind of fireworks, knives, knuckle-dusters, and any other similar weapons, as well as the construction and use of the same without a special permit from the military or police authority. Licenses given up to today cease to be of any value and those who possess the above articles are obliged, within two days from today, to hand over same to the nearest police authorities.

(5) The temporary medical treatment of persons not residing with the family which gives the treatment, if this is not stated within two hours to the nearest police authority.

(6) The possession, installation, and use of amateur radio stations and any means of receiving and transmitting.

(7) The hoarding and excess pricing of foodstuffs or of any other goods which serve the provisioning needs of the public, or the setting-aside of same for this purpose by anyone.

(8) Hunting. All licenses granted up to now are canceled.

(9) The violators of this order will be tried by the Special Courts Martial and will be punished according to the decree related to a "state of siege."

Athens, April 25, 1967

ANGELIS ODYS

Lieutenant General

Chief of Army General Staff

In the days immediately following the coup, the radio blared martial music, broadcast talks filled with patriotic fervor, and provided the Greek people with a rationale for the coup—*stability*. Of a series of eighteen proclamations, two ran as follows.

Greek men and women! The Army's action in taking over the governing of the country was the immediate consequence of all that has happened up to now against our country. For many years Greece has been undermined. And for a considerable time she breathed in agony. She was on the verge of catastrophe. And she deeply felt the need to be saved by whatever means, even strong ones. Then she acted through the National Army. And Greece now lives again. We shall leave behind us all the bad past. And we shall enter upon a period of new prosperity and glory.

Stability is the wish of all Greeks. And the Army took over the governing of the country exactly for this reason. To restore, to stabilize, and to safeguard stability. Political, governmental, social, economic, and currency stability. This it will say: *No more partisan dissension, partisan passion; no governmental crises;* no spirit of the pavement, marches and clashes; no scandals, no getting salaries without working, no excess profits for the few and misery for the many. All these "nos" make up stability. And they thus constitute a big Yes: The yes to progress. Because without stability in all sectors, there is no progress. Neither economic devolopment, nor work, nor prosperity.

No country progressed by every day changing its Prime Minister. No nation advanced by making marches and demonstrations. Only stability brings prosperity and stability is brought by the Armed Forces with a national government which we have given to the country. [Italics supplied.]

Democracy, clearly, was not to be allowed in the very country from which it sprang. Private as well as public expressions of dissent were not to be tolerated, and Greece, to use Colonel Papadopoulos' imagery, was to be strapped to the operating table and not allowed to rise until cured of her democratic ills. Article 18 of the Greek Constitution was suspended and the death penalty for political offenses was thus reintroduced into Greek political life. Systematically, and in order to "safeguard stability," all political opponents were hunted down. The leadership of the Center Union party was arrested along with those Center Union deputies known to be supporters of Andreas Papandreou. The deputies of the United Democratic Left were rounded up, as well as many other members of that party. One of the first casualties in this initial wave of mass arrests was Nikiforos Mandilaras, the brilliant Athenian lawyer who had served as the principal defense attorney in the politically inspired *Aspida* (Shield) trial involving twenty-eight army officers accused of high treason.[1] His defense made a shambles of the charges which had been manufactured by the High Command of the Greek army. He exposed their

---

[1] The Aspida "conspiracy" concerns an alleged plot by left-wing officers to overthrow the monarchy and establish a Nasser-type dictatorship. Andreas Papandreou was accused of being the political leader behind the plot. Details of the Aspida controversy will be covered in subsequent chapters. The original Aspida Report is published in Appendix IV.

fraudulent base and he paid for this humiliation of the army with his life. His body was found washed ashore on the island of Rhodes.

The Junta had expected some resistance to the coup, and, indeed, would have welcomed it as proof of a communist conspiracy to take over the country. Instead, it was greeted with a stony silence. It was caught unprepared in that it had no consistent or well-conceived social program other than the promotion of stability and public order. It began by banning all local elections. Henceforth, local officials would be appointed. Then, through the talkative Brigadier Patakos, it announced the beginning of a puritan orgy of comic-opera proportions. A ban was announced on beards and long hair for men, and mini-skirts for women, tourists included. Church attendance at Sunday Mass was made mandatory for all students. Students were soon instructed to turn in their old history books and to purchase new ones, containing a section devoted exclusively to Greek kings with a full-page picture of King Constantine toward the end. The section on modern history gave glowing accounts of rightist regimes, and George Papandreou's 1944 liberation Cabinet was described as having had six communist ministers in it. One teacher announced to his class that he had been "asked" by the Education Minister to announce that he would deliver two lectures the following week on the reasons for the coup. He then told his class that as soon as the lectures were sent to him, he would give them.

The need to maintain the racial purity of the Greek race was proclaimed, and some members of the University of Athens biology department began to revise the theories of Darwin and de Vries. Then, apparently in the belief that the fittest do not survive, the hierarchy of the Greek church was purged and the King's personal chaplain was installed as Primate of Greece. To protect Christianity and public order, it announced the revival of a 1942 law, passed during the Nazi occupation, requiring all legitimate theaters to submit scripts to a "Theatrical Plays-Control Board" for approval. The board not only was given the right to order deletions from any script, it was further empowered to *rewrite* parts of any play submitted to it for approval. Any theater faced with two rejections would be shut down, and any actor deviating in any way from an approved script would be severely punished. All plays of antiquity, by Aeschylus, Sophocles, Euripides, and Aristophanes, were to be similarly censored. The music of Tchaikovsky, Prokofiev, and all other Russian composers was banned. In the name of stability and order, new stop signs and traffic lights were installed and other enforcement measures were taken to bring the traditional chaos of Athenian traffic under control. It was announced, moreover, that any employee of a state-owned or -controlled public utility company who was late for work or otherwise not prompt, courteous, and attentive, would be fired. And in a modern variation on Mussolini's great achievement in making the Italian railroads run on time, the Junta decreed that any airplane of Olympic Airways not on schedule would be required to pay a fine.

Greece, in a classic parody of the 1930's, was being quickly transformed into the first fascist-type dictatorship to be seen on European soil since the days of Mussolini and Hitler. This was not, however, Greece's first experience with dictatorship. After twelve years of alternating dictatorships and republican governments (1923–35), and as a result of a rigged plebiscite, the present King's uncle, George II, returned to Greece. Within nine months he lost his short-lived taste for democracy and on August 4, 1936, installed one of his generals as dictator. General Metaxas died in 1941 as the Germans were invading Greece. King George then fled to London and finally to Cairo with a government-in-exile made up of royalist and conservative ministers.

George II was openly involved in the coup of 1936. The

role of King Constantine in the coup of 1967 is a bit less apparent. But one thing which will become clear, as the story of April 21 unfolds, is that Constantine was neither as innocent nor as reluctant as the American press had made him out to be. We shall be concerned throughout this book with the intrigues and the political ineptitude of this very non-constitutional monarch and his American advisers.

II

The coup of April 21 had as its primary objective the prevention of the elections scheduled for May 28. It was a virtual certainty that the Center Union party would repeat its landslide victory of 1964. It is also clear that the coup would not have taken place were it not for the rapid political ascendance of George Papandreou's son, Andreas. In the short span of two years, Andreas Papandreou had emerged as the most prominent politician in Greece and, on the basis of his program for social and economic reform, he had earned the almost pathological hostility of the Palace, the Greek army, and the U.S. State Department, along with the U.S. Military Mission to Greece, and the CIA. With this powerful array of forces against Andreas Papandreou and his Center Union party, the coup of April 21, 1967, was a foregone conclusion.

In the thirty-one years since the dictatorship of 1936, Greek politics has been firmly in the hands of the Palace and its right-wing supporters. Despite the volatility of Greek politics and its frequent excesses, this control never wavered and had never been seriously challenged. It is important to understand that Greece is a land where politics is the pre-occupation of practically everyone. With the exception of the extreme communist Left, political parties have traditionally lacked any hard-and-fast ideological base. In this ideological vacuum, Greek politics emerged as a very fluid business, with parties tending to swirl around a few dominant personalities, and with the highly individualistic politicians quick to switch their allegiances as they alone saw fit. Party structure and party discipline have always been concepts apparently alien to the Greek mind. New alignments and grand coalitions were frequent phenomena on the Greek political scene. Greek politics had become a very personal game of shells and peas with more peas than shells to hide under.[2]

In many ways this is a gross caricature of Greek politics and, like most caricatures, it exaggerates the surface of things without coming to grips with the underlying reality. But even if it were an accurate picture, it would have been more relevant for the past than for the future had not the coup taken place. A "new" politics had emerged in Greece. It threatened the old game of surface politics which never disturbed the underlying and controlling power relationships. Since the constitutional crisis of July 1965, which will be described in the next chapter, Andreas Papandreou had become a positive and major political force in Greece. He represented the "new" politics and soon became the nucleus around which a strong party was being formed with a meaningful program for reform and change. This in itself constituted a major threat to the existing economic and political oligarchies which had for so long ruled Greece unchallenged and undisturbed. The "old" game of politics had never threatened the traditional distribution of power. It lacked depth or commitment. In its very shallowness it had become a game of musical chairs, of vying charismatic leaders filled more with pomp than with achievements.

This was all changed by a former U.S. citizen of twenty years standing. Andreas Papandreou was born in Greece in

---

[2] One long-time foreign resident in Athens was moved to observe that if the American CIA had any real intelligence, it would have recalled all of its agents and replaced them with a team of clinical psychologists.

1919 and was educated at the University of Athens during the Metaxas dictatorship. During his student days at the university he joined a left-wing student organization resisting the dictatorship. He was soon caught, imprisoned, and then exiled. He came to the United States and enrolled as a graduate student in economics at Harvard, where he taught and earned his Ph.D. in 1943. He became a U.S. citizen and volunteered for service in the Navy during World War II. After the war, he became a professor of economics at the University of Minnesota, went briefly to Northwestern University, and finally settled at the University of California (Berkeley) where he served as chairman of one of the most distinguished departments of economics in the United States. During his twenty-year stay in the United States, he was very active as a liberal Democrat. In Minnesota he worked for Hubert Humphrey in his Senatorial campaigns and later for Adlai Stevenson in the Presidential campaign of 1956.

His first contact with Greek politics came in 1960 when he returned to Athens on sabbatical from Berkeley and as the holder of a Guggenheim Fellowship. While there he also served as economic adviser to the Bank of Greece. It was at his office in the bank that he first became aware of the extent of U.S. interference in the internal politics of Greece. Loughlin Campbell was then head of the CIA in Greece. He visited Andreas at the bank and asked him to arrange a meeting with his father, George Papandreou, who at the time was one of the leaders of a nucleus of parties in the process of forming what eventually came to be the Center Union. The stated purpose of the meeting was to discuss the adoption of the "kindred party system" for Greece. In the course of the discussion, it became clear that the real purpose of the visit was not to arrange a meeting with George Papandreou (which did not need the services of Andreas), but to get Andreas, as a U.S. citizen, to apply pressure on his father to accept the CIA-sponsored change in the Greek electoral system.

Under the kindred party system each political party was to be listed under one of two classifications—*nationalist* and *non-nationalist*. The two right-wing parties, the National Radical Union (ERE) and the Progressive party (KP), and the variety of center parties then in existence, were to be grouped under the first category. All remaining parties, that is, the United Democratic Left (EDA) and other socialist and communist-front parties were to be placed in the "non-nationalist" camp. All parties would go into the elections independently of each other. After the election returns were in, the sum of both camps would be compared, winner take all. The parliamentary seats would then be divided among the parties of the winning group (nationalist, of course) on the basis of their relative standing in the nationalist sub-total. This was, obviously, a crude plan for the total disenfranchisement of the Left in Greece. The CIA had become alarmed when the United Democratic Left received 25 percent of the total votes cast in the 1958 elections. A truer figure would have been 33 percent in view of the manipulation of the elections, especially in the rural areas. But this 25 or 33 percent did not represent a communist resurgence in Greece. Much of it was made up of protest votes against the police-state methods of the National Radical Union government then in power—which was subsequently demonstrated by the rapid decline of the EDA votes in the 1963 and 1964 elections when the Center Union party came into power. In any event, the CIA was alarmed, particularly because the electoral system then in operation made the United Democratic Left the *official* party of the opposition. Under the kindred party system, the Left in similar circumstances would have been denied any parliamentary representation whatever, even if it had succeeded in getting 49 percent of the popular vote!

Toward the end of the visit, Andreas Papandreou told

Campbell that he would arrange the meeting with his father, if that was what the CIA wanted, but that he doubted his father would be sympathetic to such an arrangement; though strongly anti-communist, his father still retained some respect for the democratic system. At this point the head of the CIA mission in Greece stood up abruptly and, pointing his finger at Andreas, replied sharply: "You tell your father we get what we want." The meeting with George Papandreou never took place. In this one instance, the CIA did not get what it wanted. It did much better, however, on April 21, 1967, and before that on July 15, 1965, during the well-engineered constitutional crisis which brought down the Center Union government.

From 1960 to 1964, when he officially ran for Parliament, Andreas Papandreou alternated between the Berkeley campus and Athens. Through his efforts, and with grants from the Ford and Rockefeller Foundations, the Center of Economic Research and Planning was set up under the sponsorship of the University of California. Andreas Papandreou became its first director. A highly qualified professional staff was hired and a steady flow of foreign economists came as visiting scholars. For the first time in the history of Greece, a systematic program for basic research in economics was undertaken, a plan for economic growth was developed, and a program was started to train qualified Greek economists for key posts in government and industry.

Andreas Papandreou resigned his professorship at Berkeley to enter Greek politics in the elections of 1964. A great deal of pressure was put on Andreas by his father, but the explanation is not quite that simple. During the grand coalition of the center parties early in 1963, the problem arose over who would be the party leader of the combined forces. The two main contenders were the elder Papandreou (then seventy-six years old) and the relatively younger Sophocles Venizelos, son of the famous Eleftherios, and leader of the dominant Liberal party. As in most coalitions of this sort, the leader of the major party is always feared, and a great deal of opposition arose to Venizelos' candidacy. But rather than break up the coalition, a compromise was worked out whereby the elder Papandreou was designated head of the combined forces, with the understanding that Venizelos would succeed him upon his death.

Constantine Mitsotakis, a subsequent defector from the Center Union government, led a group of deputies who also pressured Andreas into entering Greek politics—the idea being that he would act as major counterbalance to Venizelos, thereby increasing the chances of another compromise leader in the future, namely, one of themselves. As things turned out, George buried Sophocles, rather than the other way around.

The Center Union won an absolute majority of the parliamentary seats in the elections of 1964. Andreas Papandreou was given the patronage-controlling position of Minister to the Prime Minister. He quickly came under attack by the far Left, the far Right, and by members of his own party who saw him being groomed as a successor to his father. He was looked upon as an *arriviste,* an ambitious power seeker. The charge of nepotism was raised, and Andreas Papandreou didn't help matters much by exuding a self-confidence and cockiness which only served to infuriate his opponents. The Left denounced him as a puppet and tool of the United States; it even went so far as to hint that he was a CIA agent.

Andreas Papandreou was new to politics. After twenty-odd years as a professor, he was hardly prepared for the world of politics—and Greek politics is among the most intense and wildly competitive in the world. Many of his initial appointments, some of whom were professionally trained Greeks repatriated from the United States, turned out to be disastrous. His confidence in people was all too often misplaced. And he was unable to resist the flattery heaped upon him by his newly acquired camp of followers. All told, Andreas' performance as a politician was rather bad—about a grade of C, to gauge him by his prior occupation. And even if he had any innovating ideas of his own, there was always the restraining and vacillating influence of the Prime Minister, his father. In response to pressures from within his own party, he was removed as Minister to the Prime Minister's Office and reassigned as Alternate Minister to the Ministry of Coordination. This post was more in keeping with his professional training, but soon after he was assigned by his father to handle the exploding Cyprus problem.

Despite its general ineptness and its floundering, the Center Union government of 1964–65 did introduce an air of political freedom which was unprecedented, and it did undertake certain social programs in education, agriculture, and economic development which were far reaching and popular with the electorate. The government, however, could not push its programs too fast. The Center Union government had become aware of the dissatisfaction and rumblings within the Greek army, and it knew that before it could proceed any further it would have to try to impose civilian control over the army. It was this attempt to control the armed forces, compounded by the Cyprus problem, which ultimately led to the constitutional crisis of July 1965 and the downfall of the Papandreou government. Details of these developments will be given in the next chapter.

The Center Union government was in serious political trouble. It was being led by an old-time politician of doubtful antecedents. George Papandreou was known in Greece as "the Windmill"—a man who was by instinct a compromiser and capable of turning every which way with every change in the political wind—and also as a vain, gregarious, and unpredictable politician who was at the same time an eloquent orator and a powerfully charismatic leader. In the early days of the Center Union government, Andreas Papandreou was the much resented son of an aging politician who, no matter how much he might have disagreed with his father, did whatever he was told.

III

What "made" Andreas Papandreou was the crisis of 1965. From July 1965 to April 1967 he created his own independent identity by stumping the country and showing a remarkable political courage. He broke away from his father's restraining influence, and introduced something new to Greek politics—a consistent, well-thought-out, and far-reaching program for Greece. Coupling this with a sometimes strident nationalism, and helped by the hysterical and all-too-frequent attacks on him by the right-wing press, he succeeded in capturing the imagination of the young people and many members of the professional and intellectual classes—though the latter still regarded him with suspicion as something too good to be believable.

Above all, he had been dangerously outspoken against the King and had flatly stated that if the King were to trigger the army into a coup, the whole issue of the monarchy in Greece would subsequently be reexamined. He strongly implied, in other words, that in such an eventuality the entire royal household would once again be exiled and Greece transformed into a republic. He was the only politician in Greece who had dared to broach the subject publicly.

It soon became popular in Greece to link the younger Papandreou with the late President Kennedy—as a man with style, intellect, and a program to get Greece moving again. It would have been more accurate, however, to have viewed him as having been caught in the unfortunate dilemma of being Robert Kennedy plus Hubert Humphrey rolled into one. Andreas, like Kennedy, had clearly set his eyes on the highest political office his country had to offer. Like Kennedy, too, he had risen very fast and had captured the imagination of the people. But, unlike Kennedy, his father was not a man of great wealth. Andreas and his father, by way of contrast, were both active politicians in increasing disagreement with each other. More important, for comparison's sake, the former Attorney General was able to quit Lyndon Johnson's Cabinet and, as Senator from New York, dissociate himself from the President's present policies and failures. Andreas, on the other hand, was more like Humphrey, in that it was very difficult for him to criticize the political leader of his party, who, in this instance, also happened to be his father. Yet the remarkable thing is that Andreas, despite the built-in limitation of his position, was able to generate sympathy for his dilemma and to give the very distinct impression throughout Greece of being far more progressive than his father. By December of 1966, as we shall see, he was on the verge of breaking with his father.

Andreas' "radicalism," however, was nothing more than a mixture of the New Deal, the New Frontier, and the Great Society. But for Greece's semi-feudal, Byzantine structure, attitudes such as these are extremely radical, and Andreas was regarded by the far Right as a dangerous communist. The Right had little fear of Papandreou *père*. They knew him to be manipulable and a member in high standing of the old school of Greek politics; they also knew that he was a compromiser capable of adjusting his position easily under pressure. What the Right feared most was that Papandreou *fils* would someday succeed his father as Prime Minister and carry out the programs he had so frequently publicized in his speeches and in his writings. And it was for this reason that the Right and its many newspapers attacked Andreas so relentlessly and with such abandon from July of 1965 until the coup of April 1967. And it was for this reason that the coup took place.

The Right, however, was not alone in its opposition to Andreas. The extreme Left, which had stopped criticizing him since the crisis of 1965, regarded him now as a temporary expedient to be supported so long as it served their purposes, and within the Center Union party a few powerful deputies looked upon him as *the* major stumbling block to power. In all this, Andreas had eclipsed his father and had emerged as the de facto leader of his party. It was largely due to Andreas' meteoric rise, and the political ineptness of the King and his followers, that he emerged as the first serious threat to the Greek establishment in over thirty years.

Throughout the entire postwar period, Greek politics had been polarized between the extreme Left and the extreme Right. Democratic socialists, liberals, and other political parties in the center had been splintered and ineffective. The extreme Left was well organized but, since the civil war of 1946–49, lacked any real possibility of getting into power through the ballot box or otherwise. The Palace, the army, the right-wing parties, and the U.S. presence were guarantees of that. The Right, therefore, had the field to itself. Occasionally, and only occasionally, a moderate Center government would take over for a very brief period of time. But regardless of what party was in office, the levers of power were firmly controlled by the Right. Thus, a pseudo-democratic semblance of government was tolerated, so long as no one threatened to tamper with the existing institutional structure and the given distribution of power.

The Right maintained full control over the machinery of State. The bureaucracy, the police, the rural gendarmerie, and the army were staffed with their own people. Greece, for example, was the only Allied country in which the collaborators were not purged from their official positions. Indeed, in the immediate postwar period, and just prior to the 1946 plebiscite on the return of King George, the army, the bureaucracy, the university, and the security forces were purged of *republican* job-holders. It is significant that none of the Metaxas appointees or university professors who had collaborated with the Germans were dismissed. But they couldn't have found very many liberal republicans in the 1946 purge. The dictator Metaxas had done a thorough job during his reign of terror and had bequeathed the purged branches of the governmental machinery to the German occupiers, who then turned them over intact to the British who, in turn, after the purge of 1946, handed them over refurbished to the Americans.

The Center Union government of 1964–65, however, got a little too ambitious. It tried to exercise some control over this sub-level of government which was busily sabotaging its social and economic programs. The duly elected government was then summarily dismissed by the King in July of 1965. Since then, and up to the coup of April 1967, a series of Palace puppet governments were propped into power. When it became obvious that the Center Union party had not been broken and, under the de facto leadership of Andreas Papandreou, would win the constitutionally required elections, the Constitution was abrogated, the politicians were arrested, and an open military dictatorship was imposed upon Greece.

It is time now to turn to a detailed examination of the series of events which led up to the coup of 1967.

Chapter 2

The July 1965 Crisis

I

The coalition Center Union party was founded for the 1961 elections, in which it won 34 percent of the votes cast. The Center Union charged that the elections were fixed, and as dissatisfaction with the repressive right-wing government of Prime Minister Constantine Karamanlis grew, pressure built up for new elections. They were set for November 3, 1963 and a caretaker government was installed after assurances were given, and lived up to, that the elections would not be rigged, as they had been over the entire postwar period. The intimidating activities of the rural gendarmerie were severely circumscribed by the caretaker government and the elections were held under relatively free conditions.

The Center Union emerged as the major party with a plurality of 42 percent of the total vote and 47 percent of the parliamentary seats, 140 out of 300. It was 11 votes short of a parliamentary majority. The Progressive party of Spyros Markezinis, which had won only 2 parliamentary seats, was not able to provide the necessary votes. The remaining 158 seats were split unequally with 128 for the right-wing National Radical Union (ERE) and 30 for the United Democratic Left (EDA). The balance of power therefore lay with the Left.

EDA had been founded in 1951 as a front for the Communist party of Greece (KKE), which had been outlawed in 1947. EDA offered the leader of the Center Union, George Papandreou, its parliamentary votes without making any demands for any appointments in the government. George

Papandreou was therefore in a position to form a government without assigning a single ministry to EDA. The offer was turned down for the obvious reason that the Center Union would have been at the mercy of the extreme Left.

George Papandreou had a precedent for his refusal. In the elections of January 26, 1936, the royalist parties had won 143 seats and the republicans 142, leaving the Communist party with the remaining 15 seats. When the republican leader, Themistocles Sophoulis, accepted the 15 Communist votes to become President of the Chamber of Deputies, the Palace became alarmed and let it be known that it would not sanction any government based on Communist support. A "non-parliamentary" government was then formed under Constantine Demerdjes, who then proceeded to die one month later on April 13, 1936. King George immediately appointed General Metaxas, and four months later installed him full-blown as dictator of Greece.[1] But even apart from this object lesson, George Papandreou had a long record of anti-communism. As a member of the Cairo government-in-exile he bitterly opposed the major resistance movement in occupied Greece and, when the British rushed him back to Greece as Prime Minister immediately after the German evacuation, he cooperated with their intrigues to disarm the National Liberation Front (EAM), build up the royalist factions (many of whom were former collaborators), and bring back King George of Metaxas fame.[2]

---

[1] See L. S. Stavrianos, *The Balkans Since 1453* (Rinehart: New York, 1958), pp. 670–72.

[2] For a detailed account of George Papandreou's role, see L. S. Stavrianos, *Greece: American Dilemma and Opportunity* (Henry Regnery Company: Chicago, 1952), pp. 112–138.

In the winter of 1960, I had the opportunity to visit the former Prime Minister in his Athens home, at the invitation of his son, Andreas. Over dinner, I mentioned the failure of liberal politicians

Cooperation with EDA was clearly out of the question. New elections were called for and they were scheduled for February 16, 1964, under the same caretaker government which had been so scrupulously fair in the prior elections. The results were startling. For the first time in over thirty-five years a liberal Center party had won an absolute majority. The election returns and the distribution of the Greek Parliament among the Right, Center, and Left-wing parties was as follows:

PARLIAMENT

	Percent of total vote	Number of Deputies	Percent of total
National Radical Union (ERE, Kanellopoulos) and the Progressive party (KP, Markezinis)	35%	107	36%
Center Union (EK, Papandreou)	53%	171	57%
United Democratic Left (EDA, Passalidis)	12%	22	7%

The Right found itself in the unaccustomed position of being decidedly the minority party. The Center and the Left

---

like himself to get together and offer the people a viable program for social reform. I argued that by default they permitted the extreme polarization of Greek politics, and that a young man with a liberal orientation had no choice but to move to the Left. George Papandreou became livid, ignored the substance of my comment, and began re-counting the atrocities committed by the Communists during the Greek civil war of 1946–49. Rational discussion of the problem was impossible. He finally stopped pounding the table and listed how many times EDA had approached him and offered their electoral support and cooperation. And, raising his hands to his head, he related with great dramatic flare how each time he turned their proposal down by saying to them: "You offer to put the crown on my head, but when the time comes for you to remove it, you will take my head with it."

had emerged with 65 percent of the popular vote and 64 percent of the parliamentary seats. But more importantly, the Center Union now had an absolute majority and had no need of additional parliamentary votes to form a government.

The stage for the 1965 crisis was set. The Palace, the extreme Right, and the army had become alarmed, but they were not prepared to make their move at that time. They still were in complete control of the bureaucracy and the security forces. They were, in other words, in full control of the sub-level of government where the real power lay. As long as no attempt was made by the new government to tamper with it, they could afford to bide their time.

Papandreou's unprecedented victory was not in itself a direct threat to the Palace and its political and military supporters. Papandreou was well known to be a procrastinator, a moderate, a crafty politician, a rabid anti-communist and, on the basis of his role in the immediate postwar period, not an anti-royalist. Indeed, he held out the olive branch to the royal household and tried hard to please it. Without being asked, he introduced a bill to give the powerful Queen Mother, Frederika, a very respectable pension, and passed a law forbidding any criticism of her in the press or in public statements. The Queen Mother accepted the latter but refused the pension after a loud public outcry against it. Again without being asked, and in order to please the Palace, he appointed Petros Garoufalias, a Palace supporter and beer baron of Greece, to the sensitive post of Defense Minister, and he made other conservative Cabinet appointments as well.[3]

But he did other things less pleasing to the Palace. He

---

[3] George Papandreou unwittingly revealed the extent to which he played into the hands of the Palace in a speech he gave in Athens on October 11, 1966, entitled, "The Five 'Crises' With the King Which Brought on His Shameful Act." The text of his speech was published the following day in the Athenian newspaper, *To Vima.*

broke the control of the rural gendarmerie over the country-side, renegotiated contracts with large foreign monopolies on terms more favorable to Greece, and reformed the educational system. Furthermore, he introduced an air of political freedom that had long been absent from Greece by severely limiting the political activities of the dossier-keeping security forces, and by proclaiming a general amnesty for political prisoners.

But all of these pluses-and-minuses of George Papandreou do not add up to the crisis of 1965. If anything, he was playing, or thought he was playing, a clever game of balancing the Right against the Left. The important point is that the army, which had long been purged of its democratic elements, continued to remain firmly in the hands of the Palace and the extreme Right.

II

Things started to go wrong when the Cyprus crisis arose. Relations between Greece and Turkey, both members of NATO since 1952, worsened rapidly and began to threaten NATO's southeastern flank. The United States started applying pressure on the Papandreou government to resolve its differences with Turkey along lines that would have spelled political suicide for the Center Union government. Papandreou and his son were invited to Washington, but all of President Johnson's powers of persuasion came to nothing.[4] Greece continued to take an independent stand and suspicion grew within the U.S. Embassy and State Department that Andreas Papandreou was a neutralist, that he harbored anti-NATO sentiments and favored opening

---

[4] A private source recalls that at a social affair during these meetings President Johnson turned to Iakovos, the Greek Archbishop of North and South America, and said, referring to George Papandreou, "You can have him. One de Gaulle on my hands is enough. I don't need another."

relations with the Soviet Union and the communist countries on Greece's northern borders. At the same time the United Democratic Left and the more liberal elements of the Center Union were putting pressure on Papandreou to investigate the personal corruption of former Prime Minister Karamanlis —a proposal which, of course, infuriated ERE. Then began the series of errors leading to Papandreou's downfall.

The Center Union government raised no objections to the negotiations between Cyprus and the Soviet Union for the purchase of weapons. And as part of a planned squeeze on the United States and NATO, the elder Papandreou accepted an invitation to visit Moscow. This was the old political game of blackmail used so successfully in the past by small countries against the United States. But in Greece, having fought a bloody communist civil war from 1946 to 1949, this was to extremist elements tantamount to treason. The leader of ERE, Panayiotis Kanellopoulos, called for the resignation not of the government but of Papandreou himself. He asked, in effect, that the Center Union party replace him with another Prime Minister from their ranks—a most unusual interference in the internal affairs of another party. The Prime Minister retaliated by releasing the Pericles Plan, a plan (inadvertently left behind by the previous ERE government of Karamanlis) for the use of the army to rig the elections of 1961. Papandreou threatened to purge the army and, in retaliation, the Aspida "conspiracy" was revealed, implicating the Prime Minister's son, Andreas, then Alternate Minister of Coordination.

Behind the Aspida "revelation" was General Grivas, who had led the guerrillas in Cyprus against the British and who now, as a Greek general, commanded the Cypriote army. Grivas' royalist and right-wing sentiments are a matter of record. During the German occupation he had virtually a free hand in Athens as the leader of a right-wing terrorist organization known as "X." William Hardy McNeill, a former Assistant U.S. Military Attaché in Athens, gives the following evaluation of Grivas' role during the occupation.[5]

> Grivas was an ardent royalist, and his organization came to stand for the King. As the shadow of ELAS [National Popular Liberation Army] spread over the land, X came by degrees to fear more the power of the Communists than the oppression of the Germans . . . It is not certain that Grivas ever came into direct contact with the occupying authorities; more likely he dealt indirectly through the Greek quisling government, in whose ranks not a few former Army officers and Metaxas officials were to be found, who would easily lend a sympathetic ear to a man of Grivas' position and political ideas. In any case, X was able to possess itself of arms from German and Italian sources. With the weapons so secured, gangs of bravos were equipped, who made it their habit to seek out leading EAM [National Liberation Front] organizers to shoot or beat up.

On the Cyprus issue, General Grivas moved counter to Archbishop Makarios' policies and supported the cause of immediate *Enosis* (Union) with Greece. The Archbishop, a somewhat better tactician and with the support of the Papandreou government, favored independence as a first step, with the issue of *Enosis* to be decided at a later time. A struggle between the General and the Archbishop soon developed over the control of the Cypriote army. The command posts of the Cypriote National Guard are staffed by Greek army officers which, along with Greek army units in Cyprus by treaty arrangement, are under the overall command of General Grivas. The Cypriote Defense Ministry exercises no operational control over these units.[6]

---

[5] William Hardy McNeill, *The Greek Dilemma* (Victor Gollancz: London, 1947), pp. 75–76.

[6] In December of 1966, Archbishop Makarios entered into a secret arms deal with Czechoslovakia. The Archbishop's plan was to equip an autonomous and independent military force under his direct con-

When Andreas Papandreou took over the political handling of the Cyprus issue, he supported the position of the
Archbishop against the General. Grivas then struck back
with his obviously manufactured charge that Aspida was a
secret organization of army officers conspiring, under the political leadership of Andreas, to take over the Greek army,
throw out the King, and impose a Nasser-type dictatorship
on the Greek people.

The Aspida Report was written by a lieutenant colonel
of the Greek army and released in October 1966. It was followed a few months later with the military trial in Athens
of the twenty-eight officers accused of high treason.[7] The
Report was an absurdly political tract lacking any credibility
whatever. It consisted of hearsay and unsubstantiated allegations. The King, long before the issuance of the Report,
ordered the Defense Minister, Petros Garoufalias, to investigate the Aspida controversy and to report his findings directly
to the Palace.

At this point, Prime Minister Papandreou moved to implement a decision, made prior to the Aspida controversy, to
dismiss Garoufalias and take over the Ministry under his own
portfolio. Unfortunately for Papandreou, Garoufalias refused
to resign without a writ from the King, which, of course, the
King refused to issue on the grounds that a father investigating the treasonable activities of his son was not likely to
submit an objective report.

On the surface, the King's argument seemed plausible. But

---

trol and as a counterbalance to General Grivas. The Czechoslovakian
weapons were to be used to transform the Cyprus Police Corps into
such an instrument. When the first shipment arrived in Cyprus, a
political storm arose in Athens and the Archbishop was forced to
back down. (See the *New York Times,* December 5, 1966, International Edition.)

[7] The main part of the Report is reproduced in Appendix IV. It is
one of the very few copies available in English.

the Prime Minister had been forewarned, sufficiently in advance of the July crisis, that Garoufalias was to be used by the Palace, at the appropriate time, to overthrow the Center Union government. Several months earlier a wealthy Greek ship-owner approached Papandreou and told him of a conversation he had had with his good friend, John McCone, then the director of the CIA. He passed on the information that a plot existed between the Palace and the Defense Minister to bring about the downfall of the government. It is doubtful that this was a plant. It is, if anything, a testament to the indiscretions that even directors of intelligence services are capable of making.

Shortly afterward, an incident occurred that tended to support the ship-owner's information. Although, by his own admission, Papandreou appointed Garoufalias as a gesture to the Palace, the full extent of his future cooperation with the King had not been accurately anticipated. It had come to the attention of the Prime Minister that major elements of the right-wing General Staff had begun to doubt the "patriotic" motives of the Center Union government and were beginning to discuss a coup d'état should the government continue to pursue its liberal policies. A meeting of the inner Cabinet was called to discuss the gradual replacement of the General Staff. Papandreou knew this would cause trouble with the King and the matter was fully discussed in the Cabinet meeting. Garoufalias was a member of this inner Cabinet and, soon after, the Prime Minister received a well-calculated letter from the official representative of the King, Constantine Hoidas, informing him that the Defense Minister had reported the substance of the inner Cabinet's discussion and that the King would strongly resist any attempt to change the Greek High Command. When confronted with the letter, the Defense Minister denied the whole matter, but when the Palace insisted that Garoufalias was the basis of its information, the Prime Minister's hand was forced and, along with the rest of his Cabinet, he agreed that the Defense Minister had to be replaced. To ease the embarrassment of dismissal, it was decided that the Prime Minister should take over the Ministry temporarily as part of his own portfolio. At this point, the Aspida charges were made public, putting the Prime Minister in a very peculiar situation vis-à-vis his son.

In this highly unusual situation—where a Defense Minister refuses to resign and a "constitutional" monarch, using the conveniently manufactured Aspida charges as an excuse, refuses to accede to the wishes of his Prime Minister— Papandreou *threatened* to resign. That was enough for the King. He accepted the threat for fact and immediately swore in Athanasiadis-Novas, then a Center Union deputy and President of the Parliament, as Prime Minister-designate. Novas was literally laughed out of office. In his younger days he had published a poem about the whiteness of women's breasts and how much he enjoyed tickling them. Wherever he appeared, mobs of people would taunt him with, "*Gargalata, Gargalata.*" ("Tickle them, Tickle them.") After Novas' failure to win a parliamentary majority, the King tried Elias Tsirimokos, a left-of-center deputy in the Center Union party. Tsirimokos did no better than Novas.

Despite the attempts of the King to split the Center Union party, the great majority of its deputies held fast. Finally, after much intrigue and some CIA money, 49 Center Union deputies were cajoled or bought out. The 49 "apostates," as they were called in Greece, attempted to convince the remaining 122 deputies to maintain the Center Union party in power by dumping George Papandreou.

By this time Papandreou had become a national hero, and hundreds of thousands of people poured into the streets of Athens in unprecedented mass demonstrations in support of the Center Union. The Parliament was besieged each time a vote was taken. The 122 remained fast. The right-wing parties then gave the 49 defectors their combined 107 votes to form a government. But neither ERE nor the Progressive party participated in the formation of the government. Subsequently, 45 of the 49 defectors regrouped themselves into the post-election Liberal Democratic Center (FIDIK), with the remaining four listing themselves as independents, though supporting the government of Prime Minister Stephanos Stephanopoulos on crucial votes. The FIDIK government had a mere 15 percent of the parliamentary seats (for which they were not elected as members of their newly formed party) and served at the pleasure of ERE and the Progressive party; that is, at the pleasure of the Palace. In the full sense of the word, FIDIK was a *puppet* government.

The net result of all this was an intolerable situation with a general paralysis creeping over the entire legislative process. That the puppet government of Stephanopoulos survived as long as it did (until December 20, 1966) was a minor miracle and a testament to the power of the Palace to impose its discipline over the parties of the Right.

III

The *details* of American interference in Greek politics are not too well known in Athens though everyone, as a matter of course, believes that virtually nothing happens in Greece, politically, without the approval of the U.S. Embassy. But the State Department is not that all-powerful. The CIA and the Defense Department play, by far, a more important and decisive role. Military and economic aid to Greece, for example, amounts to approximately $100 million a year. The Greek army is completely integrated into the NATO alliance, with the Greek NATO command dominated by U.S. army officers. The U.S. military, in effect, makes the important decisions regarding weaponry and the structural organization of the Greek army, and exercise, through the Palace, a pronounced influence on promotions within the

Greek officer staff. The deployment of the Greek army, furthermore, is geared to NATO requirements and is not designed to cope with local contingencies.

When the Cyprus crisis broke out, the Greek government found itself in a difficult position with regard to its army. The changes it undertook alarmed the NATO command and led the United States into pressuring Greece to compromise its differences with Turkey for the sake of the NATO alliance. When Greece refused to go along with the Acheson Plan for the partitioning of Cyprus, attention focused on the Prime Minister's son as the key troublemaker, and from this it was not difficult to take the next step, and label him an anti-NATO leftist attempting to move Greece out of the Western orbit. But the real issue was that Greece refused to behave as a satellite should. She sought control over her own foreign policy and generally started taking an independent stand. When the Center Union government, playing the old power game, said it would welcome Soviet assistance in preparation for a possible war with Turkey, the U.S. Embassy demanded an explanation, and it was at this point that the wheels for Papandreou's fall began to turn.

When, on top of all this, the Papandreou government threatened to replace the extreme right-wing officers of the army's High Command with its own people, the Center Union skidded rapidly toward the debacle of July 1965. The Greek army has traditionally been regarded as the private preserve of the Palace. Indeed, the late King Paul, father of Constantine, addressed the officer staff of the Greek army in Salonika one year before his death. His statement, widely reported at that time, had a proprietary directness to it: "You belong to me and I belong to you." [8]

The present King inherited the Greek army from his father. He is possessed, unlike his father, with a mystical

---

[8] The royal household's attitude toward democracy is of equal interest. At a 1960 private dinner party at the Grande Bretagne Hotel

vision of a new Byzantium, and he fervently believes in the necessity of a holy crusade against the communists. The King, furthermore, regards all of the Left as a dangerous gang of criminals. And when we take into account the fact that the Center Union won 53 percent of the popular vote in 1964 and the United Democratic Left 12 percent, the King had a lot to be worried about, since 65 percent of his subjects were suspect. Indeed, his Christmas message of 1965, five months after the July crisis, stressed the danger of communism and warned his people against their possible "contamination." So, when confronted with a direct challenge over the control of *his* army, he naturally viewed it as a communist conspiracy to overthrow him.

The Papandreou government, in order to realize its own policies, tried to gain control of the machinery of state and, in particular, to bring the military under *civilian* control— a state of affairs usually taken for granted in most democratic states. The Greek army, however, under the long political tenure of the Right, had long been purged of its democratic and leftist officers under the Metaxas dictatorship. But many of these former officers had been readmitted during World War II out of sheer necessity. A para-military right-wing organization known as "The Sacred Alliance of Greek Officers" (IDEA) was set up in Cairo, under the government-in-exile, two years before the end of World War II in Europe. As the war drew to a close, IDEA began a new purge of the Greek officer corps. It succeeded brilliantly and has since dominated and controlled the Greek army. IDEA is dedicated to the monarchy and to NATO and is linked directly to the extreme royalist wing of the political Right.

The United States, through its military mission, fully supported the King on the issue of whether the elected gov-

---

in Athens, Queen Frederika turned to Andreas Papandreou and said, "You know, Mr. Papandreou, I would be the first to fight for democracy if I thought it had anything to offer the people other than modern bathrooms."

ernment of the Greek people should have any say on the composition of the General Staff. Shortly before the July crisis, Andrew Sinclair, the U.S. Naval Attaché in Athens, drew Andreas Papandreou aside during a dinner party at the home of a friend. He took it upon himself to inform a minister of the government then in power that too many young Greek officers lacked respect for the King. He finished his unsolicited lecture with the implication that Andreas was somehow responsible for this state of affairs, and warned him bluntly that the army *belonged* to the King.

A U.S. Assistant Military Attaché, Lieutenant Colonel Joseph L. Lipczyk, arrived in Athens one month before the July crisis. He soon became the King's favorite squash partner and was seen constantly in the King's company. One evening in his own home, Andreas Papandreou told Norbert Anschuetz, the U.S. Chargé d'Affaires, that he knew Lipczyk was the principal CIA agent in Greece and complained to the U.S. Embassy official about the agent's activities.

More intriguing, however, is the case of Richard Barhum. Barhum had spent three years in Greece as U.S. Commercial Attaché and then returned to the State Department's Middle East Division, which covers Greece and is reported to be rife with CIA agents. One month before the crisis, as in the case of Lieutenant Colonel Lipczyk, Barhum returned to Athens. His sudden reappearance was billed as an informal visit to survey the Greek economic situation. It soon became known to the Prime Minister that this suspected CIA agent had paid visits to Constantine Mitsotakis and John Tsouderos (two of the major defectors, as it subsequently turned out, from the Center Union government), and had freely circulated at Athenian cocktail parties making frequent and very audible references to the Prime Minister's son, Andreas, as an unreliable and dangerous leftist.[9]

---

[9] Barhum will reappear in our story in connection with the military coup of 1967.

The United States, in short, was not innocent in the developments which led up to the crisis of July 1965. It felt far more comfortable with the right-wing governments of the past. For one thing, they were cheaper to buy and it was thus much easier to mesh Greece's foreign policy with that of the United States. Greece provided the United States with a strategic military base not only for control of the southeastern end of the Mediterranean but for the whole Middle East, with Cyprus as an important part of the entire complex. The Center Union government tried to change Greece's status from that of an unthinking satellite to a fully participating ally. This alone was enough to bring it into disfavor with American policy makers.

For the next twenty-one months, the United States advised the King and did everything to assist him in preventing new elections. But things did not quiet down. A large majority of the Greek people felt outraged that the first truly liberal government to be elected in two generations had been toppled from power by the King with the connivance of the ubiquitous Americans. The clamor for elections grew louder, and it became progressively more difficult to continue their postponement as the constitutional limit was approached. Clearly, a way out had to be found if an outright coup was to be avoided. It was not found and the reasons for this failure make up the subject matter of the next chapter.

Chapter 3

The Interregnum

I

From July 1965 to the downfall of the FIDIK government on December 20, 1966, a delicate and unstable equilibrium existed which could easily have tipped in the direction of a coup—as it finally did in April. But in private conversations with Greek deputies, party leaders, and other members of the various political parties, the threat of dictatorship was quickly dismissed. It was very difficult, at that time, to determine how much was based on fact and how much was simply a matter of wishful thinking or self-delusion.

The reasons usually given for playing down the threat of a coup fell into three general categories. First, that conditions had changed—that the Greek people would rise en masse to quash any such attempt. Second, that the King himself was not willing to gamble his crown on such a coup and, the reasoning went, without the permission of the King, the army would not move. Third, that the U.S. Embassy, though suspicious of Andreas, was also against the coup. The first argument was a bit simplistic, the second attributed too great a rationality to the King, and the third did not take into account the role of the CIA and the U.S. Defense Department.

Despite the private beliefs that a coup would not take place, public statements by Center Union leaders and the writings of the left-wing and Center Union press drummed up the imminent takeover by the Palace and the army. For a while, a day hardly went by without banner headlines about the impending dictatorship. All told, a dangerous game of bluff was being played. Threats and counterthreats abounded in the daily press and in the political speeches of both sides. Yet neither side was sure of what the other would do. It was a stalemate—but with a difference. The forces were not evenly divided. The Center Union had the great majority of the people behind it, but the King, ERE, and the puppet government of Stephanopoulos had the power, i.e., the army.

The only reason the contest was not joined sooner was that the Right had time in its favor since elections, under the Constitution, could be postponed until March of 1968. The Right, in other words, had the power to determine when and if elections were to take place. If in this interval they saw the current running against them and couldn't chance an election or couldn't rig one properly, then the Constitution, or some parts of it, would be temporarily suspended and some kind of modified dictatorship would be imposed in the name of a national emergency. As we shall see, the King and the United States had this very much in mind when the colonels jumped the gun.

Shortly after the release of the Aspida Report in October 1966, twenty-eight officers were brought up before a court-martial in Athens on charges of high treason. The timing of the Aspida trial was significant. It had been postponed for over a year in order to push the military trial closer to the constitutional election limit. It was expected that the trial would drag on for a long time, thus affording the Right enough time to milk it for all its propaganda value. At the same time the terrorist activities of the rural gendarmerie were resumed and the para-military organization known as the National Security Battalions (TEA) covered the country-side and mountains of Greece with huge signs wishing long life to the King and warning the people of the dangers of Red Fascism. If the Center Union could be discredited, elections would be held. If not, the trial could be used as the basis for a coup.

The Aspida trial served another purpose as well: to take the spotlight away from the Lambrakis trial then going on in Salonika over the political assassination three years earlier of the EDA deputy and the deep involvement of the Salonika security police in his murder.[1] Both trials backfired. In the obviously rigged Aspida trial, two of the principal officers involved stated publicly that they were offered bribes of $100,-000 each to give testimony implicating the Papandreous, and accused another officer of having accepted $33,333 (one million drachmas) for turning State's evidence. In another startling development, one of the accused, Captain Theofanis Tombras, revealed a plot to murder George Papandreou a few days before his actual dismissal by the King. The quotation from *The Times* of London (January 23, 1967) runs as follows:

> Captain Theofanis Tombras, one of the twenty-eight defendants facing charges of revolt and high treason, indicated that a military aircraft which was to have flown Mr. Papandreou to Corfu to see King Constantine on July 10, 1965, was to have been sabotaged.
>
> The Captain . . . said that Greek Intelligence learnt about the plot while intercepting the telephone conversations of a retired Greek air force senior officer [2] who was suspected of

---

[1] It should be noted here that the murdered deputy, Gregoris Lambrakis, was a leading participant in the riots which proved so humiliating to the Queen Mother, Frederika, a few years ago when she was forced ignominiously to take refuge from the crowd in a London doorway. Speculation over who was behind the police has long been a favorite parlor game in Athens.

[2] The Greek Air Force officer involved was General Skaramarliorakis who has long been known to be a CIA agent for the United States. The original tap on General Skaramarliorakis' phone was ordered by the Karamanlis government of 1955–63. It had become aware that the General was supplying the CIA with information concerning Greek army movements in the event of a war with Turkey over Cyprus. The Center Union party retired the General when it

spying on behalf of the American air attaché in Athens.

Captain Tombras ... said that Mr. Papandreou and his party ... had been switched at the last minute to a commercial flight to Corfu.

Flight Lieutenant G. Haralambopoulos, another defendant, confirmed the captain's statement.

Other embarrassing revelations followed: that one of the prosecution witnesses, a Greek army officer, had been used by the Americans to set up an espionage network in Egypt and that, as a result, twenty-seven Greeks living in Egypt were caught in 1959 and court-martialed.

The trial, as it soon became obvious to everyone, was not going too well for the King and his supporters. The danger of a coup thus became more real. The United States, therefore, had a critical role to play. It had become all too clear that the King was running the show and that the King was unlikely to disregard any *strongly* represented views of the U.S. government. But given the U.S. role in the Dominican Republic and its apparent acquiescence in the military coups of Brazil and Argentina, one could not entertain much hope on this score. Despite Senator Javits' warning that the United States should not let events overwhelm its foreign-policy deliberations, there was no danger of this happening in Greece. The United States was solidly behind the King and knew precisely what was going on.

The possibility of a coup was now uppermost in everybody's mind. But the Center Union deputies had been lulled

---

assumed power in 1964, but the tap on his phone was continued. General Skarmarlioakis is now one of the 36 members of the *Supreme Revolutionary Council* which makes all the basic decisions to be followed without question by all the Ministers of the Junta government. He is also a member of the Council's Executive Committee along with Patakos, Papadopoulos, Makarezos, and Ladas. This raises a few interesting questions concerning the CIA's prior knowledge of the coup and its possible role in the current military dictatorship.

by their own rhetoric and by the mass outpouring of the people in the streets during the July crisis. They had reassured themselves that any attempted coup would be immediately crushed by the people. Accordingly, they made no contingency plans, and when the coup finally did come, they were unprepared and were quickly rounded up, leaving the future development of any resistance movement in the hands of the far Left by default. When faced with the counterargument that, unlike the July 1965 popular outcry, the use of troops, tanks, and the security police would be enough to keep order in the major cities of Athens and Salonika, the Center Union leaders retreated to a second line of defense, equally implausible, as it turned out—that a split would take place in the army with the defection of the younger officers, thus aborting any attempted coup.

II

That the coup did not come any sooner than it did can be attributed to one last attempt to find a way out of the constitutional crisis of July 1965. The Right (excluding the FIDIK government) and a few powerful members of the Center Union were quietly developing a plan for resolving the constitutional crisis which took into account the personal weaknesses of the former Prime Minister, George Papandreou.

The crisis of July 1965 would have long been resolved were it not for the presence of Andreas Papandreou. An Aesopian story in Athens concerned a chance meeting between the young King and the old Fox. Said the King to the Fox, "Mr. President, our differences could easily be resolved if you would only get rid of your son." Said the Fox to the King, "I am in complete agreement with you, Your Majesty, and I would gladly accede to your every wish if you, too, would exile your mother." Since it was highly unlikely that Andreas and the Queen Mother would voluntarily quit Greece, a plan was evolved to isolate Andreas politically. And this is where Christos Lambrakis comes in (not in any way related to the murdered EDA deputy, Gregoris Lambrakis).

Lambrakis is a wealthy young man in his middle thirties; a brilliant businessman and a potential and ambitious king-maker. He inherited from his father a publishing empire which included the two leading newspapers of Greece (*Ta Nea* and *To Vima*) as well as a string of other publications. Early in the constitutional crisis of 1965, Lambrakis became convinced that the King could not be forced to back down and that therefore a plan had to be devised for re-solving the conflict on terms acceptable to the Palace. The King in 1965 was confident that he could force the Center Union government to dump its President, George Papandreou. As events turned out, he was misadvised and his mis-calculation placed him in an extremely dangerous position. The great fear of the Palace was that if it allowed elections, the Center Union would get an even greater majority than it did in 1964, thus turning the elections into a plebiscite against the crown.

One way out of this impasse was to assure the King that though the Center Union party would continue to be the major political force in Greece, it would receive a plurality, rather than an absolute majority, of the popular vote in any forthcoming election. Publisher Lambrakis served as leader of a group trying hard to resolve the crisis along these lines—a group which included a small number of conservative depu-ties of the Center Union coalition, the dominant leaders of the business community (wealthy ship-owners included), and the non-extremist element of ERE. The big problem, of course, was to guarantee this outcome in *free* elections. And this, in turn, is where Papandreou *père* came in.

In a country with a government-controlled radio and with-out television, the elder Papandreou was necessarily depend-ent on Lambrakis' two newspapers. The Lambrakis papers gave the former Prime Minister a big play while, at the same time, enforcing a virtual blackout on his son. In addition to this powerful squeeze on the elder Papandreou, there was his known anti-communism. The elder Papandreou had stated in unequivocal terms his unwillingness to join forces with the left-wing EDA for purposes of forming a coalition government. But pressure was put on Papandreou *père* to take a more strident anti-communist line as one way of re-assuring the Right and the business community of his good intentions, i.e., to support more repressive police measures against the Left. Along these lines, Papandreou tried to force his party to vote for a bill, reintroduced by the FIDIK government, banning a communist-front youth group. He was immediately faced with a revolt within his own party. Andreas and his followers opposed the bill on the grounds that this was the first step in a campaign of terror in preparation for rigged elections. The elder Papandreou refused to back down and was finally given a graceful way out when EDA formally adopted the youth group as part of its political apparatus, thus removing it constitutionally from the realm of permissible legislation.

The overall strategy of Lambrakis and his collaborators was to push the former Prime Minister into alienating the marginal but important liberal voters in Greece who, in protest and out of a sheer lack of choice, had in the past traditionally voted for EDA. In the elections of 1964 many of these voters switched to the Center Union, causing EDA's vote to fall from a maximum of 25 percent in the 1958 elections to 12 percent of the popular vote in 1964. As a result, the Center Union came out, as we have seen, with an absolute majority of 53 percent. With the former Prime Minister alienating this all-important protest vote, the Center Union could be expected to fall, say, to 43 percent of the total vote, with EDA rising once more to about 17 percent, and ERE gaining the remaining 5 percent (thus recapturing a major part of the ERE swing to the Center Union in the 1964 elections). And given the elder Papandreou's fear of communism and his pledge not to join with the Left, the Center Union would be forced into a coalition government with ERE. Feeding into this plan was the split within the ERE party itself; between the more moderate Kanellopoulos faction which favored elections, and the extreme right wing of the party pushing for a harder line.

Given, therefore, the expected Center Union plurality and George Papandreou's overriding ambition to be Prime Minister, a coalition Center Union-ERE government would be formed, with Andreas Papandreou neatly pushed into a corner as an extra bonus for the King. The King, furthermore, would be spared the embarrassment of having the elections interpreted as a plebiscite against his crown.

III

The Lambrakis plan came to fruition on the evening of December 20, 1966. Kanellopoulos, the leader of ERE, announced his withdrawal of support from the FIDIK government of Prime Minister Stephanopoulos. Stephanopoulos had no alternative but to resign, and the King immediately appointed the governor of the National Bank of Greece, Ioannis Paraskevopoulos, as head of the caretaker government, with elections scheduled for May 28, 1967. The leader of the Center Union, George Papandreou, announced his immediate support of the new government without consulting his own party. This led, not unreasonably, to speculation that a pre-arranged deal had been made between Kanellopoulos and the elder Papandreou—Kanellopoulos out of fear that the extreme right wing of his party was planning to oust him and recall Karamanlis (the former head of ERE) from Paris, and George Papandreou out of his fear of a coup d'état and his impatience to become Prime Minister once again. But apparently, in the bargaining between the leaders of the two major parties, Papandreou was much in the weaker position. Under the Constitution, elections would not be held until March or April of 1968. By that time the elder Papandreou, whose health was already failing him, would be eighty years old.

George Papandreou was therefore forced to concede on certain major points. First, he was to agree to Paraskevopoulos as head of the caretaker government. Second, Parliament was not to be dissolved and elections were to be postponed for five to six months. Third, Papandreou was to give the King a free hand in appointing the ministers of the new government. Fourth, the elder Papandreou was to resolve his differences with the King, abstain from any attacks against him in the campaign, and refuse to collaborate with the Left on any terms. Fifth, the Center Union would not call for new elections in the event of its failure to obtain an absolute majority, and would form a coalition government with Kanellopoulos of ERE as Deputy Prime Minister. These were stiff demands and the elder Papandreou, in his haste to become Prime Minister, accepted them unilaterally without calling a caucus of his own party.

The terms and conditions of the elder Papandreou's capitulation became quickly known. In its bitterness, the FIDIK government released a transcript of the meetings between Kanellopoulos, Mrs. Eleni Vlachos, publisher of the two leading conservative newspapers in Athens, and Demetrios Bitsios, head of the King's political bureau. The text of their discussions was published in the January 1, 1967 issue of *Eleftheria,* the newspaper of the FIDIK government. Although *Eleftheria* claimed it had gotten hold of Kanellopoulos' stenographic notes, it was later revealed that Constantine Mitsotakis, Minister of Coordination under the FIDIK government and part owner of *Eleftheria,* had KYP (the Greek central intelligence agency) secretly tape the meetings. It had also been reported that the publisher of *Eleftheria* had been in New York several months earlier buying the latest electronic bugging devices. In any event, the text of the *Eleftheria* exposé had many references to Lambrakis, acting as official spokesman for George Papandreou, and to Norbert Anschuetz, Chargé d'Affaires of the U.S. Embassy. Although libel suits were filed, the text of the meetings as reported in *Eleftheria* are generally accepted as substantially accurate. And privileged information acquired independently of the *Eleftheria* revelations, supports in large measure the account given of the terms and conditions imposed on George Papandreou. For the record, it should be noted that Andreas Papandreou was secretly advised of Mitsotakis' plans to publish his exposé. Through an intermediary, since father and son at this point were not on speaking terms, George Papandreou was warned that *Eleftheria* was in possession of the tapes and that the Center Union would be torn to shreds if the information were made public. The former Prime Minister was urged to change his policy line and repudiate the Paraskevopoulos government before it was too late. But George Papandreou was too deeply committed by then to back out, and the warning was ignored. His attitude was that the decision to back the caretaker government had been made by him alone as president of the Center Union and he *demanded* a personal endorsement by each member of the party.

A large bloc of Center Union deputies, led by Andreas Papandreou, refused to go along and announced that they would vote against the Paraskevopoulos government. The elder Papandreou immediately issued a Diktat: *any deputy who either abstained or voted against the caretaker government would be summarily expelled from the Center Union party.*

All communication broke down between father and son and a great internal struggle for power was quick to develop within the Center Union. Messages were sent back and forth through intermediaries but in the end the elder Papandreou took an inflexible and adamant position. To test his strength and to force the issue of leadership, the former Prime Minister called a caucus of the Center Union party. When the time came, approximately 40 or one-third of the 122 Center Union deputies refused to attend, including Andreas. The younger Papandreou, prior to the caucus, was approached by other Center Union deputies willing to vote against George Papandreou. In short, Andreas found himself in the position of being able to topple his father from the party leadership. But such a defeat would have brought the elder Papandreou's forty-year career as an active politician to an ignominious end. And to have it so brought to a close at the hands of his own son would have been unbearable.

For this reason, the additional support offered was refused by Andreas.[3] In any event, as things stood at the time of the caucus, the elder Papandreou could not very well afford to excommunicate 30 to 40 percent of his party. George Papandreou's attempt to impose his will after the fact had failed. The wife of Andreas, Margaret Papandreou, was then called to Kastri, the home of her father-in-law. Several meetings were held and in the end Andreas and his followers agreed to go along with George Papandreou provided one all-important condition were met—that Andreas Papandreou would have a large measure of control in designating the party's parliamentary candidates. Since the elder Papandreou had already pledged that the 122 deputies who had not defected during the 1965 crisis would automatically stand for elec-

---

[3] My own advice to Andreas, at the time, was to split with his father and form his own party, even if this meant an ERE victory in the May elections. My reasoning was that Andreas had a unique opportunity to do so on the grounds of political *principle;* that after the elections, if his father made a mess of things as I expected him to do, it would be too late for Andreas to break away and form his own party.

tions under the Center Union banner, this meant that Andreas would now be able to fill many of the remaining 178 slots on the ticket with his own people. In this way, the influence of Christos Lambrakis and George Mavros, a conservative and powerful member of the Center Union, would be minimized, and their move to seize control of the party effectively countered.

This condition imposed by Andreas on his father was by far the most critical element in the power struggle that had developed within the Center Union party. The goal of Lambrakis was to tarnish the image of George Papandreou by maneuvering him into a compromising position vis-à-vis the King and Kanellopoulos. By doing so, the Center Union's resulting plurality would placate the King and give Lambrakis the opportunity to build up George Mavros as successor to the aging Papandreou. At all costs, in other words, Andreas Papandreou was to be blocked and forced into the arms of the extreme Left—even if it meant, in the short run, a victory for the ERE party in the 1967 elections.

Andreas' major objection to his father's policy, about which he had not been consulted, was the decision to accept a caretaker government for five months without the dissolution of Parliament. Within this period, as had so often happened in the past, the Right would have been afforded ample time to rig the elections and resort to terror and political intimidation in the countryside. The ministers of the caretaker government had been recruited exclusively from the extreme Right and supporters of ERE. Not a single minister was appointed from the ranks of the Center Union. The terrorist activities of the rural gendarmerie had been reactivated and the civilian members of the National Security Battalions (TEA), each unit headed by an army officer, had been issued army rifles and equipment and were already marching through Peloponnesian villages in order to intimidate the local population. Andreas' position was that the

King and his extremist followers should not be given the time to organize a new terror—that the King should have dissolved Parliament and declared elections in forty-five days as required by the Constitution. The feeling was that in his haste to become Prime Minister again, George Papandreou had sold out.

IV

It might be useful to conclude this particular saga with a recounting of what went on behind the scenes just prior to the downfall of the FIDIK government, and the role of the United States in bringing it about. The U.S. government had one overriding goal—to get Greece and Turkey to resolve the Cyprus problem and thus end the threat to the strategic southeastern flank of NATO. From the U.S. point of view, Papandreou and Kanellopoulos had to be brought together in order to bring the Cyprus problem to a successful close since the FIDIK government, in its year and a half of tenure, had neither the strength nor the necessary political support to do so. And as a prior condition to this, the bitter feud between Papandreou and the King had to be patched up. In any event, the FIDIK government had to be brought down.

The Lambrakis plan fitted in well with U.S. objectives since it envisaged a coalition government consisting of the moderates of the Center Union and ERE parties. The more extreme members of ERE, led by Panayiotis Pipinelis, were equally taken by surprise when Kanellopoulos moved quickly to topple the FIDIK government. Clearly, the leaders of the two major parties had agreed secretly, through the intermediation of Lambrakis, to collaborate without first consulting their respective parties. Of the two, however, Kanellopoulos was more successful in keeping his party in line. The King most probably was pressured by the United States to go along with the plan since it was not in his interest to see the moderates of the two major parties unite. Indeed, the King favored a change in the electoral laws to a simple proportional system since such a change would result in a splintering of the political parties and thus increase his power to determine and control future governments. At any rate, the King went along with the plan on condition that elections would be postponed for at least five months and that he would have complete say over the composition of the caretaker government.

The one major concern of everyone involved in the plan was how Andreas Papandreou would react. It was decided to try to induce him to go along or, failing this, to get assurances from George Papandreou that he would expel his son if he refused, thus neutralizing him as a political force. Subsequent events indicate that the elder Papandreou had agreed to this strategy.

The first step was to attempt to get Andreas' support. The FIDIK government fell, by prearrangement, on Tuesday evening, December 20, 1966. The Saturday before, an early telephone call was placed to Andreas' home by the U.S. Chargé d'Affaires, Norbert Anschuetz. Margaret Papandreou took the call. The Embassy official wanted Andreas and his wife to join him for a private lunch at his home. When he was informed that Saturdays were usually spent at Kastri with the former Prime Minister, the urgency of meeting that very day was emphasized. The invitation was accepted. After lunch, the three of them retired to the official's sitting room and the business at hand began.

Andreas was sounded out on the notion of a transitional government and it was discussed at some length. When Andreas reacted negatively to the idea and insisted on a dissolution of the Parliament with elections in forty-five days, Anschuetz lost his patience: "Damn it, Andreas, I've tried so hard to get a solution to this problem but you haven't given me any help; you insist on making things tough for me."

The discussion then took off on another tack. Anschuetz suggested that a private meeting be held at his home between the King and Andreas. When asked the purpose of such a meeting, he replied that the King was a moderate, a man of good will who was being poisoned by the people around him concerning Andreas, and that it would be a good idea if the two of them met alone for a private talk. Andreas declined for the obvious reason that the meeting could easily be turned into a political trap for him; that despite the King's good intentions the people around him could leak out news of the meeting, thus destroying his credibility and making it seem as though he, Andreas, had made a deal with the Palace. Andreas' counterproposal was to have the King invite *all* political leaders to an open meeting. Andreas was next asked to compromise by sending a personal representative to meet with the head of the King's political bureau, Bitsios, who at that time was already deeply involved in his discussions with Kanellopoulos, Mrs. Vlachos, and George Papandreou's personal representative, Lambrakis. Andreas said that he would have to think about it and the long luncheon ended at 5:00 p.m. with a statement by the U.S. Embassy official that Andreas' attitudes were demagogic and the king-army problem had to be shunted aside in order to get down to such basic problems as economic development and growth.

The Stephanopoulos government fell the following Tuesday, late in the evening. Two hours later a Greek industrialist called Andreas' office on Souidias Street and asked to speak to him. Andreas signaled to his aide that he was not in. The industrialist asked the aide to make every effort to locate Andreas since it was a matter of the utmost urgency and ended by saying that he would call back in half an hour. Two more calls were made and on both occasions the industrialist was told that Andreas Papandreou could not be located. Finally the aide was asked to transmit a message to Andreas as quickly as possible: that he, the industrialist, had been authorized by the Paraskevopoulos caretaker government to ask Andreas if he would like to name two or three ministers provided, of course, that he agreed to support the new government when it came up for a vote of confidence in Parliament. It later became known that Andreas' political aide had been thoroughly investigated, well before the actual downfall of the FIDIK government, and his dossier placed before the King who then indicated his willingness to appoint the aide as a minister in the new government if this was the price to be paid for Andreas' support.

When both of these attempts to implicate the younger Papandreou failed, it fell upon the father to discipline his son by threatening to expel him and his followers from the Center Union party. And when it became clear that Andreas' power within the party was greater than anyone had anticipated, Andreas was able to impose a compromise on his own terms—control over the party slate.

For the moment at least, Lambrakis and Kanellopoulos had been stalemated and Andreas had emerged, in effect, as the de facto leader of the Center Union, thus putting things back to where they were initially—with the Center Union party once more in a position to capture an absolute majority of the parliamentary seats. The major difference, however, was a very disturbing one for the Palace—the leadership of the Center Union had, in effect, changed, with the King now firmly committed to elections on May 28, 1967. The plan, in short, had backfired. It had underestimated Andreas' strength.

Had Andreas Papandreou been effectively neutralized, had the Lambrakis plan, in other words, succeeded, Greece would have gone on much as it had in the past and no coup would have been necessary. Greece would have continued being a satellite and the Greek politicians would have resumed their turns at the till in an orderly and serial fashion.

The fact remains that the Lambrakis plan did not succeed and Andreas was not effectively neutralized. Indeed, he had emerged from it all as *the* major political force in the country. It would not in the least be an exaggeration to say that Andreas was made by his enemies.

Chapter 4

The Coup of April 21, 1967

I

There were two major variables in the Greek crisis from July 1965 to April 1967. First was the factor of time. It was inexorable. It grew shorter and shorter as the constitutional deadline for elections approached. The other variable was Andreas' popularity—and that continued to rise in spite of, and more often because of, the attempts to destroy it. Two major efforts had been made to attack the base of his popularity, and both had failed. The Aspida controversy, followed by the official Report, and then by the trial of the twenty-eight officers, was a desperate and transparent attempt to picture the younger Papandreou as the Greek equivalent of Egypt's Nasser. The Lambrakis plan, on the other hand, was an ingenious piece of strategy which had some chance to succeed. But like most ingenious plans it was too rationally thought out; it did not anticipate the counteractions of Andreas. After all the intrigue and counterintrigue, nothing had been accomplished by way of removing Andreas from the political scene. Yet the Palace and its supporters were now firmly committed to the May elections. The Center Union had, this time, outmaneuvered the Palace and was well on its way to an electoral triumph.

The Palace, in other words, had come to the end of its line. It had no more room for parliamentary or constitutional maneuver. Elections had to be prevented by some means and a coup d'état was now the only way out. Certain events occurred indicating that preparations for the coup were well under way. The head of the Joint Chiefs of Staff and the head of the national gendarmerie, both suspected of leaning

toward the Center Union, were removed. Demetrios Georgia-
dis, the Greek army's former chief in Cyprus, was arrested
on charges of high treason. Yet the Center Union had
mesmerized itself into believing that the King wouldn't dare
allow a coup. As late as December, 1966, Andreas Papandreou, writing in the Athens periodical *Neoi Dromi* (New
Roads), dismissed the threat of a coup in these words:

> . . . objective circumstances do not allow it. Today, Greece is
> a democratic volcano. It is not 1936. And only a foolish in-
> dividual would dare it. Also the European atmosphere is
> such, today, that it would discourage even the most daringly
> presumptive Caesar. Europe of 1966 will not tolerate a new
> Spain in its midst.
>
> For these reasons, the whisper of dictatorship is a trap:
> First, it seeks to prepare the ground psychologically for recon-
> ciliation; to create an atmosphere to justify a democratic re-
> treat . . . Second, to create the subjective circumstances for a
> new terrorism, a new *Pericles Plan* to rig the elections.

In the party newspaper *Ethnos,* a few days before the coup,
Andreas had denounced as a *provocateur* a member of his
own party for having raised the issue of a military takeover.
The Center Union simply would not face up to the possibility
of a coup and for this reason made no plans for its eventuality.
In an orgy of self-delusion, it grasped at every straw that
blew its way. It gave a huge sigh of relief when an influential
newspaper five thousand miles away published an editorial
on April 17, 1967, four days before the coup. In a highly
critical editorial entitled "King Constantine's Dilemma," the
New York Times concluded: "It is the King . . . who has
wedged himself into a political corner, where the only option
to the return of a Papandreou government may be an army-
backed dictatorship. *This is not an acceptable option and
Constantine must know it.*" (Italics supplied.)

This last sentence was interpreted to imply that the United States had gotten wind of a coup and had squashed it. *Ethnos,* the Center Union paper in Athens, reported that President Johnson had sent a message to King Constantine on April 13 warning him against a coup. *Ethnos* went so far as to say that the President's message "emphasized that the United States would in no way condone, either by deed or by word, the eventual establishment of a dictatorship" and that, as a result of the President's warning, the King would now appoint a non-political caretaker government to guarantee the fairness of the May 28 elections. As proof of its report, *Ethnos* cited the *New York Times* editorial of April 17. Two days later the U.S. Embassy in Athens denied that any message had been sent.[1] And two days after the denial, the military struck.

II

We turn now to the political events, after the failure of the Lambrakis plan, which led up to the coup of April 21. With the fall of the King's puppet government in December 1966 and the appointment of the succeeding caretaker government of Paraskevopoulos, the King found himself in an impossible situation: he had committed himself to the May elections without having gotten Andreas Papandreou out of the way. Indeed, his latest in a long series of blunders had, in the end, transformed the younger Papandreou into the de facto leader of the predominant Center Union party. It was then that a new plot began to be hatched.

It may seem that altogether too much emphasis has been put on plots and conspiracies, but given the Byzantine complexities of Greek politics and a King who is living in the wrong century, they are unavoidable. The very personal nature of Greek politics and the economic concentration of

---

[1] The *New York Times,* April 20, 1967.

power restricts politics to the very few. And in this type of microcosm, as compared to the United States, the system becomes a natural hothouse for intrigues and plots.

The latest plot was to create an atmosphere of tension and chaos in order to prevent the May elections. In the record time of nine hours, in a country notorious for its leaden bureaucracy, the Athens prosecuting attorney, a staunch supporter of the Palace, had charged Andreas Papandreou with high treason in connection with the Aspida "conspiracy." He asked that Andreas' parliamentary immunity be removed so he could be tried in a civilian court.

The right-wing ERE party, under the leadership of Kanellopoulos, supported the attempt to lift Andreas' immunity, but the Center Union opposed it on the grounds that it was "justice under orders" and a thinly veiled attempt at blackmail and political intimidation. The Aspida court-martial of the twenty-eight low-level army officers was then drawing to an end, and in the closing arguments before the court, where twenty-year sentences were being asked for by the prosecution, it was announced that new trials would be scheduled to try, on similar charges of high treason, those retired generals who were in command under the former Papandreou government. It became evident that a new and broader purge of the army was in the making. The use of Aspida as a political weapon was not to be allowed to die out. It was to be continued throughout the pre-election period. The trial of Andreas Papandreou in a *civil* court was part of the plan. Andreas was informed that the charge of high treason had been brought against him on orders of the Queen Mother, Frederika. In the meantime, a war of nerves began. He was constantly beset by rumors and warnings of imminent arrest, or assassination, or that dynamite would be thrown on the lawn of his home in the Psychico section of Athens.

If the King had wanted to, he could have decreed a general amnesty, freed the air of the charges and countercharges, and thus restored the country to its normal, democratic development. Instead, stories began to appear in the Danish press (March 9, 1967) that the King had requested permission for "permanent" residence in Denmark. This gave rise to speculation that a military coup was to take place while the King was out of the country. If it succeeded, he would be called back. If it did not, his crown would be clean and, denouncing the coup, he would return to lick the wounds of his stricken country.

The Center Union's opposition to the removal of parliamentary immunity was supported by the recently deposed FIDIK party because charges under Aspida were also scheduled to be brought up against its former Minister of Coordination, Constantine Mitsotakis. Before his defection, Mitsotakis was a minister in the Center Union government of 1964–65. Now that the FIDIK government was out of power, he, too, was vulnerable and the Right was anxious to settle old scores. On this one issue, the Center Union and its "apostates" were surprisingly in agreement. EDA, the United Democratic Left, was, of course, also opposed to the removal of parliamentary immunity. The new terror building up made it the most exposed of all parties.

It is significant that the Greek Constitution requires the dissolution of Parliament forty-five days before elections. Over that period of time, Andreas would no longer be a deputy; he would be, simply, a candidate for election. There was a constitutional question of whether former members of Parliament continued to be covered for a four-week period of grace, but in any event there were still the last fifteen days during which Andreas would be subject to arrest. The arrest of Andreas could be counted on to provoke large-scale demonstrations and riots in Athens, Salonika, and Patras— thus giving the Palace and the army the needed excuse to intervene and postpone elections because of the social unrest they themselves would have created. But even so, elections under the Constitution could not be postponed beyond March of 1968, and another year of turmoil would have been unbearable. The likelihood, therefore, was that a dictatorship would be imposed within the two weeks before the elections of May 28.

The Center Union knew that the Junta existed. They knew that it met frequently and that the King was informed of its deliberations, if not actually directing them. Though Kanellopoulos, the leader of the major right-wing party, was not a part of the Junta, he had his own designs. He had planned to overthrow the Paraskevopoulos caretaker government and assume the reins himself in order better to rig the elections. He wanted, however, to provoke the Center Union party into bringing down the caretaker government by withdrawing its parliamentary support. It was for this reason, and not because of any Junta plot, that he maneuvered the caretaker government into removing the head of the Joint Chiefs of Staff, as well as the head of the national gendarmerie—both considered to be Center Union supporters. The former Prime Minister, George Papandreou, loudly protested their removal, but he did not withdraw his party's vote of confidence. There was no reason to do so, and thus bring on a governmental crisis, since the Center Union party was already assured of a majority victory in the forthcoming elections.

III

The next step in this war of political maneuver came when the caretaker government was forced, by the Right, to declare unconstitutional a Center Union sponsored amendment to the simple proportional bill pending before Parliament. The bill was drafted originally in January of 1966 by the puppet government of Prime Minister Stephanopoulos. At that time, the Judicial Committee of Parliament preparing the electoral law accepted a proposal of ERE itself that a section be included protecting the deputies from arrest during the pre-election period. It was voted on unanimously by the committee, which included George Rallis— ERE's supposed expert on the Constitution. In 1966 it was not known what government would have control during the election period, and ERE's support of the provision for parliamentary immunity reflected its concern over the ten or more ERE deputies who were themselves legally entangled. When, in 1967, they saw that they and the Palace had the government (most of the ministers of the caretaker government were either ERE members or sympathizers), the section was no longer necessary. In fact, it was an obstacle to the potential arrest of Andreas. Not surprisingly, when the Paraskevopoulos caretaker government presented its electoral law in Parliament, the section on parliamentary immunity had been removed.

During the general discussion of the bill in Parliament, the Center Union reintroduced the deleted section, word for word, in the form of an amendment. Kanellopoulos then went into a rage and, screaming that it was unacceptable, he threatened to create a crisis by withdrawing his vote of confidence in the caretaker government. When he saw that the Center Union could not be budged, he then charged that it was unconstitutional and asked that the caretaker government rule on its constitutionality. This was in itself a highly irregular procedure. The purpose of Parliament is to legislate. The constitutionality of any measure can only be determined ultimately by the Supreme Court, and then only if the measure has been brought before it in a suit.

Nevertheless, Prime Minister Paraskevopoulos obtained a ruling from one of his own ministers that the amendment of the Center Union party was unconstitutional. Kanellopoulos and his ERE party therefore refused to discuss the issue any further. The Center Union then demanded that Parliament take a vote on whether or not the issue should be discussed. ERE knew that the Center Union, supported by FIDIK and EDA, had the majority. Prime Minister Paraskevopoulos was then told to say that the disagreement between the two major parties supporting his caretaker government constituted a governmental crisis obligating his government to resign. At noon on Thursday, March 30, Paraskevopoulos met with the King for discussions. Later in the afternoon, the Prime Minister telephoned George Papandreou at his home and asked him if his stand on the amendment was still the same. The president of the Center Union party replied, "Definitely." The caretaker government resigned that evening.

With the resignation in, Kanellopoulos became hysterical that evening. He had wanted two things: the simple proportional system and the freedom to clap Andreas Papandreou in jail during the forty-five-day period before elections. As things were going, he could not have them both. So in a fit of temper he overthrew the government. He had thought that by dangling the simple proportional law before the smaller parties, which would have given them a better chance in the elections at the expense of the Center Union, he would receive their support. But the issue of parliamentary immunity was too strong a counterbalance.

On Friday, March 31, the King started his round of talks with the heads of political parties. For the sake of appearances, George Papandreou, as president of the leading parliamentary party, was called in first for a two-hour conference. The elder Papandreou summed up the situation for the King from the Center Union's point of view. He suggested a two-part solution. The first part was to dissolve Parliament and immediately form a service government with elections within forty-five days. This Parliament, he said, was a dead body, and only elections could bring some meaning back into political life. Then, since it was the desire of the King and several of the smaller parties to have a simple proportional election system, and since the Center Union had already declared its willingness to vote for such a system, the King could choose a caretaker government which could come to Parliament for a vote, pass the electoral law, and go immediately into elections. However, said the president of the Center Union party, there could be no normal elections with the threat of political persecution under the trumped-up charges of Aspida. He pointed out that every day new people were getting summonses, that four of the officers who had been declared innocent were to be retried, and that there were further threats of investigating ex-generals and air force people. Therefore, the service government, he argued, should also pass an amnesty bill or, better yet, Constantine himself should declare an amnesty and get the credit as a magnanimous King who wished to bring peace to an embattled political scene. Papandreou argued that this, in sum, was the only correct approach, but that if the King was considering a political government, then the mandate would have to be given first to the leading party in Parliament, the Center Union. He stated, further, that it would be unconstitutional to do otherwise, and if by any chance the King were to give the mandate to ERE (as he subsequently did), he, George Papandreou, would charge the King with having ceased to be a King, of having transformed himself into a "party boss." In other words, Papandreou warned the King that such an act would intensify the attacks on the court and on the King himself. Such was the substance of the private talk between Constantine and the head of the leading party in Parliament.

On Sunday, April 2, after finishing his round of talks with the party leaders (including Elias Tsirimokos, who had organized his own party with his nephew as the only other member), the King had his political adviser, Bitsios, call George Papandreou and ask him to join with the other "leaders" on Monday noon for further discussions—a sort of

"King's Council" on internal matters. Papandreou said he would not participate; that he had already stated his views to the King and that he was at his disposal any time the King thought a second meeting necessary. The Athens radio in its 9:30 P.M. broadcast announced that the King had called in all the leaders to discuss a government of "national unity" and that Papandreou had refused to come. Bitsios had said nothing about the intention of the meeting in his telephone call to Papandreou, but even if he had, the refusal would have been forthcoming since a "national unity" government implied a further postponement of the elections.

During all of this maneuvering and double-dealing, the King was being closely advised by the U.S. Embassy. Then, on April 3, the King bypassed the largest party, the Center Union, and appointed Kanellopoulos as the head of the new caretaker government. But it soon became clear that the vote of confidence in Parliament would be 101 in favor and 199 against—despite Kanellopoulos' attempt to dangle the simple proportional election law as bait before the smaller parties. The King, as usual, had gotten himself into another hopeless corner. Rather than face the humiliation of defeat, he told Kanellopoulos to dissolve Parliament, continue as head of a service government, and move immediately into elections within forty-five days. By now, however, the elections had been truly turned into a plebiscite against the crown, but then there remained the fifteen days before elections to arrest Andreas Papandreou and thereby provoke the excuse for suspending them. A dictatorship was clearly in the wind.

The U.S. Embassy, furthermore, had secretly approached Andreas Papandreou twice—on the third and seventh of April. It became clear to Andreas, on the basis of two conversations held with the U.S. Chargé d'Affaires, Anschuetz, that the United States was trying to help the King by getting the Center Union to agree to the postponement of elections and the establishment of a "national unity" government. By now it should be more than apparent that the overriding obsession of the King, the army, the National Radical Union (ERE), and the U.S. Embassy, was to prevent the elections. It had become more than obvious that the Center Union party had the great majority of the people on its side and that *free* elections would undoubtedly bring the Center Union into power in a landslide bigger than that of 1964. Clearly there was not enough time left to rig the elections adequately. When the Center Union turned down the U.S. Embassy's suggestions, its fate was sealed.

IV

The stage was now set. The Prometheus Plan for a military coup, in the event of an attempted communist takeover, has been in existence for some time as part of the NATO program.[2] Prometheus was now adapted for other purposes and was to be put into effect if it seemed that the Center Union party would win the elections, as indeed it did. To provide the needed excuse, the arrest of Andreas Papandreou for high treason, now that Parliament was dissolved, would provoke the expected street demonstrations (as in the July 1965 case), thereby *proving* that the Aspida plot for a communist insurrection was at hand. But Kanellopoulos, who had an independent and unpredictable turn of mind, came to an agreement with George Papandreou that Andreas would *not* be charged or arrested by the service government. Quite clearly, Kanellopoulos, as head of the service government, was not playing the game according to the plan— which explains his subsequent arrest and, on his release, his "retirement" from politics. When this *détente* between

---

[2] The questions this raises for NATO and the entire Western Alliance have been eloquently stated by six Italian professors in a letter to the *New York Times*. The letter has been reproduced as part of Appendix II.

the two major parties became known to the military, the army struck at two o'clock in the morning on April 21. At 6:00 A.M., as we have seen, the Greek people were informed in a radio broadcast that the army, by authority of the King, had taken over the country and had suspended certain major articles of the Constitution, including Article 18 forbidding the death penalty for political offenses. The question now is, whose coup was it? The King's or some lower-level colonels'?

The U.S. press, with strong assistance from the Palace and the U.S. State Department, has steadily maintained that the King was innocent; that he had nothing to do with the coup; that in order to prevent civil war and bloodshed, he reluctantly went along with the *fait accompli* in order to moderate it and ultimately push it toward the restoration of constitutional government. Even if this were true, the fact remains that for twenty-two months the King, with the advice and consent of the United States, had done everything in his power to prevent democratic elections. Whether or not this was a colonels' coup independent of the King is irrelevant from the point of view of ultimate responsibility for it. On this score alone the King and his American advisers cannot be absolved.

It has now been revealed that *two* Juntas existed side by side. The Big Junta involved the generals, the King, and the ubiquitous Queen Mother, Frederika. Their scheme was to take action in the fifteen days before the elections. Undoubtedly their kind of dictatorship would have been more cleverly done—less in the Gestapo-Nazi style, with more democratic-looking officers, and with established conservative politicians in the government. They would have hoped to keep the moderates of both the Right and Center Union parties with them, arguing immediately for some social reforms and an eventual return to democracy. The United States was also a part of the Big Junta, if only because it knew of its plans and went along with them. In his syndicated column of May 15, Marquis Childs wrote the following:

> As it turned out, the top-secret meeting in Washington in mid-February was like the lament of a Greek chorus for the tragedy to come. Around the table were military, intelligence, State—all the powers dealing with the Greek problem.
>
> CIA reports had left no doubt that a military coup was in the making with the knowledge if not the sanction of King Constantine . . .
>
> The solemn question was whether parliamentary government could be saved even though George Papandreou and his son, Andreas, were driven from the political scene. This last was the goal of the extreme Right among the military. To throw out the elder Papandreou would be to throw out the symbol of the democratic process. A "plot" had been worked up and Andreas was under investigation for possible conspiracy to commit treason.
>
> The consensus around the table, after some hand-wringing with agonized appraisals of the consequences, was that no course of action was feasible. Walt Rostow, the President's adviser on national security affairs, was reported as closing the meeting with these words: "I hope you understand, gentlemen, [that] what we have concluded here, or rather failed to conclude, makes the future course of events in Greece inevitable."

Rostow, of course, was talking about the Big Junta, but the Little Junta got there first, much to the distress and embarrassment of the Americans and the King. The Little Junta, however, needed the King, and using his name and the supposed communist threat to sanction the coup, finally "convinced" him to go along. The new Prime Minister, Constantine Kollias, was with the Big Junta, but was persuaded to become the front man at the urging of the Queen Mother, Frederika. In the days immediately after the coup, there was an army officer constantly at his side and four others stationed outside his office. Evidently, they didn't trust him completely. Certain of the King's army friends were retired and Major Arnaoutis, the King's military adjutant, was shunted aside and replaced by a member of the Little Junta. The initial phase of the coup was thus a "mix" of the two Juntas, with the Little Junta in fairly absolute control.

There is, however, one disturbing aspect to all this. Henry Kamm, writing in the *New York Times* (May 5, 1967), reported that "According to junta sources, General Spandidakis [a member of the Big Junta] . . . was not informed until the later stages of *preparation* for the coup. He agreed to take part, informed sources believe, in the hope of representing the King's interests. The generals who were retired stayed aloof" (italics supplied). This statement clearly implies that the King's generals knew of the Little Junta's plans *before* the coup. Can it be, therefore, that the King, and hence the United States, could not have known? If Kamm's reporting is accurate, a second hypothesis can be offered—that the Americans and the King were a part of *both* Juntas, that they knew what was going on and gave it their tacit approval. The manner in which the coup was carried out, the King's feigned reluctance, and the apparent surprise of the Americans, all become part of an elaborate scheme, in this view, to protect the King and to mask the involvement of the United States.

This is perhaps too fanciful an explanation. The truth lies somewhere in between the two arguments—that the King really knew nothing beforehand of the colonels' coup, or, alternatively, that it was all a clever act to dissociate the crown and the United States from the coup they had both secretly engineered.

What most probably happened, and what is the only explanation which fits all the pieces together, is the following. It is clearly impossible that the colonels could have pushed, or planned to push, all the buttons to start the coup without anyone on the general staff having heard about it. The colonels, no doubt, did take the initiative and having done so, the generals and the King were caught in a trap. They had the power, *technically,* to stop the coup by issuing countermanding orders. The reason they did not, we are told, was to prevent a civil war and the consequent bloodshed that would have inevitably followed. But it was not out of fear of violence that this step was not taken. It was rather that, having moved to stop the coup, or once started to reverse it, the "cat would have been out of the bag." The Big Junta would have been seen putting down a coup against the Constitution in support of the democratic process—a most unusual position for a Junta to be found in. But having done so, they could not very easily have sprung their own more moderate coup, which had been planned to take place three weeks later. Faced with this dilemma, they had either to go along with the colonels' coup and try to take it over (while the King took on the pose of innocent consternation), or suppress it and postpone their own coup until after the elections. The latter choice was far too dangerous—the democratic opposition would have been alerted and, in any case, a coup after the elections, with about 60 percent voting for the Center Union and another 10 percent for the United Democratic Left, would have been absurdly crude and would have exposed the nakedness of their anti-democratic power play. They had no choice but to go along with the coup and try to take it over. Kollias and Lieutenant General Spandidakis—both members of the Big Junta—were moved in, and the Little Junta, though keeping much of the power in its own hands, was forced to accept a façade of civilians in ministerial posts.

There is some evidence for this last interpretation of events. It concerns the activities of retired Admiral Spanidis who had formerly headed *Democritus,* the Atomic Energy

Commission of Greece, and who at the time of the coup was Secretary-General of ERE.

At 1 o'clock in the morning of April 21, Admiral Spanidis was notified of the coup by a high-ranking army officer. The telephone lines had been cut and Admiral Spanidis drove immediately to the Skaramanga Naval Base outside Daphne, toward Corinth. Saying that he represented the Kanellopoulos service government, he ordered the Navy to depart for Crete within the four hours it took to prepare the ships for sailing. The Naval Commander of Skaramanga refused to sail without an order from the King. The King was notified by wireless. His reply was to wait for orders. The orders never came.

The Air Force had also balked initially and did not fly over Athens in a supporting show of force until the following Sunday. It took two days for the Junta to get the Navy and the Air Force on its side. Had the King ordered them to Crete, the Junta would have quickly collapsed. But then, in all probability, the elections would have had to be held and this, for the King, was the greater evil.

V

At the time of the coup the Sixth Fleet, stationed in the Mediterranean, was riding anchor in Phaleron, the port of Athens. For the sake of playing games, let us suppose that the coup of April 21 had been attempted by the communist-front party of the United Democratic Left. There cannot be the slightest doubt that the U.S. Marines would soon have been patrolling downtown Athens. Another intriguing coincidence is that Ambassador Phillips Talbot's children were absent from the American Academy in the Hallandri section of Athens for several days prior to the coup. It is also probably a coincidence that Nicholas Farmakis, the official spokesman for the Junta in its first days, was in the United States about three months before the coup and let it be known to a few intimate friends in New York that he was there on a hush-hush mission. He made several trips to Washington and then returned to Athens. Perhaps he went to visit some friends. Perhaps not. In any case, there were altogether too many coincidences.

Another coincidence concerns Richard Barhum, the suspected CIA agent who played such a prominent role in the July 1965 crisis—having arrived in Athens one month earlier, along with the King's favorite squash partner, Lieutenant Colonel Lipczyk, the Assistant U.S. Military Attaché. Barhum, after his return to Washington, quit the foreign service to accept private employment with an oil company in the United States. A few months before the April coup, Andreas Papandreou was informed that Barhum had turned up once again in Athens working out of the office of Esso-Pappas. The Pappas Foundation of Boston has been identified as a conduit for CIA money, and when John C. Pappas returned from Greece, shortly after the coup, he was quoted by the *Boston Herald* as having said of the colonels, ". . . they are real patriots. Other countries would do well to imitate them." All this, too, may be mere coincidence.

On March 1, 1967, a month and a half before the coup, Andreas Papandreou gave a speech before the Foreign Press Association concerning American-Greek relations and American foreign policy. Andreas had become alarmed about U.S. involvement in the internal politics of Greece and the military considerations which gave rise to it. He used his speech to warn that future developments would be determined by the United States either overtly or with its passive blessing. Andreas was more than aware that the State Department was not in full control; that the activities of the Pentagon and the CIA were paramount. But each time he tried to warn the U.S. Embassy directly, or by special emissaries, of the clear and present danger, he was invariably told that the State Department did not consider the situation in Greece particularly dangerous or in a state of crisis. Two U.S. Embassy representatives, having seen an advance copy of his speech, got up and walked out just prior to its delivery. This was dutifully reported in the American press. What was not reported was the substance of his talk. The following is an extended quotation from that speech:[3]

> The cards are stacked in Greece . . . Ever since it became a free nation, Greece has been under the tutelage of one or more friendly powers. The sponsor nation has always seen fit not only to direct political developments within Greece, but also shape its foreign policy, more or less independently of vital Greek interests. Since the Greek civil war, the United States has replaced England as a sponsor nation. It poured funds into Greece both for the purpose of guaranteeing the success of the then government forces, and for the purpose of assisting in the reconstruction effort that followed the civil war. This gave it an all-powerful place in Greek political life. In a very real sense it participated in the process of government formation. American diplomats did and still have a very close connection with the Palace, and maintain excellent relations with rightist circles in Greece. This may explain the fact that American officials have almost always argued for the institution of a "strong" King in Greece . . . Of course, it is a mistake to think of American foreign policy in Greece as monolithic. Present In Greece are at least three distinct American agencies—the State Department, the Military Mission, and the CIA. American policy in Greece has displayed the basic characteristics of the cold-war foreign policy which has . . . been characterized by some insensitivity to the needs and the problems of the allies of the United States, especially so in the case of small nations . . . One has the feeling that somehow [the United States] has never felt secure, that it has never been satisfied with a reasonable allied relationship, but that it has always been driven to establish complete dominance in the affairs of

---

[3] Additional text of the speech is given in Appendix I.

allied states . . . The disclosures that are going on now in America concerning the role of the CIA in foreign policy should leave no doubt as to what we mean when we insist that Greece should belong to the Greeks.

Perhaps Andreas Papandreou knew what he was talking about when he addressed the Foreign Press Association in Athens on March 1. And perhaps the two U.S. representatives knew where they were going when they got up and walked out.

Part II
The Role of the U.S. in Greece

Chapter 5

The Postwar Development of U.S. Influence in Greece

I

Modern Greek history reflects all of the tragedy of ancient Greek literature. Greece has been dominated by foreign powers since she freed herself from Turkish rule in the 1820's. And in the almost 140 years that have elapsed, Greece has always been treated primarily as a vital strategic Mediterranean base at the expense of her national sovereignty.

Lord Byron's romantic attachment to the ancient glories of Greece was replaced by the less ethereal British domination at the end of the eight-year revolution. A Bavarian princeling was imposed by the British as the country's first monarch. When he abdicated thirty years later, the German-Danish Glucksburg family, which still rules today, was installed on the throne, again by the British.

Greek political leaders were encouraged by the British in particular to push what is known in modern Greek history as the "Great Idea," the re-establishment of ancient Byzantium in all of its splendor. Throughout most of the nineteenth, and at least the first three decades of the twentieth centuries, Greece was to engage in a series of wars to establish a "Greater Greece." Huge sums of foreign capital, especially British, were borrowed to wage these wars; the terms were such as to guarantee Greek dependence on Britain in both its foreign and domestic affairs.

During much of the twenties and midway through the thirties of this century, a series of coups, plots, and counterplots resulted from the failure of adventurous military activities in support of the "Great Idea." Particularly during the reign of George II, the monarchy was openly aligned with the military as it sought to strengthen its own position. Failure of these military adventures, and public opposition to a more important role for the monarchy, led to the exile of King George on two occasions prior to the outbreak of World War II. In these years Greece's anti-monarchical movement was led by the Liberals. In their relatively brief interludes of power, they sought to strengthen republican influence in the armed forces. Characteristically, however, the monarchists always purged high-ranking republican officers when they returned to power.

George II came back to Greece from his second exile following a rigged plebiscite in 1935, in which he received 97 percent of the votes. Within a year, he appointed one of his closest adherents, General John Metaxas, as Prime Minister. Asserting that a communist takeover was imminent, Metaxas staged a coup d'état ending constitutional government. Parliament was formally abolished and the political opposition was exiled or placed under house arrest. Metaxas set up his "Third Civilization," strongly reminiscent of Hitler's "Third Reich," which was then three years old.

While Hitler's successes impressed Metaxas, British appeasement weakened Britain's position in Greece as elsewhere. Through economic agreements with Germany, Greece became more and more a German colony as Europe moved toward World War II.

When Mussolini's troops invaded Greece from occupied Albania late in 1940, they expected to meet little resistance. Neither King George, nor his Prime Minister, nor the Commander of the Armed Forces, General Papagos, expected the kind of resistance the Greeks showed, and none of them visited the front lines. In what was virtually a spontaneous uprising, the Greeks threw the Italians back into Albania. All Italian counteroffensives were beaten back, and five months after the invasion began Mussolini's vaunted legions had even lost ground. By this time, however, the German timetable had caught up with Greece and in a little more than three months the Greek campaign was over. King George again went into exile, this time with his government but without the dictator, Metaxas, who died prior to the German invasion.

Collaboration with and betrayal to the Nazis ran deep among the political and military leaders in the Greek regime. Generals who had ordered their troops home when the German onslaught began were installed by the Germans as the government of Greece. Under the various quisling regimes, the Metaxas governmental machine continued to operate. It was not accidental, therefore, that widespread resistance developed in Greece. Nor was it accidental that the opposition to the quisling regimes was in large measure directed against the monarchy and its supporters.

Among the resistance movements during the German occupation, the one led by the communists was undoubtedly the strongest. Initially aided by the British, this guerrilla movement lost British support in 1943 when that country became concerned with what would happen in Greece when the Axis powers were defeated. Military support shifted to the right-wing, royalist-oriented guerrillas. Given the understanding with the Russians at Teheran concerning Greece and the later agreements among the Big Three at Yalta, the British acted to make certain that their dominance in Greece would not be seriously threatened by the Left after the war.

Outside the Greek mainland, the British acted to insure the return of King George to the Greek throne, or at least a more amenable postwar government. Mutinies in the Greek armed forces in the Middle East in 1942 and 1943 were put down with the aid of British forces in the area, and republican officers were interned or dismissed.

In the midst of these conflicts inside and outside of

Greece, the British sponsored a conference in Lebanon which was attended by representatives of all guerrilla forces and the government-in-exile. As liberation approached, the conference led to the formation of a National Unity government. It became clear to the British that whoever controlled the Greek military forces controlled the country. It was therefore necessary for them to contain the massive military strength of the Left-led guerrillas in order to prevent them from taking over and to insure the continuation of British preeminence in Greece.

To guarantee that Greece's postwar government would be in good hands, the British chose George Papandreou, a virulent anti-communist, as Prime Minister. Greek armed forces outside the country (consisting exclusively of royalists after the purge of mutinous elements), and the guerrilla forces inside the country, were placed under the command of British General Scobie. The British force that landed in Greece early in October of 1944 was a small one and there was no heavy fighting. In fact, British figures on losses list two dead between disembarkment and the start of the post-liberation insurrection in December 1944.

The government that returned to Greece faced severe economic and political problems. Although the former were critical to Greek reconstruction little attention was paid to them and political tension increased without letup. The Left dominated most of the country by virtue of the military agreement reached just prior to the British landing. All of Greece, except for the northwestern enclave of Epirus and Athens itself, was to be administered by the communist-led guerrillas. However, two principal issues continued to divide the National Unity government:

1) The Left insisted that immediate action be taken to punish wartime collaborators, including members of the police force and the gendarmerie. This would clearly strengthen their hand and they asserted the necessity of

such action as basic to Greece's future. They questioned whether a repetition of the past could be prevented as long as positions of power were maintained by those who had aided first the Metaxas dictatorship and then the quisling governments.

2) Disagreement existed over the steps to be taken to disband guerrilla forces and create a Greek national army, as had been agreed at Lebanon. Papandreou insisted that all guerrilla forces, Left and Right, be disbanded. The Left countered with a demand that the largely rightist and royalist armed forces, recently cleansed by the purge, be simultaneously disbanded as a prelude to the formation of a national army.

In the bickering over these two issues, it became clear that the initiative was in the hands of British General Scobie, and not the Greek Cabinet. Rather than let the Greeks settle their differences among themselves, General Scobie insisted on the dissolution of guerrilla forces. An order to that effect was issued by him on December 1, 1944. On the same day he declared his determination "to achieve, as far as I can, the realization of the aims which have been assigned to me by my government." Three days later, Downing Street announced that General Scobie had acted "with the full knowledge and the full consent of His Majesty's government."

The British stake in Greece was summed up by William Hardy McNeill, postwar U.S. Assistant Military Attaché in Athens, as follows:[1]

> Their first and principal concern was that the government of Greece should always be friendly towards them; and the men who shaped British policy for Greece were by this time firmly convinced that an EAM (Left) government would not be friendly. Exactly what "friendly" meant was not clear. Prob-

---

[1] McNeill, *op. cit.*, pp. 134–35.

ably it meant in part the re-establishment of economic concessions to British-owned public utility and other companies;
but in the last analysis, and far more important, it meant a
government in Greece that would side with Great Britain in
case of another war.

The British decision, as noted above, was taken in 1943, at
a time when England switched support from the Left guerrillas to those of the Right.

The issue was drawn. The Left resigned from Papandreou's Cabinet and the stage was set for the Battle of
Athens, which was to start in a few days. If anything
strengthened the determination of the Left it was the ineptitude of the traditional political forces in Greece, and the
compromised position of almost all of Greece's non-Left
political leaders. By their actions in Greece while the Second
World War had almost six months to go in Europe, the British
made clear their concern not for Greece, but for their own
interests. Behind the rationalizations and explanations of
policy actions in terms of preserving democracy in Greece and
preventing a communist takeover, the British established a
pattern of support for the Right. They did so regardless of the
limited support the Right enjoyed among the people.

II

These, then, were the underlying causes of the insurrection in Greece. The immediate cause was the firing on what
all observers have described as a peaceful demonstration by
the Left against the actions of the Papandreou government.
Papandreou resigned and negotiations were begun to form
a new government. At this point, Prime Minister Churchill
intervened and insisted that Papandreou remain in power
and he readily agreed. The British Embassy in Athens and
General Scobie warned would-be aspirants that it was not
the desire of the British Prime Minister to see a change in
Greece's government just then.

British intervention increased as General Scobie declared martial law and active fighting began in Athens. Outside the city there was calm, and it continued throughout the hostilities. Churchill instructed General Scobie "to take over command of Athens and to restore and maintain order by whatever measures are necessary." As the fighting progressed, British reinforcements were brought in to offset the military gains of the Left in Athens. Hostages were taken on both sides as fruitless negotiations took place between the Left and General Scobie. Meanwhile, the United States government, through Secretary of State Stettinius, dissociated itself from British actions in Greece. The United States urged that the liberated nations be allowed to work out their problems along democratic lines, "without influences from the outside."

On a visit to Athens on Christmas Day, 1944, with Foreign Secretary Anthony Eden, Churchill maintained his hard line against the Left. On his return to London, he expressed his readiness to support a temporary regency in place of the monarchy and prevailed upon King George to appoint the Orthodox Archbishop Damaskinos as Regent. Papandreou resigned, this time with Churchill's approval. The new government, headed by General Nicholas Plastiras, was dedicated to continue the all-out fight against the Left until it complied with General Scobie's orders. By the end of the first week of January, British forces had successfully ousted the Left from Athens and were in hot pursuit of them. By mid-January fighting had ceased, and early in February, 1945, an agreement was reached which called for the development of a "free and normal political life."

The major political questions in the agreement provided that:

1) A plebiscite be held within the year to determine whether the monarchy would be continued;

2) Guerrilla formations were to be abandoned and a new national army, based on universal conscription, was to be formed.

In the year between the February agreement and Greece's first national elections in ten years, the cleavage between the Right and the Left intensified. The badly beaten Left gave up its weapons, as called for in a special protocol to the agreement, and disbanded its guerrilla forces. The Right, on the other hand, followed British troops into all parts of Greece and freely took retribution on their enemies. As the government's National Guard units spread throughout the country, quasi-military, pro-monarchist bands sprang up with British-supplied arms given to them by the Guard units. So serious and disruptive had rightist band activity become that British Prime Minister Attlee cabled the Regent in August, 1945, that he was "disquieted at the information of new excesses on the part of the Right."

Between the agreement ending the Battle of Athens and the elections in March 1946, an estimated 85,000 Greeks were arrested and 1,300 killed. Neither the police nor the gendarmerie were purged of wartime collaborators. Graft and favoritism spread and inflation began to develop. The new national army called for in the agreement was never formed, and the army was enlarged by recruiting officers and men whose political convictions were previously ascertained and approved. Efforts of the Prime Minister to limit royalist control of the army were blocked by the British Military Mission, which accused him of trying to play politics with the army, and by General Scobie and the British Ambassador. Control of Greece's air force and navy was in the hands of other special British missions.

British troops remained in Greece long after the end of the war, despite constitutional provisions which required a special law to permit the stay or passage through Greece of foreign armies. No such law was ever promulgated. To have done so would have necessitated stating the nature of the "national need." The Greek government's control over the country depended heavily upon the presence of British forces.

Prewar concessions to British capital were re-established, including Athens streetcars and the electric-power company. In short, the Right accepted Greek economic bondage in exchange for political and military support against "communism." As government succeeded government and the terror was intensified throughout the countryside, undernourishment, inflation, and corruption spread concurrently.

Although the February agreement had called for a plebiscite on the monarchy prior to a national election, the British government decided in the fall of 1945 to reverse the order. While the agreement specifically called for a plebiscite during 1945, both the plebiscite and the election were put off to 1946. Aside from the royalists, all other groups, including the traditional republican Liberal party, opposed hasty elections on the grounds that rightist terror and disorder precluded really free elections. This again created a government crisis and for three weeks no government could be formed. In behind-the-scenes maneuverings, British intervention was so blatant that the Regent first resigned, and then resumed his Regency at the urging of the United States Ambassador.

Greece had become, in the words of one American official, "a client state" of the British, who had "effectively limited (one might say terminated) the sovereignty of the Greek government."[2] British policy changed in form, but not in content, when it imposed a Liberal party government over the objection of the Regent. The Liberal Prime Minister, Themistocles Sophoulis, who had pledged to hold elections in March, was no more allowed to act independently than had any of his predecessors. In an effort to deal with Greece's growing economic problems, the British imposed a permanent Economic Mission and the control of the issuance of currency was taken over by a joint Anglo-American mission.

As had been expected, the elections resulted in a victory for the royalists, particularly the Populist party, which barely

---

[2] McNeill, *op. cit.,* p. 184.

existed in 1945. Despite its overall favorable report on the elections, the Allied Commission for Observing the Greek Elections, composed of representatives from the United States, England, and France, could not help but admit "serious intimidation" against voters and irregularities in the electoral registers. It recommended "a complete revision of registration lists" before "the opinion of the Greek people is again sought on matters of national import."

The government which stemmed from the elections was recognized in the West as the legal and democratically chosen spokesman of the Greek people. One of its early actions was to provide "retroactive ratification" of legislative actions taken by the occupation governments. Its greatest programmatic emphasis, however, was to announce a plebiscite in September, 1946, on the restoration of the monarchy. As the date neared for determining the future of the monarchy, rightist terror in the countryside continued to grow and communist-led guerrilla bands began to be formed in the mountains. King George was brought back to Greece with 69 percent of the votes in the September plebiscite, a figure considerably less than the 97-percent vote announced after the 1935 plebiscite.

No longer in power in his own country, Churchill's views continued to set the tone of Greek royalist policy. His "Iron Curtain" speech in Fulton, Missouri, in 1945, delivered with the President of the United States at his side, and at a time when East-West relations were worsening, gave the Greek Right not only justification for its policies, but direction as well. Conflict intensified between Greece and her northern communist neighbors, Yugoslavia, Bulgaria, and Albania, and allegations of border incidents were made by both sides. As the guerrilla movement spread, the communist countries were accused by the Greek royalist government of supplying the guerrillas militarily and providing a haven for them when necessary. "Communism" was the principal issue, but also involved in this conflict were the complexities of historic Balkan conflict, and charges and countercharges were freely exchanged.

Political and economic deterioration ran deep in Greece at the beginning of 1947. Former Prime Minister Papandreou summed up the bankruptcy of Greece's political life when he spoke in his 1945 monograph, *The Liberation of Athens,* of "a people worthy of their history" and "a leadership unworthy of the people."

In December 1946, the Greek government charged at the United Nations Security Council that Albania, Bulgaria, and Yugoslavia were threatening Greece's internal security and integrity by arming and supporting guerrilla activity. It called upon the Security Council to take the necessary measures to stop this intervention and, thereby, put an end to internal disorder. The Security Council endorsed an American proposal to send a special commission to Greece to investigate these charges.

On February 24, 1947, while the U.N. Commission was meeting in Greece investigating the charges and countercharges, the British Ambassador in Washington informed the United States government that his country would be obliged to terminate all aid to Greece on March 31. He said that Britain would also withdraw its troops soon thereafter. The action brought an end to more than one hundred years of British economic and political tutelage in Greece. It ushered in a new phase in both Greek history and American policy. Sixteen days later the President of the United States delivered to a joint session of the Congress a statement that has since become known as the Truman Doctrine.

III

The Truman Doctrine (March 12, 1947) was a frank statement of America's involvement in Mediterranean affairs as a result of Britain's partial withdrawal from that arena because of her weakened economic position. In a sense, it was a statement of the evolution of American policy since the end of the war. Its purpose was the containment of communism. In practice, this meant that the United States government had decided to throw its weight against any leftward change in a non-communist country. With no other alternative in Greece but the Right, this policy could only result in backing a kind of dictatorship of which the State and Defense Departments would approve. It marked a sharp departure from President Roosevelt's policy that had condemned British intervention in Greece's internal affairs.

Despite President Truman's protestations that the United States was acting to protect Greek democracy, *New York Times* writer Raymond Daniel noted three weeks after the President spoke (April 5, 1947): "Greece is beginning to take on some of the aspects of a police state . . . There is a security law which enables the police to deport, without trial, persons suspected of subversive activities." And Walter Lippmann observed in the *New York Herald Tribune* (April 1, 1947): "We have selected Turkey and Greece not because they are specially in need of relief, not because they are shining examples of democracy and the four freedoms, but because they are the strategic gateway to the Black Sea and the heart of the Soviet Union."

The Truman Doctrine represented a new departure in American policy. It also reflected the fact that the friendly relations developed among the Great Powers during World War II, particularly those between the United States and Russia, had completely broken down. In retrospect, the Truman Doctrine was a relatively mild document. However, it laid the essential groundwork for intensification of American involvement in support of undemocratic and militaristic governments in various parts of the world. Today, it seems obvious to say that the United States government is not adverse to backing a police state which it can control, while at the same time condemning as police states regimes over which it exercises little or no control. In 1947, such a policy shocked most Americans concerned about our posture abroad.

In some ways, the dilemma facing American policy makers in 1947 was similar to certain of the problems in United States policy in South Vietnam today. For whatever historical reasons—some of which have been sketched above—there existed little hope in Greece for the creation of a democratic government as we understand it. Ineptness, corruption, and a history of collaboration with the enemy characterized most of Greece's traditional political leaders. Resistance to the Germans and Italians had been led by the Left and, although the Left had been compromised by some of its policies and by its defeat in the armed conflict of December 1944, it was still the only organized political force of any significance. The American decision was to try to shore up whatever existed outside the Left and to hope that, with substantial American economic support, a viable Greek government could in time be created.

Although bypassing the United Nations has now become a matter of habit, in 1947 there was still hope in many diplomatic quarters that the U.N. could deal with the problems of war and peace. The authoritative Foreign Policy Association, which supported the new American policy, observed at the time: "The most serious error committed in connection with the presentation of the Greek-Turkish aid bill proved to be the President's failure to give a full explanation of the reasons why the U.N. could not cope with the internal aspects of the Greek crisis."[3]

The State Department sought to explain why the U.N. had been ignored by asserting that international economic agencies were not equipped to handle loans on the scale

---

[3] *Foreign Policy Reports* (September 1, 1947).

needed by Greece and Turkey. More than two weeks after President Truman's speech, the U.S. delegate to the U.N. denied that U.S. action was inconsistent with the U.N. Charter and declared that "in due course" it would be superseded by international action. In the Congress, bipartisan leaders expressed "regret" that the U.N. had not been notified of the planned U.S. action. An amendment to the Greek-Turkish aid bill was adopted allowing the President to suspend or change the enabling legislation if the U.N. Security Council or the U.N. General Assembly decided that action or contemplated action by them made further unilateral U.S. action unnecessary or undesirable.

The bypassing of the U.N. was a major blow to that organization. Its ineffectiveness as a peace-keeping body stems from such unilateral actions about which the U.N. is powerless to do anything. The extent of American cynicism resulting from its new policy of containing communism was revealed in the attitude of the United States government to the U.N. Commission of Investigation.

The Commission had been set up by the Security Council after the Greek government had charged Greece's northern neighbors with responsibility for internal disorders in that country. The American representative had proposed the enabling resolution, which specifically noted that setting up the Commission reflected no prior judgment on the Greek situation.

The Commission assembled in Athens on January 29, 1947. On March 21, drafting committees were set up and the first meeting of these committees took place in Geneva on April 7. The report was presented to the Security Council for action on June 27. The dates are important: 42 days after the Commission arrived in Athens, 25 days before it began to write its report, and 107 days before the report was presented, the United States had already reached its conclusion via the Truman Doctrine and was active in support of its own policy.

Prejudgment by the United States prevented the theoretical possibility that the American delegate might express other conclusions on the basis of his own findings. It removed any possibility that the Commission might possibly find Greek domestic policies, rather than action by its northern neighbors, responsible for internal conflict. Although good taste is not necessarily involved in international diplomacy, the timing of the Truman Doctrine precluded an impartial study or report. The majority report was written by the United States representative on the Commission and reflected the conclusions concerning Greece reached by the White House. It followed the vagaries of President Truman's "I don't like you, but I'll back you to the hilt" policy.

In essence, the majority of the Commission attributed partial responsibility to the Athens regime for the unrest and discontent. It criticized Greece for its discriminatory policies toward the Slav minority in Macedonia and pointed to its venal politics and economic disintegration. as causes for disorders within the country. In general, however, it followed the Greek regime's charges that disorders within Greece resulted from intervention by Greece's northern neighbors in support of the guerrillas.

The Commission's proposals could only be considered as sanctions and punitive measures, according to the French delegate. To have accepted them, Greece's northern neighbors would have had to accept the Commission's conclusions, and their rejection therefore was hardly surprising.

IV

Initial reaction in Greece was just what might have been expected. The Right hailed the Truman Doctrine. America, after all, was far richer than England and the British departure without another country filling the gap would have meant their collapse. The initial reaction of the Right was an orgiastic outburst of increased terrorism against its opponents.

The Center was also enthusiastic about the Truman Doctrine. Despite its overwhelming defeat in the March 1946 elections, the Center felt that America's support of "third force" movements in Europe would lead to its ultimate leadership of the government. Political maneuverings by such Center leaders as the octogenarian Themistocles Sophoulis continued with renewed enthusiasm, and six months later the aged leader became the head of a reconstituted government.

The moderate Left was taken aback by the President's statement. One of its leaders, a former Foreign Minister, John Sophianopoulos, wrote of conversations with American leaders prior to the announcement of the Truman Doctrine. He spoke of assurances given him that the United States government would back moderation. He pointed to a speech by Secretary of State Marshall urging that Greeks forget "bygone differences" and embark upon a "dynamic policy of amnesty, coupled with the disarming of illegal bands, just and rigorous tax reform, modernization of the civil service, realistic financial control and the even-handed dispensation of justice."[4] The extreme Left vigorously condemned the Truman Doctrine, and declared its intention of intensifying guerrilla warfare against the government and its policies.

Of the $300 million initially appropriated by the United States for Greek aid, half was to go for the army and the other half for reconstruction. The United States, as Britain had been, was invited by the Greek government to send

---

[4] Referred to by John A. Sophianopoulos, "Le Problème Grec," *Politique Etrangère,* No. 4 (September 1947). Marshall's speech was given on February 14, 1947.

experts to administer the relief program and to participate in working out policies connected with finance, trade, exchange control, civil service, and price and wage regulation. Experts were also assigned to government ministries in an advisory or supervisory capacity.

Guerrilla activity increased following the announcement of the Truman Doctrine. In part this was the Left's answer to the United States and to the Greek Right and Center. In part it was a reaction to the government-supported spread of terror, as the former Minister of Justice in the centrist postwar government, Constantine Rendis, declared.

Under pressure from the United States for a more palatable government than the one led by the royalists, a coalition government was formed in the autumn of 1947 with the old Liberal leader, Sophoulis, as Prime Minister. Populists, however, dominated Sophoulis' three successive governments and the absolute majority they held in the Parliament prevented the government from taking any action with which they disagreed. The façade of representative government belied the fact that no real change had occurred in Greek politics.

Sophoulis had come to office to diminish public doubts in the United States concerning the regime and to ensure the continuation of American aid. His three governments were wrought with conflict because of Populist efforts to control them. The background leading to the formation of his first government is indicative of the extent of American intervention in Greek politics, as well as of the bankruptcy of the traditional political leaders.

Prompted by the Americans, three of the mildest right-wing ministers demanded the removal of Napoleon Zervas as Minister of Public Order in the royalist government. Zervas, the right-wing guerrilla leader who had won British backing in 1943 to the exclusion of all other guerrilla movements in Greece, had been accused of being the principal supporter of rightist terrorism throughout the country. When Foreign Minister Tsaldaris, a royalist and the government strongman, refused to accede to the demand, the government fell and King Paul asked Tsaldaris to form a new government.

Differences existed between U.S. Ambassador Lincoln McVeagh and Dwight Griswold, Chief of the American Mission for Aid to Greece. The former wanted to broaden the new government, while the latter sought to liberalize it. Sophoulis rejected McVeagh's proposal that a new coalition be formed and demanded that his party alone form the new government. The U.S. Embassy then announced that to support a solely Liberal government would be the same as supporting a "communist minority," since Sophoulis' party held only 48 out of 354 seats in the Parliament.

Considering this a tacit endorsement from the U.S. Embassy, Tsaldaris then sought to form a completely Populist government. He was, however, thwarted by Griswold, who privately warned that such a government would be "inadmissible." Tsaldaris then asked McVeagh to state in writing if the United States had any objection to the government he proposed to set up and, if it did, whether formation of such a government would result in any change in American policy toward Greece. McVeagh publicly denied any intention of intervening in Greece's internal affairs and said that Griswold should have used the word "inadvisable" rather than "inadmissible." Announcing that "the Americans are not interfering," Tsaldaris set up an all-Populist government.

At this point, Loy Henderson, the State Department's Chief of the Division of Near Eastern and African Affairs, was rushed to Athens. Henderson talked Sophoulis into an agreement wherein the aged Liberal leader would become Prime Minister, but would not himself select all the members of his Cabinet. Tsaldaris, on the other hand, was told bluntly that unless he agreed to a government led by Sophoulis, American aid would be withdrawn. That Sophoulis was largely a façade for the Populists is shown by the fact that Tsaldaris' party held the important Ministries of Interior, War, Navy, Finance, Welfare, Reconstruction, and Coordination.

Guerrilla warfare continued until the latter part of 1949 when government forces defeated their armed opposition. As long as it lasted, the effective seat of Greek administration was the General Staff, rather than the Cabinet and the Parliament. The death of Sophoulis in June, 1949, led the then U.S. Ambassador, Henry F. Grady, to announce publicly that now was the time to hold new elections. This act of direct intervention by Grady was apparently motivated by two factors:

1) Sophoulis' death created a government crisis: the Populists would accept no other Liberal substitute for the deceased Prime Minister. The American Ambassador also recognized the faulty base on which the Populist majority rested and hoped that in new elections less compromised Greek politicians would become more important.

2) The differences between Marshal Tito of Yugoslavia and the Cominform led to a feeling that an amicable settlement between Greece and Yugoslavia was now possible, providing the Populists were no longer the dominant political force in Greece. An understanding between the two countries would strengthen America's anti-communist front in the Balkans. In fact, after lengthy negotiation, Greece and Yugoslavia re-established friendly relations in November 1950.

The principal issue between the Populists and the Liberals in 1946 had been the monarchy. By 1950, none of the major parties questioned the monarchy's legitimacy. The Liberals, however, were split into three groups, although there were no real differences among them or with the Populists. All three Liberal groups were led by political figures each of whom thought that he was the proper bearer of the mantle of the prewar Liberal leader, Eleftherios Venizelos. To each, politics was the kind of game in which personal as well as political power, public recognition, and even monetary wealth were the end results. Politics was viewed as a method of advancing one's personal fortune and the wealth of one's family and close supporters, while economic and social affairs would take care of themselves. Such an approach could hardly be expected to deal effectively with Greece's desperate economic and political situation. Nor, for that matter, could the United States continue to tolerate it indefinitely in view of its own conception of Greek problems.

Although the monarchy was not at issue in 1950, neither King Paul nor his close advisers were politically neutral. The King's political sympathies were never announced publicly, but in all of its years of operation, as at present, the monarchy was intimately involved in politics.

The army's General Staff, as observed, was of decisive political importance. Its commanding officer, General Alexander Papagos, had recently conducted the successful government operations against the guerrillas. While there has been some question of the effectiveness of his leadership in the 1940–41 campaign against the Italians, much of the credit for Greek heroism went to him. Ostensibly nonpolitical, the army was unquestionably royalist and conservative. It was anything but neutral in the political struggles and squabbles, and only the pressure of American officials restrained the army's historic proclivities for coups d'état.

V

United States efforts to find a non-Populist solution to Greece's troubled political situation seemed to have succeeded, following the 1950 elections. Though continuing their control of the government's administrative mechanism, the Populists lost substantial support at the polls and, even with the aid of the smaller rightist parties, they were no longer a majority in the Parliament. The three centrist parties together had a clear majority and they agreed to combine their forces in support of General Plastiras, leader of one of the three parties. Plastiras' social outlook and his political program were confined to vague generalities and his primary claim to fame was as an associate of the elder Venizelos in anti-monarchical movements dating back to the early 1920's. Plastiras had been Prime Minister for a short time after the December 1944 hostilities, and had some reputation as a peacemaker because of his role in the agreement ending the post-liberation conflict. The other centrist leaders were former Prime Minister Papandreou, who had headed the post-liberation government, and Sophocles Venizelos, the son of the founder of the Liberal party.

An announcement on March 12, 1950, publicly confirmed the rumors of a Plastiras-led coalition government, to the consternation of both the Populists and the King. Early election returns had indicated that Plastiras would have the largest number of deputies among the three parties. Final returns, however, gave the younger Venizelos a larger number of deputies. It did not take much appeal to his vanity to convince Venizelos that he, rather than Plastiras, should become Prime Minister. The same kind of vanity precluded Plastiras stepping down. Venizelos turned to the Populists for support, and ten days later formed a coalition Cabinet with them. Although it is doubtful whether one coalition would have been much different from another, the Venizelos-Populist Cabinet meant control of the government apparatus by precisely the same group that had controlled it before.

Despite all of his maneuverings, the Greek politicians had out-foxed U.S. Ambassador Grady. Grady, in turn, made public a letter to the new Prime Minister in which he outlined a program of government reform and intimated that if the reforms were not carried out American aid might be reduced or discontinued. Indicating his belief that the new

Cabinet was unable to meet the country's needs and questioning its stability and popular support, Grady, in effect, demanded a broadening of the coalition to include Plastiras.

No Greek political force, be it a party or the monarchy itself, was in a position to challenge the United States. The Populists, the King, and, of course, Venizelos, were outraged. Commenting on Grady's letter, the text of which had been made public, a conservative Athens newspaper, *Embros* (April 7, 1950), declared: "Without warning, Washington uses methods which show up Greece as a protectorate and provide Red propaganda with anti-American arguments."

Venizelos reluctantly resigned three weeks after triumphantly announcing his Cabinet. Plastiras formed a government the following day, including members of the Venizelist party as ministers. Venizelos went abroad for "reasons of health" and blamed "the allied factor" for his resignation. Six weeks after the election, the American representatives in Greece had exactly the kind of centrist government they had been seeking. It was with this tenuous coalition that the United States sought to put into effect its plans for Greece outlined three years earlier in the Truman Doctrine.

Plastiras did not justify the hopes Grady had placed in him. His reform program turned out to be more words than action, and his parliamentary support was tenuous. Within six months he resigned and Venizelos was back in office as Prime Minister. Shortly thereafter, Grady was replaced by the well-known "Cowboy Ambassador," John Peurifoy, who publicly declared America's neutrality in Greece's internal politics. The maneuverings of the State Department had resulted in none of the changes the United States thought necessary for Greece. The government structure was the same as ever, government expenditure and corruption were still rampant, and the economy was as sick as it had ever been.

The U.S. government then embarked upon a program of economic pressures. It publicly announced a sharp reduction in the Greek aid program, blaming the action on the Greek government's lack of fiscal and economic responsibility. Counterpart funds were no longer to be used to balance Greece's fiscal budget.

Venizelos promptly and graciously promised to comply with the American demands and did not resign, as he had done following Grady's intervention six months earlier. By this time the U.S. Embassy had exhausted the list of potential Prime Ministers and, perhaps, Venizelos was as good as any of the traditional politicians.

The American plan to stabilize the Greek economy through a severe reduction in Greek military expenditures was forgotten when the Korean War broke out. It became difficult for the United States to urge on Greek politicians the necessity to reduce the cost of the military on one hand, and to assert elsewhere that the outbreak of the Korean War resulted from a lack of preparedness.

Obviously, then, the plan to stabilize the Greek economy by 1952 would have to be postponed and U.S. economic aid to the Greek regime would have to continue on a vast scale for a while. American policy in Greece became a two-fold one: economic reconstruction was to be on a longer-range basis, while Greece's military position with respect to her communist neighbors would have to be strengthened. American influence on Greek internal policy ranged from day-to-day direct intervention in the country's economic and political affairs to less direct control through fiscal supervision.

In 1952 Greece joined NATO, and Greek military policy became part of overall NATO planning. The dominant position of the American military in the Greek aid program meant that the fears of civilian American economists concerning such problems as inflation were to be put aside in favor of military needs. Greek government leaders, of course, found this to their satisfaction, as did the military.

The 1950 election had led to unstable coalition governments, which pleased no one except the politicians who held office. New elections in 1951 left the political situation largely unchanged. In 1952, therefore, and under strong pressures from the United States, the electoral law, based on proportional representation, was replaced by a majority system. The Parliament was reduced to three hundred members. Candidates receiving the largest vote in each constituency were to be declared elected, rather than basing representation on the popular vote of each party. With Greece's plethora of political parties, this led to the formation of pre-election coalitions. Although the coalitions did not preclude internal conflicts, they effectively limited to two the major contending electoral forces.

Following his retirement from the army in 1951, former Army Chief of Staff, General Papagos, who had dissociated himself from politics, founded a new political movement, the Rally of the Greek People. Aimed as a "protest" against "politics as usual," Papagos pointedly refused to use the word "party" for his "rally." He had the support of conservative politicians who, like the upper echelons of the Greek army, distrusted democracy. The majority system of choosing deputies resulted in Papagos' Rally winning overwhelming support in the Parliament, much to the satisfaction of the U.S. Ambassador and the U.S. Mission in Greece. They viewed the new Papagos government as one with which they could do business. U.S. purse strings were loosened, credit to private business was relaxed, and grants for new projects were discussed with the government.

Because of American control of Greece's finances, efforts were made by Papagos' economic planners to find alternative sources of financing, and some German money went to Greece through credits from the Krupp firm to a private Greek firm. The new regime, however, concentrated most of its economic policy on governmental financing of industrial development. Despite its efforts to strengthen the economy and its export segment, the Papagos government, like its predecessors, never succeeded in halting Greece's ever-growing inflation.

As the economic situation became more acute in the fall of 1955, Papagos died and the usual political quarrels again broke out among his would-be heirs. The King chose a comparative unknown, Constantine Karamanlis, to succeed Papagos. The new Prime Minister organized his own party, the National Radical Union (ERE), and new elections took place in February 1956. Gerrymandering of electoral districts as the election approached resulted in Karamanlis' party winning a small majority in the Parliament, although it received a minority of the total votes cast. The brief period of military authoritarianism under Papagos was followed by the return to the Greek scene of the old "politics as usual" attitude. The election of Karamanlis also set the stage for another long period of conservative rule. Although Karamanlis was to lead the government until the early summer of 1963, at the end of the period Greece's economy was in no better shape, and inflation and corruption were as rampant as they had ever been.

The Karamanlis era, however, witnessed two important political developments. One was the emergence of the Left as the principal counterweight to the conservative-royalist coalition. The second was the formation of the centrist coalition. In a short time this center coalition emerged as the principal political force in the country and, in the process, drew from the Left a substantial part of its protest support. The sequence will be described briefly.

Defections from his tenuous majority in the Parliament led to Karamanlis' resignation as Prime Minister in the spring of 1958. New elections were held within two months and because of the peculiar election laws then in force, Karamanlis' ERE party won a 58 percent majority of the parliamentary seats (173 out of 300) on the basis of 41 percent of the popular vote. The Left coalition of the United Democratic Left (EDA), in large part a substitute for the illegal Communist party, became the second largest political force in the country, with seventy-eight deputies. The traditional Liberal party, now led by Papandreou and Venizelos, had thirty-six seats. The remaining thirteen deputies were scattered among the other parties, mainly those of the Right. Early in 1959, Kanellopoulos, a convert to royalism who was to play an important role in the events leading up to the military coup in 1967, joined Karamanlis' Cabinet.

A new national election in October 1961 consolidated Karamanlis' position, and ERE obtained for the first time a majority of the popular vote, 50.8 percent, and with it a slight increase in its parliamentary representation. Karamanlis had no spectacular success in solving Greece's social and economic problems, but the "stability" and "steadiness" of his government won for him the enthusiastic backing of the U.S. State Department. In Karamanlis, it would seem, the State Department had gotten what it had been looking for since the promulgation of the Truman Doctrine in 1947.

The 1961 election, however, witnessed the emergence of the new Center Union (EK) coalition. On the ballot for the first time, the Center Union garnered slightly more than one-third of the popular vote and a third of the parliamentary deputies. The vote for the United Democratic Left (EDA), meanwhile, dropped sharply to under 14.7 percent of the popular vote, and the number of its deputies declined from seventy-eight to twenty-four. Clearly, the Center Union had drawn off a substantial part of EDA's popular support, particularly that segment of EDA's vote which was unwilling to support the rightist ERE but until then had had no alternative but to vote for EDA in protest.

Karamanlis resigned as Prime Minister in mid-1963 because of personal differences with the royal family and conflict within his party. A caretaker government again organized new elections, this time in the autumn of 1963. The events subsequent to the elections of 1963 have been described in earlier chapters.

Chapter 6

U.S. Reaction After the Coup

I

Writing about the British role in Greece in the immediate postwar period, L. S. Stavrianos came to the following conclusion:[1]

> [The] resources of the British Empire were thrown against ELAS [The National Popular Liberation Army]. And the rightists were lifted from political eclipse to a position of authority which they retain to the present day.
>
> Why did the British government adopt their policy? One reason was the biased intelligence coming from Greece. British representatives did not comprehend or appreciate the significance of the new forces at work in the country. Churchill accepted their distorted reports without question because they fitted in with his own preconceptions. He was convinced that imperial interests and a radical resistance movement were incompatible . . .
>
> In the end it left Britain saddled with puppet rightist regimes which were entirely dependent on British bayonets and British pounds.

History seems destined to repeat itself in Greece. The danger of biased intelligence reporting from the field is, of course, not new. Arthur Schlesinger, Jr., in his description of the Bay of Pigs invasion, reported that Washington was not kept apprised of developments in Guatemala, where the Cuban refugees were being secretly trained by the CIA.[2] At

---

[1] *Greece: American Dilemma and Opportunity* (Henry Regnery Co., Chicago, 1952), pp. 137–38.

[2] *A Thousand Days* (Houghton Mifflin, New York, 1965), pp. 236, 268, and 274.

one point, when refugee discontent broke out into open mutiny, the CIA was sending back reports to Washington about "the splendid morale in the camp." And contrary to President Kennedy's explicit order that no Americans were to be used in the invasion, the first man to set foot on the beach was a U.S. frogman. The series of events described by Schlesinger led him to observe that though "top CIA officials . . . were civilized and responsible men . . . the CIA operatives in the field *and their military colleagues* were a different breed . . ." (Italics supplied.)

These two problems—biased intelligence reporting from the field, and a sub-level of government free to follow at times its own independent foreign policy and able, if need be, to *countermand* the orders of the highest political authority, the President—both were equally visible in Greece. Both the CIA and U.S. military representatives in Greece sent back biased reports to their superiors which led Washington to regard a Center Union election victory as an unacceptable solution to the constitutional crisis of July 1965. The State Department and the U.S. Embassy, however, were not far behind.

II

The role of any ambassador is to represent his government and to report back to it, through the State Department, all relevant developments in the country in which he is stationed. In the two years since the July 1965 crisis, Andreas Papandreou had clearly developed into *the* major politician in Greece. Yet the U.S. Ambassador, Phillips Talbot, refused to have any contact with him whatever.

One evening in the middle of August 1966, the U.S. Chargé d'Affaires, Norbert Anschuetz, was a dinner guest at the home of Andreas Papandreou. It was a long evening lasting until two in the morning. It was also an unusual evening, in that an open and frank exchange took place between Andreas and Anschuetz on the issue of the Ambassador. When Andreas complained of the gross distortion of his position by the Embassy and the refusal of the U.S. Ambassador to try to assess at first hand Andreas' position on NATO, Cyprus, and other related items, Anschuetz replied that Andreas had been frequently invited to Embassy functions and that on each occasion he had refused the invitation. Andreas replied that the invitations had all been to official functions, such as cocktail parties, receptions, and Fourth of July celebrations where members of the "apostate" (FIDIK) government would be present; that Anschuetz knew full well of a Center Union policy decision to boycott any functions, Greek or otherwise, where even a single member of the puppet government was present; and that in the light of this knowledge, the Embassy's invitations were a hollow gesture.

There was, of course, the technically legitimate counter-argument that even though Andreas and his party regarded the FIDIK government as illegitimate, the fact remained that the United States recognized it as the duly constituted government of Greece. The U.S. Ambassador, therefore, as the representative of his government, could hardly be expected to take the Center Union party's position. Andreas recognized this, but based his complaint on the Ambassador's refusal to see him on a *private* basis. Anschuetz stated flatly that this was not so and that when Andreas returned from his political tour of northern Greece he would arrange a private dinner with the Ambassador at his, Anschuetz's, home. The invitation never came. Anschuetz had no doubt approached Ambassador Talbot and been rebuffed.

H. Daniel Brewster, formerly chief of the political section of the Embassy and currently country director for Greece in the State Department's Middle East Division, visited Greece in his latter capacity early in 1967. Together with his State Department colleague, John Patrick Owens, he exercises an inordinate influence on U.S. policy toward Greece. Both Brewster and Owens are fluent in Greek and have made

Greece their professional area of specialization. Both are to be counted as arch-enemies of the Center Union and of Andreas Papandreou in particular. And both were involved in setting up the April 10–12, 1967, University of Wisconsin symposium on "Greece Since the Second World War" in honor of the twentieth anniversary of the Truman Doctrine. The funds for the conference came from the State Department and the leading participants were carefully screened. Two were CIA agents, and several Greek professors well known for their rightist sentiments were invited, expenses paid, to attend. Many of the American participants were unaware that the entire program had been carefully managed. When Greek students studying in the United States tried to raise current political issues, they were denounced as communist trouble-makers.

When Andreas Papandreou learned of Brewster's arrival in Athens he tried to arrange a meeting with him through Anschuetz. Anschuetz again said he would try to bring it about and again he failed. Brewster, either on his own initiative or on instructions from Washington, refused to see Andreas. This was part of a general pattern to isolate Andreas and, in large measure, accounted for the biased reports coming out of Athens.

Andreas had repeatedly taken the public position that Greece would remain within NATO, but at the same time he insisted that she should reap some of the benefits as well as the obligations of membership. He insisted, furthermore, that Greece be treated as a country with opinions to which she had a right, and not merely as a satellite country expected to execute mechanically the foreign policy of the United States.[3]

Andreas Papandreou was not a "dangerous leftist," to use that convenient euphemism for "a communist." Competent field work would have shown that Andreas Papandreou had

---

[3] See Andreas' foreign-policy paper reprinted in Appendix I.

done more to weaken the communist position in Greece than any other politician, and more so than the repressive police measures of the rightist governments had ever been able to accomplish.

The fundamental issue, however, was not Andreas' misrepresented views on communism and NATO. The United States was out to maintain the status quo by continuing to manipulate the internal political affairs of Greece. They supported the King's proprietary claim to the army and considered him far more tractable and more in keeping with the U.S. interest in Greece as a military base. The decision to strengthen the southeastern flank of NATO was considered necessary now that France had all but withdrawn and the Middle East was once again on the verge of another violent eruption. The United States therefore required a government in Greece completely subservient to American foreign-policy interests. And when the Center Union party started taking a more independent line, while still maintaining its treaty obligations under NATO, the Pentagon became alarmed. It viewed Andreas Papandreou as the key troublemaker—and in the Pentagon mind, a troublemaker *is* a "dangerous leftist." The Right, and its military supporters, know enough not to make trouble for the Pentagon. Indeed, the Right and the Pentagon feed upon each other and thrive as a result.

Even the U.S. Chargé d'Affaires, who should have known better, viewed Andreas Papandreou through the eyes of the Right. One month before the coup, Margaret Papandreou asked Anschuetz point-blank if he regarded Andreas as a demagogue. Without hesitation and with a candor unusual for a diplomat, he answered, "Yes." And Anschuetz was the only intermittent contact Andreas had with the U.S. Embassy.

III

Andreas Papandreou was aware of the biased reports concerning him which were being fed back to Washington by that "different breed" of U.S. field operatives whose partisan position colored everything they saw or heard. Early in January 1967, Andreas decided that a trip to the United States would be necessary in order to bypass the barrier that had been erected between him and high administration officials in Washington.

At that time I was asked by Andreas to contact Carl Kaysen when I returned to the United States in February and to arrange, through him, a series of appointments with members of the Johnson administration. Kaysen and Andreas had started their academic careers as instructors in economics at Harvard. Andreas looked upon Kaysen as a friend. Kaysen, now Director of the Institute for Advanced Studies, was a former OSS man and Deputy Special Assistant for national security affairs to President Kennedy in 1961. He is still active in this area and has continued as an adviser to President Johnson.

On February 24, 1967, I met with Kaysen at his home in Princeton. The meeting lasted approximately two hours. Kaysen stated flatly, and with a marked tone of disappointment, that over a two-year period he had tried to influence Andreas without any apparent success. He used the words "cynical" and "realist" as those virtues which Andreas lacked and which were so necessary for a politician to be successful.

During his stay in Athens in the early fall of 1965, shortly after the July crisis, Kaysen was in frequent personal contact with Ambassador Talbot and Anschuetz.[4] He knows Anschuetz well and regards Talbot as a good friend. Clearly, his conversations with Andreas at that time were discussed in detail with these two top-level Embassy officials. Kaysen's main complaint was that Andreas was too much the "rebel" and the "revolutionary" for the United States to regard him as trustworthy. He then went on to state that Andreas could

---

[4] Kaysen was also in Athens in 1960 when he spent part of his sabbatical leave from Harvard in Greece.

restore himself to the good graces of the United States by coming out unequivocally in his public and political pronouncements with a strong anti-communist line. He would, in other words, be expected to make speeches denouncing the extreme Left and the communists, thus placing himself squarely behind U.S. policy and the NATO alliance.

I pointed out to him that the cost to Andreas, in terms of the Greek political situation, would be enormous. What might be desirable from the U.S. point of view might not be optimal for Andreas, given the political realities of his own existence. The long-run interests of the United States as well as Greece would be better promoted if these impossible demands were not made. I then emphasized that he, Carl Kaysen, and I knew full well that Andreas was *not* a communist and that, at least from my point of view, the prospects of political stability and economic development would be brighter under Andreas than with anyone else currently on the scene. Kaysen, however, maintained his position—Andreas had to take a strong anti-communist line if he was ever to succeed politically. I got the very distinct impression at that time that the United States would intervene *sub rosa* to prevent Andreas' rise to Prime Minister or, should he achieve it, to bring him down.

Kaysen, McGeorge Bundy, and Bundy's replacement at the White House, W. W. Rostow, are administration men who exercise a large amount of influence within the Johnson administration. They make up a select and influential group of "end-of-ideology" intellectuals who pride themselves on being cold, cleareyed, and unemotional pragmatists. Past friendships are not allowed to intrude on their policy considerations.[5] Andreas had first to prove his "loyalty" to the

---

[5] Though it should be mentioned that, after the coup, when word was received of Andreas Papandreou's imminent execution, Kaysen was very helpful in seeing to it that U.S. pressure was sufficiently applied to assure Andreas' safety as a political prisoner.

United States. Apparently, the United States has not learned much from the past and it continues to insist on measuring a person's loyalty in direct proportion to the virulence of his anti-communism. This explains why the Right is so naturally attractive to American officials, and accounts for the frequency with which the United States is to be found on the side of dictatorial and military regimes in the underdeveloped countries.

I suggested to Kaysen that one way out of this impasse was to have Andreas come to the United States and express his views directly in private conversation with a few highly placed people in the administration. I was surprised to find Kaysen resistant to this idea. I pressed him on this point, saying that since there were great misconceptions about Andreas among people who should know better (no doubt because of the slanted reports coming out of the U.S. Embassy and the CIA, which were available to Kaysen), it would serve to get things into better focus if Andreas did come. I then exceeded my authority and on my own initiative suggested that this might be one way of getting the assurances the United States wanted in *private* without subjecting Andreas to a political setback in his own country.

It then became clear what was bothering Kaysen. He suspected that what Andreas really wanted was to come to the States in order to be photographed with top U.S. administrators, thereby building his image up in Greece for the forthcoming elections in May by giving the impression that the United States favored the Center Union party. At this point I used his remarks to emphasize how little administration-Americans knew about the Greek political situation—that Andreas' major problem at the beginning of his political career in 1964 had been to remove the stigma of his long stay in the States and his identification with it. Indeed, he had been openly suspected of being a puppet of the Americans, and I hardly thought Andreas wanted to bear that particular cross once again. In this context, I stressed that the meetings were to be private, whereupon Kaysen asked about the efficiency of Greek intelligence at the Greek Embassy in Washington. I replied that I could in no way evaluate this, though I would expect them to get wind of any meetings Andreas had with administration officials. In any event, I said that I doubted that Andreas wanted to exploit his visit here by turning it into a publicity junket. Kaysen then gave in a bit and said, with obvious reluctance, that *if Andreas wanted it* he would set up appointments with Nicholas deB. Katzenbach in the State Department, W. W. Rostow in the White House, and, at my own insistence for the long run, Robert Kennedy. He flatly resisted the idea of a meeting with Senator Fulbright for all the obvious reasons—the foremost of which is (though Kaysen did not state it) that Fulbright is regarded as the arch-enemy of the Johnson administration and any meeting of Andreas with him would only serve to poison his other contacts.

Kaysen clearly had a great deal of interest in Greece and though he felt some friendship for Andreas, he had great reservations about his reliability and responsibility as a politician. He very definitely regarded Andreas as somewhat of a demagogue though, unlike Anschuetz, he was careful not to use that word openly. He was also under the impression that Andreas had direct access to Ambassador Talbot; that Talbot was too experienced a diplomat not to keep his lines open with the major politicians of any country in which he was stationed.

The breakdown in communication between the United States and an important political segment of Greece was only too well reflected in the attitudes and convictions of Kaysen, a Presidential adviser on matters affecting national security. It should come as no surprise that the receiving end should reflect the attitudes of the biased intelligence reporting coming in from the field. What is disturbing, in short, is the extent to which a country's foreign policy in a critical area is in the hands of what Schlesinger recognized as "a different breed" of men.

As things turned out, the Greek political situation quickly deteriorated and Andreas Papandreou was not able to make his planned trip to the United States. It is doubtful that it would have made any difference. The United States, with the Palace and the Big Junta, had already opted for a coup which would have been much less crude and far more subtle than that of the Little Junta which took place on April 21.

IV

The next part of this story has to do with the counter-manding of a Presidential order both in the field and at home. Five days after the coup, I received a telephone call from Paris informing me that the Athens airport had been closed and that Andreas Papandreou was to be tried by a kangaroo military court and executed within forty-eight hours. This confirmed what had been expected all along. Efforts to prevent Andreas' execution had started from the day of the coup and, with the President out of the country attending the Adenauer funeral, intense pressure was applied to the State Department. For the four hectic days immediately following the coup, the people involved got virtually nowhere. A few academics with direct lines to the President even had bouts with their consciences about using their influence with the President when he returned; as though it were a scarce commodity in fixed supply to be rationally allocated. Vice-President Humphrey was contacted three times, once in Washington and twice in Minneapolis. He refused to intercede.

As a last resort, John Kenneth Galbraith was contacted at 10:30 in the evening. His first reaction was that he was "counter-productive" with the Johnson administration, but that he would see what he could do. Within two hours he achieved what everyone else had failed to do battering on the doors of the State Department and pressuring their more "productive" academic friends with direct lines to the President. Johnson was informed by Galbraith's White House contact of the possibility of Andreas Papandreou's execution and of the fact that in the entire history of the State Department it had never received such an outpouring of telegrams and telephone calls from the academic community on any single issue.

The President acted quickly. Through the Undersecretary of State, Katzenbach, he issued three orders: (1) that Ambassador Talbot was to go out, find Margaret Papandreou (a native-born American citizen) and her four children, and offer them sanctuary in the American Embassy; (2) that the Junta's Prime Minister, Constantine Kollias, was to be informed of the President's personal concern over Andreas Papandreou's safety—that he was to be regarded as being virtually under the protective custody of the U.S. government; and (3) that Galbraith was to inform his academic contacts down the line of the President's personal intervention. In view of the unprecedented uproar of the academic community and his already bad relations with it over the Vietnam war, Johnson was anxious that he not further alienate it with the political murder of Andreas Papandreou.[6]

Galbraith called late that same evening of April 26, to inform me of the President's three orders, which he described as being "as far as the President can go short of calling out the Marines." He asked that I inform others in the academic

---

[6] One prominent economist telephoned W. W. Rostow and when Rostow started giving out the threadbare CIA line that Andreas Papandreou was a "dangerous leftist," the economist lost patience with Rostow. Before slamming the receiver down, he told Rostow to inform President Johnson that if anything happened to Papandreou the academic community would hold Johnson personally responsible.

community. The information was quickly relayed through Minneapolis to the West Coast. The orders of the President were confirmed ten minutes later when Kaysen, who had also been in contact with the Undersecretary of State, called independently of Galbraith had repeated them almost word for word.

The President's intervention had its effect. Andreas Papandreou was not executed. But the President's first order was apparently ignored by the U.S. Embassy, since it must be assumed that the Embassy was properly instructed by Katzenbach. On May 6 a telephone call was placed to Margaret Papandreou in Athens. She was asked if Ambassador Talbot had invited her to move into the Embassy. The answer was "No" and immediately the line was cut. When Kaysen was informed of this, his reply, quite logically, was that the Ambassador was unquestionably much too busy to attend to the matter himself and had most probably delegated the task to a subordinate. The next day a second call was made and was taken by a friend of Mrs. Papandreou. In the middle of the conversation, the caller switched abruptly into French and quickly asked if *any* contact had been made by the Embassy. The answer was, *"Rien du tout."* It has since been confirmed that, contrary to the President's order, Margaret Papandreou and her children were never offered the protection of the U.S. Embassy. There are two possible interpretations: either the President willfully misinformed the academic community or, as is more likely, his order was countermanded either in the field or in the State Department.

There is, however, an even more sordid side to the story. "Counter-productive" Galbraith succeeded in achieving what the academic "ins" either could not or would not do. John Roche, the "intellectual-in-residence" at the White House, was approached by at least two former colleagues and asked to intercede with the President on Andreas Papandreou's behalf. Clearly, one of his responsibilities is to advise the President of the sentiments of the academic community and the intellectuals-at-large. But strange things happen to academics who sniff too deeply at the hem of power. For one thing, they read too many CIA reports. At any rate, both Roche and his erstwhile colleague in the White House, W. W. Rostow, were unsympathetic to Andreas Papandreou's cause and refused to intervene. Roche, whose responsibility to the academic community is greater than Rostow's by virtue of the nature of his appointment, was apparently responding to Johnson's known anti-intellectualism when in fact the President was anxious to redeem himself with the academic community. The President, in other words, reacted to the pressures politically and in power terms. If Roche had his ear to the ground he was apparently deaf to the thundering herd of the academic community as it ran past him to the President. It is a testament to his instinct for survival that he was not trampled to death. It appeared that his usefulness to the President had, at long last, come to its expected end. It had not.

V

The saving of Andreas' life was as far as the United States was prepared to go. It certainly did not wish to re-establish the status quo ante, and it soon became evident that the United States would not exert itself any further on Andreas Papandreou's behalf. But even this minimum attempt to prevent his immediate execution was put in jeopardy when the President's orders were totally misrepresented to the Defense Department.

A few days after Galbraith's intercession, an associate editor of *Newsweek* was told about the story as background for other information he was seeking on Greece. He asked if he could print it and was refused. He then argued that the President could not be trusted and that it would serve a useful purpose to put him on public record. When he was again refused he asked if he could call up Galbraith and confront him with the story. An agreement was reached that if Galbraith was willing to go on public record, there would be no objection. Galbraith agreed. The *New York Times* picked the story up from *Newsweek,* contacted Galbraith, and ran its own feature story on the first page of its May 8 issue. The Texas White House refused to make any comment and the incident was generally accepted as having occurred the day before, when in fact it had taken place twelve days earlier. On May 5 or 6, however, a top-level meeting took place at which the Defense Department was informed that the President wanted a "hands-off-entirely" policy to be followed with respect to Greece, and, by implication, to Andreas in particular. When the *Times* story came out a few days later, the Defense Department was caught by surprise. It then checked directly with the White House to determine the President's actual wishes—which turned out to be exactly the opposite of what had been passed on to them. This raises the following questions: Who misinformed the Defense Department and why? And why had not the Defense Department been advised directly of Presidential actions taken as early as April 26?

The biased intelligence reporting to President Kennedy and the countermanding of his orders on the Bay of Pigs invasion came very early in his administration at a time when he was new and inexperienced in the wondrous ways of the bureaucratic machinery of government. But President Johnson is an old hand at the ins and outs of government. That his orders could also be nullified by underlings testifies to the power and the strength of the bureaucratic underworld. It is well known that certain people in the State Department, in the White House, and in the U.S. Embassy in Athens would just as soon have left Andreas Papandreou to his fate at the hands of the Greek military Junta.[7]

---

[7] An American, visiting the U.S. Embassy in Athens on a legal matter, got into a conversation with an Embassy official connected

At this writing, Andreas Papandreou has yet to be brought to trial. But this is only a technical matter. Whether he is tried or not, the Junta faces two immediate choices. Either to exile him, or to keep him locked up in prison. Unless the United States insists on it, the Junta will not banish him, out of fear of his political activities abroad. He would become the natural focal point for a government-in-exile and for the growth and continuation of a resistance movement within Greece. This, of course, makes U.S. insistence problematical despite the heavy pressure put on Washington by the academic community. If, as is more likely, Andreas is not banished, he will be a constant irritant and the subject of constant international pressure for his release. There is therefore the very real danger that the Junta will opt to kill him either by undermining his health or by shooting him in an arranged attempt to escape. The Junta knows of Andreas' 1965 bout with tuberculosis and that he suffers from a potentially dangerous blood allergy. And, strangely enough, Andreas' cell in the Averoff jail has a window facing the street. This in itself is a very suspicious arrangement for a maximum-security prisoner. But all this is a matter of conjecture and it is impossible to predict what in fact will happen. Yet on purely analytical grounds his murder seems more probable than his freedom. It is common knowledge that there are many who would like to see Andreas Papandreou removed from the Greek political arena on a permanent basis.

VI

Once the immediate safety of Andreas had been achieved, many of his American academic friends moved, without suc-

---

with the commercial section. The Embassy official expressed the hope that the Junta would "get Andreas." When the visiting American asked, "What do you mean, 'get'?," he received the one word reply, "Execute."

cess, to counter the biased reporting on Greece by a vast majority of the newspapers and the network television newscasts. Senator Fulbright was asked, as Chairman of the Senate Foreign Relations Committee, to hold open hearings so that much of the information that was being suppressed could be aired publicly. Letters and telegrams were sent to the Senator, and to other members of his Committee, by many individuals and organizations concerned with the Greek situation. The Senate Foreign Relations Committee declined the many requests. Fulbright was coming up for re-election in 1968 and he was already in serious trouble in Arkansas for his outspoken criticism of the President's Vietnam policy. It is possible that he did not wish to broaden his foreign-policy opposition any further and thus increase the risk of political defeat.

Except for a few moderate protests in Congress, the imposition of a neo-fascist dictatorship in Greece was accepted with equanimity on virtually all levels of government. And with the failure to obtain a public forum in the Senate Foreign Relations Committee, the Fourth Estate continued molding American reaction to the coup along State Department lines. Compared to the European press, the American press was too busy whitewashing the King to protest or to be concerned with the first reappearance of a fascist government in Europe after an absence of thirty years. But the most disturbing aspect of this particular development was the influential role of the august *New York Times*. The *Times* was not content merely to report the news. Through one of its owner-correspondents, it stirred the muddy waters of Greek politics.

Chapter 7

The Oracular C. L. Sulzberger and the New York Times Coverage of Greece

I

The main purpose of a responsible newspaper in an open society is to engage in free inquiry independently of the government. The American press, however, has willingly allowed itself to be used as an adjunct of foreign policy—usually in the name of a blinding anti-communism and the need to safeguard national security.

Arthur Schlesinger, Jr., relates how Gilbert Harrison, the editor of the *New Republic,* submitted the galleys of an article to the White House for prior approval. The article was an exposé of the CIA's activities with the Cuban refugees. When President Kennedy asked that it be suppressed, Harrison complied without question. "A patriotic act," wrote Schlesinger, "which left me oddly uncomfortable." [1] Schlesinger also tells how James Reston advised the managing editor of the *New York Times,* Turner Catledge, to suppress a similar story filed by the *Times* reporter Tad Szulc—again for the sake of not interfering with national policy. Schlesinger then "wondered whether, if the press had behaved irresponsibly, it would not have spared the country a disaster." [2]

In the case of Greece, there was no need for the *New York Times* to suppress any stories. Through C. L. Sulzberger, the *Times* was *creating* national policy.

---

[1] *A Thousand Days* (Houghton Mifflin, Boston, 1965), p. 261.
[2] *Ibid.*

II

At first glance, the proclamation of a military dictatorship seemed to be but one more of the minor political unpleasantnesses that make up our daily bread—a sudden coup, reportedly against the will of the Greek King; a suspended Constitution; the leaders of political parties arrested along with several thousand other persons; a surprised United States administration, according to the *New York Times;* appeals from the American government to the military Junta in Greece "that politicians seized in the takeover . . . be treated in accordance with democratic standards of imprisonment and trial." On the whole a deplorable, if all too familiar, situation.

In a special news report from Washington in the *Times* of April 23, 1967, United States officials, moreover, were said to maintain:

> that there is no question of breaking diplomatic relations with the new [military] government since King Constantine has remained as the constitutional chief of state; the military takeover is thus a matter of domestic, rather than international politics.

The logic is instructive, especially in view of American foreign policy during the last twenty years. As long as there was still a king, it seemed to be of little import to the U.S. administration whether the general elections in Greece, which were scheduled for May 28, 1967, took place, or whether a military junta which would prevent such democratic procedures for an indefinite time to come had taken over. Indeed, the Junta proclaimed martial law and assumed dictatorial rule over almost every area of public and private life. Where the constitutional rights and liberties of a people are thus suspended, the argument of a "constitutional chief of state" becomes sheer legalistic rhetoric. The dubious value of such political syllogisms becomes evident if one imagines a situation in which the political inclinations of the Junta had tended instead toward the extreme Left, instead of the extreme Right.

The tolerance extended by the United States toward a right-wing dictatorship seems only to have been exceeded by its reportedly almost total lack of foreknowledge of the events. On April 22, the *Times* related the following:

> From other Washington sources, who declined to be identified, it appeared that the administration had been surprised by the swift military move. In government circles here, there had been an awareness of tension since the dissolution of Greece's Parliament on April 14 by the caretaker government of Mr. Kanellopoulos.

Announcements such as these may have been meant to persuade the American public of the genuinely indigenous quality of the coup. Yet they were hardly convincing, since anyone could have known from as early as October 5, 1966, that a coup was being seriously considered. And it was on April 15, six days before the actual event, that it became certain the coup was imminent and that Greek democracy, with whatever little it had to show for itself was, at least for the present, doomed.

The source of what might at first appear to be an extraordinary gift of political foresight was no less public and accessible than the *New York Times*. The most instructive pieces of information were supplied in the columns of C. L. Sulzberger. It is with these columns in particular, and the coverage in the *Times* of the developing crisis in Greece in general, that this chapter concerns itself. A careful study of the *Times,* from October 1966 to May 1967, reveals that its editorial policies vis-à-vis Greece had been gravely defective with regard to its impartiality and objectivity. Furthermore, it becomes evident that the *New York Times* did not only attempt to engage itself actively in foreign-policy making, but also that its columns and news reports revealed to some degree the attitudes of the U.S. administration toward the "domestic" crisis in Greece and the solution contemplated for that crisis. The full history of the coup can hardly be written yet. It might be worth recording, however, how the *New York Times,* an important American institution, and one of its owners and editors, C. L. Sulzberger, were actively implicated in the Greek tragedy. The evidence comes from the pages of the *Times* itself.

III

BEFORE THE COUP

5 October 1966

This was the day on which C. L. Sulzberger's column, "Conspirators and King," appeared. In it the reader is introduced to a contemporary version of Scylla and Charybdis:

> Greece's political situation is once again polarized dangerously toward Left and Right. The amorphous center is being impelled to choose between leaders who wish closer relations with the communist world, neutralism and withdrawal from NATO, and *those ready to go to extremes in support of conservativism and the monarchy. Communism* on the one hand and the *crown* on the other are being made into *distorted symbols.* (Italics supplied.)

Although Sulzberger proceeds to elaborate at great length on the conspiratorial intentions of the Left and its most dangerous leader, Andreas Papandreou, he neither mentions any names nor any specific programs of those who are "ready to go to extremes in support of conservativism and the monarchy." Having referred to them once, Sulzberger then instantly loses interest in them. Throughout the rest of the column "young Constantine" is the sole object of Sulzberger's unrestricted praise and admiration, and is depicted as valiantly struggling against the sinister machinations of leftist conspirators. The twenty-six-year-old King of the Hellenes is presented to the reader (or built up, as it would be called in public-relations language) as "an up-to-date, sensible young man," who, since he inherited the throne in 1964, "has proved himself stubborn, gritty, and ready to fight for his rights and concepts of the national good." (Did Sulzberger, by any chance, have Constantine's dismissal of Prime Minister George Papandreou in July 1965 in mind?) "Although his opponents try to paint him as reactionary," Sulzberger assures the reader that Constantine is nothing of the sort. On the contrary, he "is more liberal than his enemies concede and tougher than they suspected. He is a fighter by nature and, incidentally, was just awarded a third-degree black belt in karate." Reference to this extra-curricular proof of royal valor might seem odd or supererogatory. Yet its further significance may be detected in Sulzberger's subsequent oracular, but scarcely mysterious utterance:

> If Constantine feared the country faced disaster I suspect *he might even temporarily suspend some of the Constitution,* should he think this necessary to meet the challenge. (Italics supplied.)

In karate language the suspension of the Constitution would imply an act of simple self-defense, executed without weapons, and directed at the most sensitive parts of the attacker's body. Despite its oriental logic, the statement revealed inadvertently who was ready to go to what extremes. Sulzberger failed to explain here the essential difference between a Constitution suspended by a liberal King and the measures that might be taken by an extreme Right. Both would lead to a dictatorship; both would mean an end to democracy; and both would fortify the position of the King *as well as* the position of his allegedly non-allied supporters. This statement broke down the isolation Sulzberger had attempted; and it left little doubt about the identities of the supposedly disparate actors in this political dream. We will meet this dream again, but in a more successfully elaborated version.

What was troubling at this moment was the ease with which Sulzberger made his prediction. What was even more troubling was one's impression that Sulzberger's political forecast seemed to be founded on highly dependable information. The context, tone, and argumentation of the entire column left little doubt about this. Sulzberger's statement which directly preceded the prediction, "he [the King] is convinced the army will now be loyal to the state and crown in any test," is not written as a piece of ordinary journalistic guesswork. In addition, the excessively favorable description of the King on the one hand and unfavorable portrayal of Andreas Papandreou on the other, left little to speculate about as to whose side Sulzberger was on. In contrast to the virtuous King, Andreas Papandreou emerges as "an engaging but arrogantly ambitious power seeker, increasingly linked to the far-out left." He is obviously highly suspect of having been a party to a leftist plot to oust the King. Another instance of clairvoyance on Sulzberger's part confirms this suspicion almost beyond doubt: "The King seems to view Andreas as the real source of danger. He appears to think that Andreas, were he in political power, would swing Greece Eastward and out of NATO, *pushing the country over a cliff whose edge it has approached but so far escaped.*" (Italics supplied.) With a situation so neatly divided into black and white, guilt and innocence, who could question Constantine's wisdom in suspending some of the Constitution?

Yet the year 1936 came to mind, when the Greek Constitution also had been suspended and when the monarchy, as Churchill put it, "had sanctioned the dictatorship of General Metaxas." All the subsequent years of murderous political turmoil also came to mind: German occupation, guerrilla warfare against the Germans, British intervention in Greece's internal affairs after the liberation, civil war, American intervention, concentration camps, and further sundry oppression. Greece: a country with its political backbone broken, which after all the pacification and liberation were over needed some breathing space to allow a new and young generation to begin developing its intellectual capacities. Sulzberger's prediction sadly brought to mind the lost opportunity for relative political .and economic improvement after the Center Union's electoral majority of 53 percent in 1964, and the light-handed ouster of its Prime Minister, George Papandreou, in 1965, by that sensible young man, the King. In the midst of all the ensuing uproar and crisis, along comes C. L. Sulzberger and intimates with no discernible apprehension that the King might finally clear up matters by merely suspending "some of the Constitution." Whatever abysses such royally democratic acts might throw his vassals into, Sulzberger assures us, "Constantine is in his palace— where he intends to stay."

7 October 1966

Two days later, another dispatch of Sulzberger's from Athens reminded one of the jolly 1950's. "The Bourgeois 'Barbarians'," is another installment on Greek affairs in which "barbarians" equals "communists." It is this bourgeois-barbarian-communist threat Sulzberger is concerned with. EDA (United Democratic Left), a front organization of the outlawed Communist party (KKE), "has gained steadily in strength and might even speak for a third of the nation's voters now." As to the accuracy of his statistics, Sulzberger says that "this cannot, however, be checked, as EDA has chosen to support Center Union candidates [that is liberal-moderate candidates] in many electoral districts. It is trying to scramble to power on the backs of the Papandreou clan, the Center Union's popular and demagogic leaders." All these assertions may suggest that Sulzberger was privy to CIA information, or its Greek equivalent, or that such an estimate simply suited his purpose. If one considers that EDA received only 12 percent of the popular vote in 1964 (a fact not mentioned by Sulzberger), he is actually saying that approximately 40 percent of those who voted for the Center Union were communists. This is not enough. Sulzberger goes further. "Whether consciously or unconsciously, the Center Union has gone along with EDA (i.e., communist) objectives, although old George Papandreou . . . is anti-communist." This in effect would mean that two-thirds of the Greek deputies are either communists or fellow-travelers.

In order to leave no doubt as to the EDA objectives, and the overall communist conspiracy, Sulzberger quotes one of the principal KKE exile leaders, Leonidas Stringos . . . "As far back as 1956 the party, proceeding from the realities of Greece, proclaims its strategic objectives to be the realization of far-reaching national democratic reforms as the first stage in the transition to socialism . . . The party pointed to the possibility of a peaceful transition to democratic and, subsequently, to socialist reforms."

Anyone familiar with communist language [Sulzberger continues], knows what this means. EDA appeals for neutrality, Greek withdrawal from NATO, and an end to "penetration of American monopoly capital" while paying scrupulous homage to the Center Union.

In case the reader had not seen his column of two days earlier, Sulzberger points out that these are also Andreas Papandreou's goals, which can mean nothing but that he is a communist.

Communist language or no, anyone familiar with Sulzberger's language knows what such remarks mean, or whither they tend. With communists everywhere, behind every claim for democracy and for economic or political reforms, a royal dictatorship is surely the only democratic solution. And all this rhetoric is being spilled over a country as desperately poor and miserable as modern Greece.

9 October 1966

Two days later Sulzberger proposes "A Greek Lesson For Vietnam." He contends that there are "many resemblances" between the Greek civil war in the forties and the war in Vietnam today. "Before being defeated," the lesson reads, "the Greek insurrection had to be stifled on five fronts: military, political, security, diplomatic, and propaganda." How does Vietnam now compare to this splendid example? Sulzberger records that "the *military* tide is turning," and that "*politically* an election has been held." The successes on the third and fourth fronts seem to fall short of both the Greek example and Sulzberger's expectations. "The *security* issue is being faced with a pacification program still less coherent than Greece's. Diplomatically we hope to reduce the open flank through which Vietcong aid pours across Laos and Cambodia as it once poured to Greek rebels across Bulgaria, Yugoslavia, and Albania."

In this column, Sulzberger's foremost concern, however, has to do with security, the operation of which he calls a pacification program. This is how Sulzberger recalls the propaedeutic Greek situation:

> Encouraged by heavy American arms shipments and an extensive military mission under General van Fleet, the Greek army started to win. At this point Athens realized it could never triumph without a comprehensive pacification program.

Sulzberger illustrates the nature of pacification with a quotation from Professor D. George Kousoulas, a well-known supporter of the Palace:

> Under the new system, all those eligible for military service were inducted without exception. Those of questionable loyalty

were placed in unimportant posts. The most dangerous of them were held in a concentration camp on the island of Makronisos off the coast of Attica, where they received intensive indoctrination. Some of the most celebrated anticommunist military battalions came out of this camp.

With approximately one-third of the Greek people belonging to EDA, as Sulzberger's previous report had it, it seemed that the time was ripe for the start of a new "comprehensive pacification program." The Greek lesson for Vietnam, including the concentration camps, may have to be learned all over again by the Greeks themselves. Or, as they used to say at those public schools in which collateral relations of the Greek royal family were once miseducated, *verbum sap.*

26 October 1966

As it was to be expected, Sulzberger's ominous remark on October 5 about a possible suspension of the Greek Constitution by the youthful King set off a political crisis in Greece. The reaction of the Greek press was instantaneous. Sulzberger's revelation made all the front pages. The Greek press was very much aware of Sulzberger's close ties to the Palace and, accordingly, they interpreted his remark as a threat issued directly by the King that unless the results of the elections could be guaranteed they would not be held at all; that a Center Union victory was unacceptable. A dictatorship was clearly in the wind. What else could Sulzberger have possibly expected? Did he seriously believe that such prospects as he casually jotted down for that country's future were to be met with either enthusiasm or indifference? His column, "Behind the Smokescreen," published on October 26, was a piece of journalism that Sulzberger could hardly take pride in. It was a piece disrespectful of another people; behind its claim to objectivity or dispassionateness, it was extremely partial; and it was a piece, as was to become evident later, that contained blatant falsehoods. In response to the political events following the publication of his earlier column, Sulzberger wrote:

> Greece's imaginative genius has been limitless since the days when it raised the Parthenon on a forbidding outcrop and sponsored Perikles, Phydias, and Plato. Now once again it displays a capacity to manufacture Olympian fantasies. I refer to the current political crisis deriving from a column I wrote Oct. 5.
>
> This column contained the phrase: "If [King] Constantine feared the country faced disaster I suspect he might even temporarily suspend some of the Constitution should he think this necessary to meet the challenge." *This mild and subjunctive conjecture* has touched off during the past three weeks *idiotic* accusations and denials concerning whether Constantine, a remarkably sensible young sovereign, might or might not be planning to impose a dictatorship upon his excitable realm. (Italics supplied.)

The "Olympian fantasies" of a people who seem, according to Sulzberger's accounts, to have only one sensible person among them, namely the "young sovereign," had put forward claims to the effect that Sulzberger had had private exchanges with that sensible young man, from which he derived certain expectations about an impending dictatorship. Sulzberger flatly denied these reports as "untrue," and referred to himself as merely an "American columnist" or "American journalist." From this column one might have concluded that Sulzberger was nothing but an insignificant little newsmonger, who simply happened to have a "mild" divination when he wrote his column of October 5.

The real reason for the storm in Athens Sulzberger saw not in his remarks, but in a *plot*. Up to the present moment, the Aspida plot is one of the most referred-to items of recent Greek history; and the wealth of comments is in inverse proportion to what is known about it—almost nothing. Yet it was this still mysterious conspiracy which was, reportedly, the main reason for Constantine's rude dismissal of the Prime Minister in 1965, and his refusal to agree to elections —events which, in turn, led to puppet governments installed by the King, political disorder, and upheaval. In Sulzberger's columns, and in later news reports in the *New York Times,* this plot served simultaneously to prove that leftist conspirators in the Greek army wanted to kill Constantine's private secretary and dethrone the King; that Greece was, at that time, teetering on the brink of a communist takeover; and that the Center Union party was deeply involved in the plot as well.

In order to demonstrate further the innocence and unimportance of his remarks, Sulzberger comes back to his chief target: "the Papandreou clan." He remarks that George Papandreou is thought to be "senile" by his opponents— although in an earlier column he granted him remarkable vigor and characterized him as "the country's most popular demagogue." But then the elder Papandreou is also "a charming old rabble rouser," and an "anti-communist" who had been led astray by his dangerous son, Andreas Papandreou. It is the latter who comes in again for the roughest treatment. Epithets such as "political hatchet man," "loudest mouth," "ruthless," "unrestrainedly vain and ambitious," adorn Sulzberger's column. Moreover, Sulzberger lightly asserts that Andreas Papandreou's "talent for fulmination is not equaled by his reputation for veracity." With respect to the Aspida conspiracy Sulzberger simply states that "some suspicion, still to be legally proved, points at the Papandreou clan." Later on in the column this suspicion firms up to "very serious charges of conspiracy."

These "very serious charges of conspiracy," along with the involvement of the Communist party, which has "openly boasted that it is using the Papandreous to try and take over the country," as well as the senile and sinister personal qualities of George and Andreas Papandreou, form Sulzberger's case, for which, it need hardly be said, he produces no substantive evidence. He ends his column: "All this is of graver import than what an American journalist suspects a King might contemplate doing *in extremis.*"

14 November 1966

On this day the *Times* published a letter to the editor by Andreas G. Papandreou. In it Andreas Papandreou hypothetically asked Sulzberger whether the American people should or would condone a situation in which President Johnson, out of fear of a Republican victory, decided to suspend the election and part of the American Constitution. Papandreou further asserted that "the Greek people are determined to uphold the Constitution and fight any attempt to impose a dictatorship. A Constitution is a precious document in a democracy, guaranteeing as it does the civil liberties of the people and their protection from the potential tyranny of the state. In Greece's case it also guarantees the rights of the King." However, since these statements emanate from someone who is ambitious, ruthless, and whose veracity is to be doubted, one cannot expect that Sulzberger would regard them as anything more than empty words.

But what about Andreas Papandreou's statement that "Mr. Sulzberger's wife is Greek; her aunt, who is the wife of a former *Times* correspondent, A. C. Sedgwick, now living in Athens, is an intimate friend of the Queen Mother Frederika, and he maintains the closest personal relations with the King." Is this another instance in which Papandreou cannot "distinguish truth from fiction," as Sulzberger contended? Now, who is closer to the truth: Sulzberger who, only a few weeks before, flatly denied having any communication with the King, and who made himself out to appear as an American journalist who is reporting from a brief visit to some foreign country—or Papandreou, who has allowed "his ambition to befuddle his judgment," as Sulzberger had kindly remarked of him.

15 April 1967

The truth of Hazlitt's statement of 1823, "I knew all along there was but one alternative—the cause of kings or of mankind," was to be borne out again literally in 1967. On the front page of the *Times* of April 15, Richard Eder reported from Athens that Panayiotis Kanellopoulos, Prime Minister of the not quite two-weeks-old conservative service government and leader of the National Radical Union (ERE), had dissolved Parliament on the day before and ordered elections for May 28. In order to lift the almost total amnesia which has taken hold of the *Times* since April 21, it may be useful to follow closely the events as they were reported on April 15.

On page one it is stated that the dissolution of Parliament was ordered by the Prime Minister "after efforts to solve Greece's political crisis collapsed." One wants to know which crisis this is and what efforts these were.

Eder then continues:

> Thus, despite *attempts* to moderate the situation, including *private appeals by King Constantine and the United States,* the way was open for a political confrontation that, responsible political and diplomatic observers believe, will represent *serious danger to Greece's democratic institutions.* (Italics supplied.)

This sentence raises the following questions: What sort of moderating measures had the King and the United States in mind? What forms would the "political confrontation" take? And which were the endangered "democratic institutions"?

The news story as it was continued on page four provides some answers to these questions. When it is compared to what was to be put forward as information in this same paper from April 21 onward, this news report must be considered as a last and remarkable effort to inform the American public. Its last paragraph, moreover, contained Cassandra-like news, not quite a week before it actually came about.

One of the most recent "efforts" to "solve Greece's political crisis" quite obviously consisted in the fact that the "King named it [the National Radical Union] to form a minority government on April 3." The task of this caretaker government was a very special one. "There is but one question in the hearts of monarchs—whether mankind are their property or not," said Hazlitt; and having been provided with the constitutional opportunities to test this assertion, Constantine and his supporters proved Hazlitt right. The efforts of appeasement to be undertaken by this new minority government were suggested by the following:

> According to most accounts, the King believed that Mr. Kanellopoulos would get the support of the small parties, and that this would allow Parliament to pass a law establishing proportional representation before the elections were held.
>
> Not only the King but a broad spectrum of political opinion here holds that the election of parliamentary deputies on a proportional basis would diminish the win-all, lose-all character of the elections, and thus blur the dangerous confrontation between the National Radical Union and the Center Union.

The peace mission of the National Radical Union, which in 1964 was able to win only 35 percent of the popular vote together with the Progressive party, as against a majority of 53 percent of the total popular vote won by the Center Union under George Papandreou, thus represented nothing more than an attempt to prevent similar results in the elections scheduled for May of 1967. In view of the fact that the King had "maneuvered the elder Papandreou out of power" in July 1965 (as the *Times* once characterized this event), it stands to reason that the King's attempt to reverse the rather unequivocal election results of 1964 would hardly find an enthusiastic welcome among his subjects. To put a duly elected minority into power over a duly elected majority without the voters' consent, and, in addition, have this unduly governing minority hastily assure more favorable results for itself in the next election by changing the electoral laws, seems scarcely a likely way of setting out to find a solution to a political crisis.

A further moderating measure on the part of the Kanellopoulos government was also reported by Eder: After having dissolved Parliament where it could only "count on a bare third of the votes," it had made known its intentions to "remain in office during the campaign and the elections." "This is a highly controversial point," Eder comments, "since there is a tradition here that party governments resign during an election period in favor of non-political caretaker regimes."

Toward the end of the news story Eder has occasion to mention that "a series of visits by the United States Ambassador, Phillips Talbot, to party leaders, to urge moderation and some kind of agreement, was also unavailing." In connection with these visits one contribution from the American side in particular must have proved rather helpful: "After Mr. Talbot saw Mr. Papandreou yesterday, word began to leak out that the seventy-nine-year-old leader had warned that if the King allowed the National Radical Union to run the elections, the Center Union's campaign would become an attack not only on its political rivals but on the King as well." To attack a political opponent during a democratic election campaign on the grounds that he has violated democratic principles and that he continues to do so would be part of the right granted to any party in a genuinely democratic system. In Greece, however—to whom the Allies left a dubious legacy in the form of a "democratic" Constitution which bestowed extraordinary powers upon a monarch and therefore inevitably also upon a privileged part of society—such warnings as Papandreou is said to have made could only have imperiled the position of the privileged even more, as well as their idea of democracy. A stratum of Greek society which had enjoyed the spoils from the end of the civil war in 1949 onward could not have been expected to place much belief in a democratic process which reduced their power considerably. As soon as the chips fell differently, the specter of communism and the threat to the crown were the best and most effective weapons to be used against the majority of the Greek people and their representatives.

Eder felt impelled to clear the Center Union of the most serious charges used not only by the extreme Right in Greece, but also publicized widely with the help of Sulzberger in the United States. He writes: "This does not mean that the Center Union, a large, sprawling party whose members range from conservative to moderate left, has decided to depose the King."

The following sentence then modifies the preceding one in the saddest of journalistic fashions:

> But many of those close to the King—army leaders, some extremist members of the National Radical Union and other court advisers—believe that this is in fact what the Center Union would do if it won the elections, *as seems likely.* (Italics supplied.)

If this sentence identified the cast of characters in the impending drama, the subsequent two sentences which end the report outlined the course of action to be taken presently:

> What is widely feared here is that the King may become convinced by his advisers that there is no other way to preserve the monarchy *except to prevent a Center Union victory.* This argument becomes, in effect, *a plea for suspending the Constitution and establishing a dictatorship.* (Italics supplied.)

There it was again, clear and unmistakable, the *mene, mene, tekel.* No Daniel was needed to do the interpreting.

16 April 1967

After the alarming report the day before, the front page of the *Times* was searched for more news from Athens.

Only on page thirty-one was a sketch found on "Spring in Athens; Politics in Bloom." The caption read, "With Ballot Due, Balmy Air Has an Effect on Logic." Eder then remarks upon the tourists' wash-and-wear "mini-dresses" and tells the reader that the base of the building in which Parliament used to meet before it was dissolved on the previous day is "lined with flower stalls," in which

> there are masses of brilliant reds, yellows, lavenders and whites —roses, carnations, gladioluses, sweet peas, lilies, and wisteria. Their fragrance even penetrates the exhausts of the blue buses that crowd one another along the avenue.

Touching rather languidly on political scenery in the second half of a whole-column article, Eder describes a conversation with "one party leader." Eleven printed lines are spent on the description of the party leader, his suit, his eyebrows, his hair, and the like. What the reader is allowed to take away from this conversation is that in this leader's opinion the government of Kanellopoulos "cannot hope to win the elections," the reasons for which the reader must supply himself.

> "This proves," he [the anonymous party leader] concluded in a blend of distress and pride of logic, that "either they are engaged in a policy of lunacy or they are preparing a dictatorship."

This statement prompts Eder, whose report of the previous day had spoken categorically of a widely spread fear that the King would prevent an election victory of the Center Union and would therefore establish a dictatorship, to the following remark:

> Logic, Greek style, immaculately leads to five different conclusions by five rival politicians.

This sentence, in turn, is designed to dissolve the "party leader's" assessment in a whiff of spring air; and, together with the caption about "balmy air" and its effects on logic, communicates unmistakably the notion that the Greeks are soft in the head, especially that Greek party leader who, like Mr. Eder the day before, and Sulzberger months before all of them, had predicted the course of events.

The journalistic practices of Sulzberger in particular, and of other writers in the *New York Times,* made several things extensively clear in their reporting on Greece: the editorial policy on the *Times* regarding this subject consistently overruled the facts. The *Times* very clearly was, for reasons which are only partially evident, actively engaged in foreign-policy making. For one essential part of the foreign policy of any country is the accurate or inaccurate, the full or incoherent, information of the public. It is from these facts that public opinion in part develops. A news medium like the *New York Times,* however, which seems to assume that its readers have forgotten what they had read the day before, must presuppose a reading public of considerable softheadedness. A news medium in which writers of columns and editorials are permitted to attempt to mold American public opinion into conformity with its editorial preferences—and even with the political games of a Greek King—by the means the *New York Times* resorted to, is irresponsible. Irresponsibility is hardly a defect these days, so long as it is not committed by such unwelcome groups as leftists, peace-marchers, black-powerites, and their kind. Yet actions are not without their effects. In the case of Greece, the *Times* has its share of the liability that is entailed in the present dictatorship. A better-informed American public might have exerted pressure *before* the events. One can be sure that a United States administration, with all its largely self-assumed obligations toward the world in general and Greece in particular, would not have allowed a genuine communist takeover in Greece. But it allowed a King, who would hardly be there had it not been for the active support of the Allies during and after the war, to contemplate a suspension of the Constitution in the name of democracy and thus facilitate the dictatorship of an extreme right-wing group. It seems once again that for the United States there is only a danger on the Left.

A better informed and less biased public might have assured such diplomatic activities of the United States as might have prevented the coup. Instead, the American public was provided by its leading newspaper with information and expert opinions of such a character that one cannot avoid suspecting something about the ties between the editorial policies of the *Times* and U.S. foreign policy, at least in the instance of Greece. A correspondent and columnist who is not only confided to by a King but who also recently acknowledged in print that he transmitted secret messages between a Russian Premier and an American President in the past, could hardly have been altogether ignorant of the nature of U.S. policy toward Greece. To what degree this conjecture is sound can only be inferred from the *Times'* coverage of the events in Greece after April 21.

IV

THE AFTERMATH

Once the takeover in Greece had been successfully completed, King Constantine's part in it faded out of existence in the pages of the *Times*.

The news reached the public on April 21 under the headline "Army is Reported Ruling in Greece on King's Order." The Associated Press report from London stated in its first paragraph that, according to an army radio station in Athens,

> the military had taken control of Greece under a royal proclamation signed by King Constantine, [Prime Minister] Panayiotis Kanellopoulos, and his Cabinet.

On April 22 we find the *Times* stating that the new Cabinet in Athens was sworn in in the presence of the

King, nineteen hours after the coup. Another paragraph reads: "Official and unofficial informants were unable to say to what extent the takeover had had the support of the twenty-six-year-old King Constantine." The editorial of the same day goes one step further than the "official and unofficial informants":

> It is doubtful that young King Constantine ordered the coup that has been carried out in his name.

From this moment onward Constantine's innocence was to increase daily in the *Times,* a process that was equaled only by the *Times'* systematic inability to recall anything that had ever been said previously on this matter in its pages.

On April 23 the *Times* carried the headline: "Greek Monarch is Said to Refuse to Support Junta." In the report beneath it, Henry Kamm writes that the Junta "is ruling Greece, apparently against the will of King Constantine." The reader is told that "reliable sources" provided Kamm with the information, contradicting the claims of the Junta, that the King had not signed the "decree declaring a state of siege and suspending a broad range of constitutional liberties," but had "refused to sign" the decree when he was presented with it early Friday morning. Later in the morning he once more refused to sign it, according to the same reliable sources, and moreover he tried "in vain to persuade the highest-ranking officers to resist the takeover." However, according to *Der Spiegel* (May 1, 1967), the Queen Mother, Frederika, ordered her son in German and in the presence of the Junta to sign in these words: *"Halt's Maul und unterschreib."*[2] Whatever the case, this did not prevent the "sensible" King from attending two swearing-in ceremonies, one on April 21 and the other on April 22. But

---

[3] "Shut your trap and sign."

since he had not yet made a speech to the nation, the "King's continuing silence is viewed here as indicative of his un-happiness over the takeover."

The correctness of the "reliable sources" in Athens was further corroborated by the "analysts" in Washington. In no less than one day they became "convinced that King Constantine had no part in organizing the takeover. He is said to be 'still sorting it all out' and seeking to evaluate this latest crisis in a two-year-old series of political crises in his country." Thus reliable sources, analysts, and other un-identifiable fountains of information, attested to the purity and misfortunes of a youthful king.

Whereas the news reports disclaimed Constantine's accept-ance of the coup and pointed to his two refusals to sign the decree, Sulzberger's column in the *same edition* (April 23) informs us that "the role of the crown in the present sad crisis was at least initially passive. The conspiracy seems to have been started by colonels, imposed on the generals and ultimately *accepted* by young King Constantine." (Italics supplied.) As regards the headlines of page one, the reliable sources in Athens, and the analysts in Washington—all of them were at odds with Sulzberger's news, namely that the King had accepted the coup.

After the events Sulzberger summarized Constantine's non-implication in the coup and tried to render some coherence to his own reporting over the last seven months.

> Constantine himself resolved months ago that he would do everything possible to prevent his country from *"going over the cliff"*; that if he felt the extreme Left was likely to change Greece's regime and policy, he would act by any means to save the nation *"from disaster."* Obviously the officers who led this coup have similar aims—but their gamble, thrust on the sovereign, could mortally embarrass him. (Italics supplied.)

The first thing that becomes clear, without much possi-bility of doubt, is that Sulzberger's report on October 5 of the King's thoughts and intentions was not merely based on "what an American journalist suspects a King might contemplate *in extremis*" (column, October 26), but resulted from a conversation with the King. On April 23, Sulzberger supplies this evidence himself. Not only does the form of the paragraph quoted above leave no doubt about it, but the quotations can within this context only be attributed to Constantine. Furthermore the quoted phrase "'going over the cliff'" also appears in the October 5 column where the King "appears to think Andreas" is in the process of "pushing the country over a cliff." Now, however, Sulzberger makes no secret of his intimate knowledge of what Constantine's resolutions were "months ago." It was months ago, on October 5, that Sulzberger, in the form of a suspicion on his part, gave us a more concrete idea of these means when he said that Constantine "might suspend some of the Constitution" if he "feared the country faced disaster." The conditions for Constantine's coup—namely, the country facing disaster—are now reported in the form of direct quotation. The "mild and subjunctive conjecture" about what a King might do, had become a certainty.

What this belated and backhanded acknowledgment on Sulzberger's part suggests is that his column of October 26, "Behind the Smokescreen," and the total denial it contained of any intimate knowledge of the King's resolve at the time, was written at the expense of truth, decency, and responsibility. He replied to the claims of a "pro-communist paper" that he had "met secretly with the Defense Minister and the King's private secretary," with the categorical statement, "This is untrue." To George Papandreou's remark that "I had had 'two recent conversations with the King'" on the topic of dictatorship, he also answered, "This is untrue." The charges made by Andreas Papandreou were obviously not worth mentioning or even denying. Sulzberger simply denigrated him: "Andreas Papandreou, whose talent for fulmination is not equaled by his reputation for veracity, has gone still further afield." In brief, Sulzberger maintained that he had no direct communication with the King or with one of the King's confidants; indeed, that there was no material basis at all for his remarks. His disastrous forecast of the future was simply to be considered an outgrowth of "what an American journalist suspects a King might contemplate *in extremis.*" Having flatly denied everything, Sulzberger then felt free to characterize the responses in Athens to his column as "Olympian fantasies," "idiotic accusations and denials," and pro-communist machinations and inventions.

Someone who maintains such delicate relations with "veracity" as Sulzberger can hardly be trusted. And since the news reports from and about Greece throughout these months largely pursued the same line laid out in Sulzberger's columns, grave doubts appear as to the adequacy of the information the reader received from the *Times* on this subject.

In another passage of his April 23 column, Sulzberger fully subscribes to Constantine's "disaster" theory of the recent events and prepares the reader for an even more dismal future. At the same time the reader is supplied with the *correct* explanation of such a future:

> In regarding the events that will now unfold in Greece we must be careful to avoid being deceived by inflammatory slogans. In the 1940's, when communist guerrillas made a power grab, many Americans were confused by a propaganda drumfire that represented the quarrel as one between "democrats" and "monarcho-fascists." In fact, it was an outright communist assault.

The lessons the reader is asked to learn from this and the whole column are: first, that the King, although he had "similar aims" to the army officers who executed the coup, had nothing to do with it. Since these events were the doing of the "extreme Right, represented by the army" alone, no conclusions are to be drawn about a " 'monarcho-fascist' " plot. As for the " 'democrats' " of the sixties, they are still the same sheep in wolfs' pelts that they were in the forties, and it is they, according to Sulzberger, who provoked "the counterplot of the former."

Finally Sulzberger achieved what he had been after all along. We now know the full version of the whole story. And we are back in the heyday of anti-communism. Even with the little information one had gotten from the *Times* during the last two years, it ought to have been clear that the ouster of George Papandreou by the King, and all the subsequent events, had to add up to trouble. To cover the political blunders of Constantine it was necessary for Sulzberger also to implicate heavily the Center Union in the conspiracy from the Left. It was equally necessary for him to support a political system in which the Right-extremist National Radical Union "had rigged an election in 1961" (*New York Times,* April 22, editorial) with the help of an officer organization in the army, which today has taken over in its own name. And it was just as necessary for him to support a situation in which a king can prevent democratic procedures indefinitely and, if need be, suspend them altogether. In such a situation, in such a country, the majority of Americans, if they had the misfortune of being Greek citizens, would now be denounced by Sulzberger and his extremist friends in Athens as fellow-travelers or outright communists. It cannot come as a surprise to anyone that leaders should emerge in such a country who would want to end the political and economic arbitrariness which continues to be perpetrated in the name of democracy. There certainly were and are leftists and communists in Greece. But it seems to be equally certain that their numbers and their intentions were grossly exaggerated. The real threat to those now in power—according to all one can know at the moment—were those who believed in democracy and its realization. The real threat to genuine democracy has been the King, his army, his advisers, and his followers. And it is this group which has had the support and sanction of the United States.

When Sulzberger writes on April 23 that the "United States has [a] special interest in Greece and a commitment that transcends even the close bonds of the NATO alliance," he is, sadly, correct. It was here that the "Truman Doctrine of American intervention was first applied," and that "we established a precedent for our subsequent and far more intensive actions in Vietnam." It stands to reason that a U.S. administration is better off with a King and his dictatorially inclined supporters than with a democratic government which eventually might urge large-scale economic reforms to overcome their country's extreme underdevelopment and poverty, and which, if necessary, might even declare itself neutral and leave NATO.

5 May 1967

By this time, not quite two weeks after the coup, the reporting had become increasingly comic. In the April 23 edition of the *Times,* the King was "under house arrest," (sources in Copenhagen), "virtually a prisoner" (AP London); the same source reports that he had said to some "foreign envoys in Athens" that "he would rather risk his personal safety, and that of his Danish-born Queen, rather than legitimize a military dictatorship." According to a story of *The Times* of London printed in the *New York Times,* it was reported from Athens that when he went to the Ministry of National Defense on the day of the coup he "was applauded on arrival by those young officers who had taken charge, and who maintain that they are saving the country from communism and political corruption." Moreover, these accounts state that not only had the King failed to legitimize the Junta; he had also, at the same time, "decided to use the possibility of limited cooperation with the military Junta as a bargaining counter to moderate the new government."

All this together in one issue of the *Times* does not mean that the confusion was simply part of the crisis. The American Ambassador had seen the King, and it could have been easily established whether Constantine was under house arrest or not, especially when one takes into consideration that he already had participated in two swearing-in ceremonies. The confusion was a mock confusion.

On April 25 we were told that the King had explained to the U.S. Ambassador that he was "resisting the military dictatorship." He also was reported to be "apparently distressed." However, "diplomatic observers feel, if he resists the military Junta too forcefully or openly, he could lose his throne or cause a civil war." The "diplomatic observers" should have saved their worries. If the King had lost his throne, Americans would surely have restored matters; and it would not have been the first time that a Greek King was put onto the Greek throne with foreign help. Here, as in other reports, the fact that the King had not yet made a public statement supporting the coup was taken to prove his resistance to the Junta.

On April 26 the *Times* reported that it "is becoming increasingly evident . . . that he will go along with" the results of the coup d'état. Impressions such as that the King was "markedly unenthusiastic and has displayed unmistakable reserve" were intended to convey his continued resistance. It was also reported that the U.S. aid shipments were *under review* since, as one "informant" in the Defense Department was quoted to have said, "'Our military aid program [\$78.7 million in 1966 alone, as against \$6.8 million in economic aid] has been predicated on the existence of a democratic Greek government and we shall watch closely to see *how the new regime meets this standard.'"* (Italics supplied.) To expect democratic standards from a right-wing dictatorship which had just suspended civil rights and liberties is like waiting for an apple tree to sprout pears. But the "sensible young King" himself seems to be engaged in a similar charade. The omnipresent and omniscient diplomatic sources have revealed that the "King's efforts are directed to moderate" the Junta and "to keep it within *democratic bounds.*" (Italics supplied.)

The *next day* finds the King attending a Cabinet meeting of the military government, a meeting which was held in the Royal Palace, no less. And this time the King was "described by a witness as pale and depressed." The King's statement, which was issued after the meeting, reportedly did not endorse the military takeover; moreover, it was supposed to provide "dramatic evidence" of the King's inner conflict. The quotations from it offered by the *Times* failed to convey any inkling of conflict, much less "dramatic evidence" of one.

> "Greece has gone through very hard trials recently," he said. "The democratic institutions have been undermined. The nation, the monarchy, the armed forces, justice have been continuously assailed, and most of all, the true interests of the people have suffered."

> [Addressing himself to Prime Minister Kollias, the King said:] "As you have rightly observed, [Mr. Prime Minister,] it is also my fervent wish that the country shall revert to parliamentary government as soon as possible. For myself as King of the Hellenes, I shall do my duty toward my country and toward my people."

This is all the *Times* quotes. In the first quotation Constantine merely condemns once more those who are now behind prison walls. The second quotation from the statement cannot be taken seriously, since it comes from someone who had precious little respect for parliamentary government when it still existed.

In other reports the *Times* continued to be sorry for the King. He is referred to as the "troubled monarch," and on April 28 the *Times* commented on a photograph of the King with his Cabinet: It "showed the twenty-six-year-old King looking tense, in contrast to the pleased expressions of the Junta members." This "contrast between the main actors of the drama, and between the purpose of the occasion and the atmosphere conveyed by the picture, made a deep impression on many Greeks." The fact remains that the *New York Times,* unlike the European press, never published the picture. On other official occasions the King again is "pale and tired"; he is still referred to as reluctant, and the like.

In the meantime, as was reported on April 29, "724 people arrested on charges of being communist organizers and militants had arrived on the island of Yioura in the Cyclades group, a traditional place of political exile. The announcement [of the Greek government] said that 1,810 were on their way to Yioura and that 2,347 were to be sent later." The assurances given previously to the U.S. government concerning "democratic standards of imprisonment and trial" were apparently being followed to the letter.

On April 30, in a commentary on Greece, the *Times* declared categorically:

> It was a coup that no one foresaw, not the Palace, not the political leaders, and not the United States, whose intelligence service had been regarded by the Greeks as all-knowing. A coup had always been a distinct possibility in the volatile political climate of Greece, *but not a coup like this.* A King's coup would not have come as much of a surprise. (Italics supplied.)

Who has to be convinced? By now it is the reader who is weary, pale, depressed, and fatigued. Nevertheless, let us assume for a moment that this statement is correct and contemplate what the less surprising coup of the *King* would have looked like. From all we know—and Sulzberger and the *Times* were not excessively stingy with such information before the non-King-coup—the effects of a hypothetical King-coup would have been exactly the same. The Constitution would have been suspended, and along with it the scheduled elections, civil liberties, the parties, freedom of expression, etc. Leftists, communists and all those who resisted the king's "democratic" actions, such as dismissal of a Prime Minister, the prevention of elections for almost two years, etc., would have been sent to the "traditional" islands for "pacification," or put in prisons. Now, what would have been the difference? Except for a few small details, none. The King would not have been "pale," "depressed," "reluctant," "distressed," and so forth, while he was performing such official functions as attending swearing-in ceremonies, Cabinet meetings, and Easter celebrations with the army. And he also would have known before 2:00 A.M. on April 21, instead of right after 2:00 A.M. on April 21.

On May 3 then, Sulzberger's column "Prometheus Unbound" relates in detail the inside story of the coup. The coup, the reader is told, was the sole doing of three colonels who used "Prometheus," a "General Staff contingency plan drawn up under NATO and envisioning war with a communist country." Even Spandidakis, the Chief of Staff who was essential to putting "Prometheus" into action, was brought in only "about one hour" before the coup actually took place. Yet on April 27 Kamm had written about Lieutenant General Gregory E. Spandidakis' role in the plot:

> He was not one of the original sponsors of the coup, but apparently gave his support *early in its preparation*. (Italics supplied.)

If one follows the reporting of the *Times* from April 21 on, one sees that the people responsible for the coup keep diminishing steadily until finally only three colonels remain, leaving the King and generals and everybody else altogether unimplicated.

Now, even if one accepts the theory of two coups—the royal coup which was planned and the colonels' mini-coup which took place—the question still arises as to how a royal coup (which would have resulted in essentially the same measures as the so-called colonels' coup) could have avoided an undemocratic and dictatorial appearance. It seems to be safe to assume that Constantine would have wanted to avoid such an appearance. In the case of a royal coup something would have had to happen to blur the total picture and largely justify the King's action.

Not only Sulzberger's columns before the coup, but especially his column of April 23, in addition to other references in the *Times,* suggest the following: repeatedly and with increasing eloquence Sulzberger emphasized the overwhelming communist threat to Greek democracy. On April 23, he explained "the events that will now unfold in Greece," in analogy to the events of the 1940's, not as a quarrel between "'democrats' and 'monarcho-fascists'" but as "an outright communist assault." Quite clearly Sulzberger must have expected something for which he was providing the explanation beforehand, something which was, however, not going to take place: civil war. Instead of fighting the dictators, the Greeks remained quiet.

On April 29, Eder says in his report, "Lack of Protest Noted in Athens," that "a member of Greece's political aristocracy" had noted "the lack of protest after the military coup." This politician is quoted as having said:

> The colonels' coup, as a military operation, was beautifully done. But it was too quick for them. They crashed against a door and saw it was open. Suddenly, *instead of having two or three days to put down resistance,* they found that they had to

make decisions—political decisions—sooner than they thought. (Italics supplied.)

References such as these suggest that armed resistance against the coup on the part of the Greek citizens was a circumstance anticipated by those who planned the coup. Only against a background of a totally quiet and oppressed people did the coup, royal or otherwise, become a monstrosity impossible to justify before anyone with even a minimum of belief in freedom and democracy. The "events that will now unfold" never unfolded. It was this important circumstance which left the coup without a rationale.

In the unexpected quiet of the post-coup days, Sulzberger found the time to visit Andreas Papandreou in the Pikermi motel where he was temporarily being held prisoner. Sulzberger told of his visit in his column of May 5 and of Andreas' request for reading material. The following table pairs past evaluations of Andreas by Sulzberger and the books sent by Sulzberger to Andreas—a political prisoner in danger of execution.

EVALUATION	BOOK
That Andreas Papandreou had despoiled Greece politically	*The Splendor of Greece,* by Robert Payne
That he was a demagogue	*Ethics,* by Dietrich Bonhoeffer
That he was implicated in the Aspida Conspiracy	*Judgment on Deltchev,* by Eric Ambler
That he was faced with a maximum sentence of death for treason	*The Masque of the Red Death,* by Edgar Allan Poe
That he was a dangerous leftist	*From Russia With Love,* by Ian Fleming

After this, further comment on C. L. Sulzberger is hardly necessary.

Chapter 8

Greece and the American Conscience

I

In the more than twenty years since the liberation of Greece some two dozen governments have held power. Part of the explanation lies in a basic difference between Greek political parties and those of other European countries. With the exception of the extreme Left, Greek parties are not formed around a political program or an ideology. They spin, instead, around a particular political leader and move in and out of power according to the magnetism and durability of his charismatic personality. Intrigue festers in this type of hothouse politics, and the constant efforts to disrupt the parliamentary support of whatever party happens to be in power leaves little time to deal with the country's basic problems.

The monarchy in Greece has fed on this general chaos and has used it to promote its own ends. It keeps a firm hand on the army, the bureaucracy, and the gendarmerie, making sure at all times that its own people man the relevant ministries regardless of the political party in power. The power of the Palace, furthermore, has been written into the Constitution. The king has the constitutional right to choose the Prime Minister. Yet the king's choice, in the absence of a majority, is not *required* to reflect the largest parliamentary plurality. In those instances where the king ignores the results of an election and chooses the Prime Minister from the party with the second largest number of parliamentary seats, he is in clear violation of the spirit and intent of the

Constitution. And it is on this basis that he and his close advisers are constantly involved in the machinations of the politicians. The Greek king is not, and never has been, a *constitutional monarch* as this term is generally understood and accepted in England and the Scandinavian countries. The Greek king is a walking anachronism and the only one still extant on European soil.

The major supporters of the Greek monarchy, apart from the United States, are to be found among Greece's old families. Contrary to their counterpart in Western Europe, the Greek aristocracy is not hoary with tradition nor is it based on extensive land holdings. Its major pursuit is trade and business. The *nouveaux riches*, many of whom were collaborators who enhanced their position during the occupation and the early postwar years, have also allied themselves with the monarchy because of its being, traditionally, the strongest base for political power.

Given this economic oligarchy, the fealty of the army, the loyalty of the machinery of State, and, since the Truman Doctrine, the support of the United States, the Palace has reigned supreme in the Halls of Parliament. In the postwar period, the power of the King and his followers was never seriously challenged until the emergence of the Center Union party. And even this new coalition could have been corrupted and manipulated, or even tolerated, were it not for the rise within it of a group of deputies led by Andreas Papandreou. For the first time a new style of politics was introduced and a viable program for economic and social reform was proposed which threatened the interests of the economic oligarchy.

When, in order to implement its program, the Center Union moved to bring the bureacracy, the army, and the gendarmerie under civilian control, the Palace and the extreme Right attempted to remove the threat by parliamentary maneuver leading, finally, to the King's summary dismissal of the Center Union government in 1965. And when, despite everything, the Center Union was once again on the verge of an electoral sweep, the only remaining alternative was a military coup d'état. And that was brought about, as we have seen, at two o'clock in the morning of April 21, 1967.

II

The reaction in Europe was immediate. The Junta's claim that it had moved to thwart a communist takeover was dismissed as transparent propaganda. It was evident that the coup had taken place in order to prevent the victory of the Center Union at the polls. The supposed "innocence" of the King, which was so trumpeted in the United States, was heavily discounted.

Europe soon became the center of activity for the formation of anti-Junta organizations. Greek politicians who had escaped the Junta's dragnet soon turned up in Europe, some of them under mysterious and rather suspicious circumstances. The representatives of the United Democratic Left (EDA) took the initiative in forming the committees and pushed for a Pan-European Conference to elect a Central Committee for a Popular Front. As in the organization of the EAM/ELAS resistance movement during the wartime occupation, the extreme Left was once more in the driver's seat.

The few Center Union representatives who had managed to get out, and who were followers of Andreas Papandreou, were very much at a disadvantage. The Center Union had been destroyed in one fell swoop by the coup. Its leaders were among the first to be rounded up, and whatever initial resistance was being organized within Greece was being led by the only remaining party with any semblance of structure and organization—EDA.[1] The question in Europe now

---

[1] See Appendix III for the resistance manifestos of the Greek underground.

was the composition of a Popular Front to include subsidiary organizations in England, France, Italy, West Germany (which had absorbed the largest wave of Greek emigration to Europe, approximately 150,000), Austria, and all the Scandinavian countries.

Western Germany, Italy, and, ironically, Denmark, which is the mother country of the present Queen of Greece, became the focal points of Center Union activity.[2] The Center Union representatives insisted, but without much success, that all resistance organizations should reflect the pre-coup political conditions in Greece; that is, 55 percent for the Center Union, 30 percent for ERE, and 15 percent for EDA. The underlying problem was one of financial assistance. The Social-Democratic parties of Europe were unlikely to support a Popular Front controlled by the communists, and if Andreas Papandreou's followers in the Center Union failed to achieve leadership, the monies would not be forthcoming. The issue of funds had become critical since the underground leadership had been calling for assistance to finance the resistance movement then in the process of development.

Pressure was put on the Center Union in Europe to go along with the establishment of a non-party Front. The argument used was that national liberation struggles are not led by parties but by cooperative resistance movements. The Center Union representatives, however, were unwilling to go along with the dissolution of parties out of fear of being absorbed and controlled by the extreme Left. The Center

---

[2] Of all the European countries, the Danish government alone has denounced the coup officially and in unequivocal terms, and has continued to apply pressure on all of the NATO countries for the restoration of democracy in Greece. When the bravery of the Danish people is recalled during the Nazi occupation and their heroic efforts on behalf of the Jewish people, it is evident that Denmark is one of the few remaining countries with a soul. For their denunciation of the Greek Junta and the Greek Embassy's reply, see Appendix II.

Union also felt that any resistance front organized along the lines suggested by the EDA representatives would in the end wind up being financed by Russian funds since the European Social-Democratic parties would be unwilling to contribute. The Center Union then decided to attempt a Pan-European League for Democracy in Greece consisting of the various Socialist and Christian Democratic parties of Europe.

With the anti-Junta forces in Europe in such a state of disarray, and with new Greek politicians appearing in Europe under suspicious circumstances, new pressures began to be applied, behind which the Center Union representatives of Andreas Papandreou sensed the heavy hand of the United States. Suspicion began to mount that Greek agents of the CIA were infiltrating the Greek resistance movement in Europe with the aim of bringing about the *Second Phase* of the coup. The United States had been visibly embarrassed by the neo-fascist triumvirate which had wrecked the plans of the Big Junta, of which it was a part. The problem now was to get them out without touching off a civil war between the Little Junta and the King's supporters which could easily get out of hand if the Center and the Left joined in.

The Little Junta had been modified in the early post-coup days by forcing it to admit Lieutenant General Spandidakis and Constantine Kollias into its ranks, and to assign other ministries to non-political civilians. The next step was to broaden it further by introducing several former ERE politicians and the right-wing, anti-Papandreou members of the Center Union party who, not surprisingly, had not been arrested. This further broadening would tend gradually to undercut the power of the military triumvirate and ease the country into the kind of pseudo-democratic, national-unity type of government the Big Junta had planned all along.

Early in July of 1967, Major Arnaoutis, the King's military adjutant, turned up in London as Military Attaché to the

Greek Embassy. The Center Union representatives suspected that Arnaoutis was engaged in secret negotiations with Pavlos Vardinoyianis, a former Minister and Center Union deputy (now living in Paris), who had been implicated, together with Andreas Papandreou, in the alleged plot to overthrow the monarchy. Vardinoyianis' subsequent activities served to confirm the suspicions of the Center Union in Exile. With Athanasios Papadopoulos, the only other Center Union deputy abroad, Vardinoyianis started recommending a new policy line. Strangely enough, key EDA representatives backed Vardinoyianis' stand. All attacks against the King were to be stopped. He was to be pictured as having been totally innocent of any knowledge of any coup, and all efforts were to be focused on achieving a *détente* with him for the purpose of bringing about the Second Phase. The Papandreous, at the same time, began to be charged, by some members of this group, with a failure of leadership and with full responsibility for what happened because of their extremist and intemperate attacks against the King and the army, which served only to provoke the coup. Both, it was argued, were to be removed from the post-coup political scene.[3] To promote these ends, a Popular Front was to be created and located in Paris. Attempts were then to be made by the Paris Front to get the underground leadership in Greece to go along, and all factions were to cooperate with the United States in bringing about the Second Phase.

The Papandreou leadership of the Center Union Party balked. The EDA representatives then met secretly with some of the Papandreou supporters and pressured them to defect and go along with the plan, including the halt of

---

[3] Vardinoyianis, however, in private conversation with me in his Paris apartment, has dissociated himself from this attack on the Papandreous. The substance of this conversation will be outlined in the next section of this chapter.

all attacks against the King. The objective of EDA was to discredit the Center Union party in Greece and thereby absorb the Center-Left followers of Andreas. For this reason they played into Vardinoyianis' plan, intending all along to denounce him and the Center Union party at the appropriate time. EDA was clearly playing for the long run, and was cynically willing to go along with the Second Phase as a pure matter of short-run strategy for strengthening their hand and their influence among the now thoroughly disillusioned Greek people.

The United States and the King are, of course, opposed to the Andreas Papandreou wing of the Center Union party and would want to make sure that it does not get control of any European Popular Front. They would prefer to see some successor to the Center Union party emerge led perhaps by Vardinoyianis and George Mavros, which could then be brought into a national-unity government as the Little Junta was pushed more and more into the background.[4]

The counterstrategy of the Papandreou wing was to continue their discrediting attacks upon the King and to do everything possible to sabotage the Second Phase. They reasoned that if they could thus force the United States to turn to them for a solution, then, at the negotiating table they would agree, as a bargaining point, to allow the King to stay regardless of his past meddling in politics, on condition that his future role in Greece would be strictly constitutional and ceremonial. And, to strengthen their hand, they would stress the need for a solution along these lines if Greece were not to be turned into a second Vietnam; that the Soviet Union and the communist countries on Greece's northern borders might find it expedient, given the U.S. involvement in Vietnam and the outbreak of war in the

---

[4] Whether the Little Junta will cooperate is another matter, but it is doubtful that it could successfully resist the combined pressure of the Palace and the United States.

Middle East, to apply counterpressure on the United States by aiding and supporting a communist-led guerrilla movement in Greece.

III

Having decided to strike off on their own, it became necessary for the Center Union representatives to reorganize themselves on a Pan-European basis in order to coordinate their activities. In the immediate post-coup period, however, a leadership struggle developed between Vardinoyianis and Nicholas Nicolaidis, who had also escaped Greece and who had been the head of the Center Union youth group (EDIN) in Greece prior to the coup. Many of the Greek students studying at the various European universities had been members of EDIN. With Nicolaidis now in Europe, and the parent party in a complete state of disarray, EDIN in effect reconstituted itself as the Center Union Party in Exile. Nicolaidis then began representing himself to the European governments as the General Secretary of the party. This was immediately challenged by Vardinoyianis, who was quick to point out that such a post had never existed within the Center Union party in Greece.

Had Vardinoyianis himself assumed the leadership upon his arrival on the European scene, most of the Greek Center Union sympathizers in Europe would have closed ranks behind him. But when Vardinoyianis was interviewed in Turkey a few days after the coup, he assumed a conciliatory tone and absolved the King of any responsibility for what had happened. And for more than twenty days thereafter he failed to make a single public statement concerning the events in Greece.

It was out of the failure of Vardinoyianis to act that Nicolaidis was able to fill the leadership vacuum. Nicolaidis had made contact with most European governments and had succeeded in getting financial support from the Italian

Socialist and Christian Democratic parties and from the large community of 170,000 Greek nationals working in Germany. As a result of his activities, Nicolaidis had his citizenship canceled by the Junta. The next step, in view of Vardinoyianis' challenge, was the legitimization of Nicolaidis as General Secretary of the party-in-exile. The issue had become virtually a matter of Apostolic succession. It was then decided to hold a party convention in Bonn, West Germany. The Social Democratic Party of Germany (SPD) offered its headquarters in Bad Godesburg and provided most of the financial assistance for the meetings. The conference was scheduled for July 29–30, 1967, and representatives were sent by the local Center Union chapters of France, West Germany, Italy, Austria, England, Sweden, Belgium, and Denmark. All told, including observers, 75 persons were in attendance. Vardinoyianis also arrived for the conference as well as the only other deputy-in-exile, Papadopoulos.

Papadopoulos had been visiting in West Germany when the coup took place. He immediately condemned the Junta and implicated the King, and had his citizenship removed at the same time as Nicolaidis. But Papadopoulos, a former butcher and tavern owner, lacked the necessary qualities of leadership and he soon fell under the complete sway of Vardinoyianis—the well-educated, wealthy, and articulate politician from Crete. From that point on, Papadopoulos stopped his attacks against the Junta and the King and took all of his cues from Vardinoyianis.

The first day of the Bonn Conference was dominated by Vardinoyianis. In a lengthy speech, at times cajoling and at other times threatening, he laid down his policy line. He announced that he and Papadopoulos, as the only deputies-in-exile, had the exclusive right to speak for the Center Union party. He then demanded that all attacks on the King be stopped—that Greece was a "crowned democracy" and that the King could not be removed by a rump caucus of doubtful legitimacy passing resolutions in a foreign country. This was in flat opposition to the sentiments of the young Center Union Turks gathered in Bonn, most of whom were students with strong socialist and republican tendencies. When Vardinoyianis sensed the tenor of the conference, he became adamant. He challenged the authority of the conference to speak for the Center Union or to extend in any way the ideological position of the party.

In the name of the President of the Center Union, George Papandreou, he reiterated the basic principles of the Party: (1) the people rule; (2) the army belongs to the nation; and (3) Greece for the Greeks. These alone defined the ideological limits of the party and without express approval from the President, then under house arrest in Athens, Vardinoyianis insisted that no one had the authority to redefine or extend them in any way. He accused the conference of usurping the powers of George Papandreou and declared that he, Vardinoyianis, would in no way be bound by any decisions or policy positions promulgated by the Bonn Conference.

The conference quickly erupted into a shouting match with Papadopoulos literally screaming at the delegates and then marching halfway out of the hall only to return to his position at the head table when he saw Vardinoyianis holding his ground amid the turmoil. When things quieted down it was pointed out by some of the delegates that the three tenets of the Center Union party had been formulated before the coup, and that the time had now come to apply them to the concrete situation of a military dictatorship—that, in other words, the people were not ruling, the army was running the nation, and Greece no longer belonged to the Greeks. In view of this state of affairs, it was argued, the Junta, the King, and their foreign supporters were to be denounced publicly. The whole institution of the monarchy had to go.

Vardinoyianis stood firm. The coup was in no way to be used to give any new ideological direction to the Center Union party. The three principles of George Papandreou had to stand as they were without deletion or addition. Then in an impassioned voice, Vardinoyianis declared, "I know suspicions exist about how I escaped, but I am not going to give any account of who helped me and thus cause still others to be imprisoned. I have been made to feel as though I am here to get my clearance from you. My position is clear—the three principles of the Center Union party as stated by our leader, George Papandreou."

The next day, Vardinoyianis boycotted the meetings and stayed in Bonn, secretly locked up in a hotel room issuing orders and receiving periodic reports from his supporters at the conference.[5] The resolution extending the ideological base of the party roundly condemned the King and was passed by a vote of 53 to 4. Vardinoyianis had been repudiated and Nicolaidis was duly appointed General Secretary and official spokesman for the Center Union Party in Exile.

Four days later in Paris on August 3, I received a telephone call from Vardinoyianis, who invited me to his apartment. For three and a half hours in the late afternoon, Vardinoyianis explained his position in some detail. He identified himself with Andreas and pointed out that Margaret Papandreou had served as "koumpara" (best woman) at his wedding. He then went on to denounce the Center Union supporters at Bonn as political amateurs who, out of their inexperience, were sabotaging his efforts to work out a political solution for Greece. He described the King as an uneducated playboy who had made a mess of things. He was quite aware of the King's unpopularity with the

---

[5] After telling me that he was leaving Bonn at the end of the first day, we were both visibly embarrassed when at 2:30 the following morning I turned up inadvertently in his hotel room in the company of two of his supporters. I had been under the impression I was going out for something to eat!

people and shared their antipathy to him, but he stated that he was convinced that no solution to the crisis in Greece could be worked out which did not include the King—at least for the short run. He argued that an all-out attack on the King would only serve to drive him deeper into the arms of the Junta, thus precluding its overthrow; that, therefore, the King had to be encouraged in his resistance to the coup particularly since Colonel Papadopoulos, the real power in the Junta, favored the exile of the King in order to assure the long-term tenure of the Little Junta.

Vardinoyianis then made it quite clear that he had been, and continued to be, in contact with representatives of the King and the United States, and that his primary objective was to bring about the Second Phase before Colonel Papadopoulos could consolidate his position. At this point, the real purpose of the meeting emerged. He stressed emphatically, and pledged his "word of honor," that he would not enter into any deal which would not absolve Andreas Papandreou of all charges; that, indeed, the "national unity government" of the Second Phase would have to include Andreas as Minister, if not as Prime Minister. Vardinoyianis then denounced Nicolaidis and presented himself as Andreas' true friend who would best serve his political interests.[6]

The Nicolaidis wing of the Center Union party, however, regards Vardinoyianis' actions as a sellout of the Center

---

[6] I received a second telephone call from Vardinoyianis in Paris and met with him again on the 26th of August for two hours. He informed me that he was leaving shortly for Washington and would be there at the same time as the King (who was scheduled to meet President Johnson on the 11th of September). Again he reassured me of his loyalty to Andreas Papandreou and agreed that he would not enter into any deal concerning the Second Phase which did not provide for (1) the release of *all* political prisoners, (2) the retention of their civil and political rights, and (3) a National Unity Government of Center Union and ERE representatives pledged to free elec-

Union, and of Andreas' leadership in particular. They look upon Vardinoyianis as the official spokesman for the right wing of the party outside of Greece, with George Mavros handling matters within the country. They point out that most Center Union deputies arrested in Greece have been the supporters of Andreas, and that Vardinoyianis' pose as a friend of Andreas is a fraud designed to lull his supporters until the Second Phase is consummated—at which time Andreas will be sent into exile stripped of his civil and political rights. The Nicolaidis wing is, therefore, concentrating on building up a resistance movement in Greece, with the FLN movement in the Algerian War serving as its model. It has already sent in trained experts in the manufacture of plastic bombs and is also planning to send in radio equipment and small arms for the resistance Center Union cadres being formed in Crete, Epirus, and Thessaly. By autumn, the Center Union in Exile expects its resistance movement to be in full operation. It is counting on the support of the Greek people to bring down the Junta and to square its account with the King and the entire institution of the monarchy.

What the final outcome of this leadership struggle will be is hard to predict at this moment. The Second Phase must count on a quick solution by the winter of 1967, before the various resistance movements in Greece become operative. Failing this, with Colonel Papadopoulos more than ever entrenched in power, civil war is a likely prospect with the distinct possibility of its being turned into another Vietnam should the communist bloc countries decide to support the resistance movement of the far Left. The fact remains, however, that the blame for the current

---

tions within a year. He also stressed that this would be the King's last chance to save his crown and that he intended to tell him so if they met in Washington. To my knowledge, Vardinoyianis did not show up in Washington.

crisis within the Center Union Party in Exile must be placed squarely with the party itself. The Center Union had all along expected a coup, yet it made no plans for resistance, nor did it provide for the succession of command in the event of a coup.

IV

It remains to make some judgment of the overall situation and the moral as well as political responsibility of the United States for what happened. United States involvement in Greece dates back twenty years to the Truman Doctrine. In his historic message to Congress (March 12, 1947), the President contrasted two ways of life:

> One . . . is based upon the will of the majority, and is distinguished by free institutions, representative government, free elections, guarantees of individual liberty, freedom of speech and religion, and freedom from political oppression.
>
> The second . . . is based upon the will of a minority forcibly imposed upon the majority. It relies upon terror and oppression, a controlled press and radio, fixed elections, and the suppression of personal freedoms.

U.S. intervention in Greece was in response to the threat of a communist takeover. A full-scale civil war was then in progress. Yet President Truman found it necessary to voice certain reservations about the Greek government he was asking Congress to support:

> The extension of aid . . . does not mean that the United States condones everything that the Greek government has done or will do. We have condemned in the past and we condemn now, extremist measures of the Right or the Left. We have in the past advised tolerance, and we advise tolerance now.

With U.S. military aid the communist insurrection was finally put down in 1949. And after the expenditure of $2 billion in support of Greek democracy, the *second* way of life has triumphed. This *dénouement* after twenty years of American influence was not in spite of, but *because of* the American presence. The details of this presence and this influence have been described in earlier chapters. It remains to attempt to offer some explanation of why the United States is to be found so often on the side of the military and the extreme Right in so many of the underdeveloped countries.

With the exception of the McCarthy period, there has generally been a separation between domestic and foreign policy. In our international relations, we seem to be in the grip of a paranoid fear of communism; that it is somehow our sacred duty to protect the world from this scourge. We see it everywhere, like a hot lava oozing quietly into every unprotected corner of the world. And everywhere barriers for its containment are erected, even if in the process we must ally ourselves with the far Right. Yet our reactionary policies abroad seem inconsistent with our liberal posture at home. This apparent inconsistency impressed Andreas Papandreou who, after twenty years as a liberal Democrat in the United States, was now faced in a very direct way with the reactionary interference of the United States in the internal affairs of Greece. His explanation for this state of affairs follows:[7]

What makes for the progress of democratic forces in its internal life is the balance of power among organized groups, be they regional or functional. In the end, both parties that govern the country on an alternating basis must pay heed to the needs of the various groups in a deeply pluralistic society. When it comes to foreign policy this balance is lost. With the exception of involvement in war, the average American displays, in general, little interest in foreign affairs. And then the pressures and counterpressures on the government are

---

[7] See Appendix I for the full text of Papandreou's speech.

limited fundamentally to approximately three groups. First, there is the Pentagon which, with the advent of the cold war, shaped American foreign policy as a tool for the containment of the Soviet bloc. It gave primary emphasis to strategic considerations in all dealings of the United States with other nations. Second, the CIA, as an outgrowth of the Office of Strategic Services which functioned during the Second World War as the key war intelligence unit, expanded beyond its initial purposes, and established an independence from the control of the government that made it possible for it virtually to chart a parallel foreign policy for the United States. Last, but not least, there are the American investors abroad and the exporters to the world market who have played an important role as a pressure group in the formation of American foreign policy. Under the circumstances it is not surprising that a military, bureaucratic, intelligence-oriented, and business-dominated foreign policy failed to keep pace with democratic developments at home.

Though change and reform in domestic matters are the result of democratic forces within the United States, they are treated with suspicion and distrust when they occur in other countries. U.S. foreign policy; in the postwar period, has thus degenerated into the apotheosis of the status quo. And when other people, in the underdeveloped countries, also wish to bring about reform and change and, as a result, are forced to oppose an entrenched oligarchy, they are soon regarded with deep suspicion as "dangerous leftists," "demagogues," or untrustworthy neutralists harboring anti-NATO sentiments. We tend, in the process, to support things as they are which, in many of the underdeveloped countries, means supporting the extreme Right. We find ourselves distrusting change because we fear that we may not be able to control it or, what is more, because we sense we cannot sell it to the Congress. And all too often, when we do grant economic aid, we insist on tying it in with the promotion of private enterprise in the recipient countries, as though private enterprise and democracy were causally and inextricably linked. Rather than assess the political and economic realities of the dependent nations, we insist willy-nilly in recasting them in our own image.

In Greece, for the first time in over thirty years, a non-communist political party had emerged with a program for reform. It quickly earned not only the hostility of the entrenched and the privileged, which was to be expected, but of the United States as well, which ought not to have been expected but was. The "new" politics of Andreas Papandreou was being built along Western European lines of party structure, organization, and discipline. This in itself strained the cohesion of the Center Union coalition and threatened its continuation. And it was this set of circumstances which led King Constantine into believing, in 1965, that he could accelerate its dissolution by arranging for mass defections. Instead, he wound up strengthening the very thing he had set out to destroy, by rallying the Greek people to the Center Union's cause.

V

The coup of April 1967 has provided the Greek people with an object lesson they are not likely to forget: that a reasoned and moderate-liberal attempt to reform a thoroughly corrupt society by peaceful means is not feasible. Young people with a social conscience and a sense of outrage will now feel that they have no choice but to move toward the far Left. The great experiment of a viable liberal Center working within the constitution has failed, and the lesson of this failure has been driven in hard. The Greeks will have to fend for themselves, and in the last analysis, it is they alone who will either have to live with the dictatorship or bring it down in a civil war. A Second Phase, which would exclude Andreas Papandreou, even if it is successfully brought about, will fool no one. The only hope for avoiding, sooner or later, the catastrophe of another civil war, is a reversal of U.S. policy in Greece. One cannot be sanguine about the prospects of such a reversal, yet the long-run self-interest of the United States demands it.

It is instructive, however, to note that after the coup the United States never officially suspended military assistance to Greece. It imposed what it called a "selective embargo" by *slowing down* the delivery of tanks and jet fighters. On July 7, 1967, the following dispatch appeared in the *New York Times*:

> The administration, encouraged by the apparent movement of the military Junta in Athens toward the restoration of constitutional government, is considering relaxing restrictions on United States military aid to Greece.

The full flow of tanks and jet fighters might now be needed as the resistance underground develops—leading, possibly, to civil war. As was not the case in the Dominican Republic, this time the United States will be able to collect an *accurate* list of communists leading the revolt. The United States seems destined repeatedly to create the very opposition it seeks so desperately to overcome. In the name of anti-communism it insists on sacrificing the long-run for the sake of a few ephemeral short-run gains.

Though the manifestoes of the Greek underground have already begun to appear,[8] the tanks and the jet fighters may be needed for another purpose. The July 7 news story in the *New York Times* masked a high-level interdepartmental conference that took place a few days earlier in the State Department. With representatives of the CIA and the Defense Department in attendance, the future policy for Greece was set down.

---

[8] See Appendix III for the text of a few that have been brought out of Greece.

Apart from the Second Phase of the coup, there still remains the Cyprus problem. Discussions are now taking place between the Junta and the United States to resolve the crisis along some variant of the Acheson Plan. One possibility is the partitioning of Cyprus into a Turkish and Greek sector to be followed immediately by double *Enosis* (Union). The only obstacle to the plan is the Cypriote leader, Archbishop Makarios. If he should refuse to go along with the plan for double *Enosis,* it is likely that a coup will take place in Cyprus to depose the Archbishop. The United States will at last have what it wanted all along—the security of the southeastern flank of NATO through Greece, with a military base on Cyprus as well. The U.S. presence in the Middle East will thus be militarily assured.

Whether the Second Phase or the plan for Cyprus will succeed is problematical. Events are too current, at this final writing, to venture any hard predictions. It is fairly certain, however, that virtually all of Greece's problems, past and present, stem from its constant vassalage to one great power or another.

Since 1947, the United States has had its turn. And the results have turned out to be disastrous for the Greek people. The fate and the future of Greece weigh heavily upon the American conscience.

Appendices

Appendix I

Foreign and Domestic Policy Positions of Andreas G. Papandreou

The following is a combination of two articles written in Greek and originally published in the Athenian newspaper, To Vima, on August 23 and 24, 1966. The text is the authorized translation into English in a revised draft. The final text was approved by Andreas Papandreou.

OUR COURSE AND OUR FUTURE: NATIONAL RENAISSANCE AND FOREIGN POLICY

by Andreas G. Papandreou

I

The foreign policy of Greece is of critical importance for the future of this country. It determines the conditions as well as the possibilities for internal development. Political and economic decisions in the area of foreign policy affect, moreover, the freedom of the Greek people and determine in large measure their future welfare. Who makes these decisions and on the basis of what principles is of the utmost importance if Greek independence is to be maintained. Without this independence in foreign policy, we cannot control our own destiny. Our position in the community of nations will then be determined by foreigners, as it has indeed been in the past, and not by ourselves.

The primary and proper function of Greek foreign policy

is to promote the interests of Greece and to implement Greek objectives and Greek ideals. We are aware, of course, that independence is not without its constraints; it is not to be confused with abandon. It carries with it grave responsibilities. But we must insist that Greece be treated as a full ally and not as a satellite whose foreign policy becomes subordinate to that of another nation.

There is a style of action and a mode of thought that is distinctly Greek. It is deeply rooted in tradition and in Greece's long and historic struggle for independence. This will for independence is part of the Greek heritage and must be recognized as such. It cannot be destroyed. The Right, however, flouts this spirit of independence and seeks its dissolution. The ideology which guides its thought and its actions is a mixture of defeatism and rampant individualism. Its views are provincial. It engages in easy accommodations. And it invariably follows the lines of least resistance—all of which lead to the betrayal of our national sovereignty. It rewards and encourages the flatterer and the conniver. It mimics the consumption patterns of other countries. And it promotes an individualistic and personal myopia which is incompatible with the national welfare. It is, furthermore, deeply rooted in the past and believes that Greece fulfilled its duty to the world and to itself in antiquity; that we have, in other words, settled our accounts and have no grounds for pride on the basis of our present or future achievements.

Above all, the Right has bargained away the national sovereignty of Greece. It has become the overseer of foreign interests in return for their protection and support. This Greek oligarchy and its foreign masters are bound together, and together they will fall. They and they alone are responsible for the political deterioration of Greece and for its failure to take its proper place within the community of free nations. Greece no longer has an independent voice in international affairs. It speaks as dictated to and does not decide or attempt to resolve its own urgent problems as it sees fit. Instead, it has surrendered its rights to the political and commercial claims of outside parties.

We have been led by the Right into a false and ephemeral security and have been forced to purchase it by paying the price of submission. These servile tendencies of the Right were reinforced by that portion of the Center Union which defected and betrayed its own party and its electoral mandate. That is why today's great struggle in Greece is a national struggle cutting across past party affiliations. It is a struggle for the unity of the Greek people. It is a struggle against those who would sell off the interests of Greece cheaply for their own immediate profit. In the great national and liberal camp of the Center, there is no room for such thinking. The Center Union is open only to progressively minded Greeks.

One problem which the Right has neglected to deal with is the mass exodus of young Greeks to other countries. Indeed, the Right has contributed to this costly outflow of human capital by virtue of its failure to include the youth of this country in the economic development of the nation. Discouraged, devoid of any hope, and with no future prospects to hold them, many young people have sought their fortunes abroad. Should this pattern of emigration continue, Greece will within thirty years be transformed into a country of old people catering to the many tourists who have even now become the main economic prop of Greece. Greece will by then be reduced to a picturesque Monte Carlo where the only vestige of Greek color will be the trooping of the Palace guard. But Greeks, by their very nature, are not servile. They will fight this denial of their long and distinguished past. Greece is a proud country. Its destiny is nobler and far greater than that envisaged by the Right—Greece merely as the Florida of the Common Market.

We here in Greece are grateful to the Right and the betrayers of the Center Union for the blow of July 15 [1965].

They have convinced us that we as Greeks must have as our national goal the democratic rebuilding of Greece in such a way as to preclude its manipulation and exploitation for the benefit of a closed indigenous oligarchy and the foreign interests they so capably serve. The idea of a *National Renaissance* must become our major preoccupation. It must become the basis of our political existence. Everything must be determined in relation to it. A claim will be just if it promotes it; unacceptable if it is contrary to it. A party will be national if it supports it; unpatriotic if it fights against it. Only in this way will we be able to reclaim our national honor by calling an end to the usurpation of the term "nationalist" by those who make a mockery of it.

One who expressed well the idea of a democratic national renaissance was Ion Dragoumis. In 1905 he wrote:

> The knowledge that Constantinople is being lost is cruel, but I am not so much shocked by Byzantine dreams as I am by the notion that whether we possess Constantinople or not, we are mediocre, moribund, wretched, and asleep. The words "Let us take Constantinople" symbolize not "Let us rebuild the Byzantine Empire," but rather *"Let us be strong."*

Thus must the idea of size be transformed into an ideal of quality. One is an idle dream; the other a potential to be seized. Let us indeed be strong! As Greeks we must not bear our nationalism as a burden or something to be ashamed of. We must mobilize it and set for ourselves great and bold objectives for the rebirth of Greece as a modern and independent nation. But this cannot be done without freeing our foreign policy from the dictates of others. By determining our own foreign policy we will, at one and the same time, be free to decide our own domestic policy for the economic and social development of Greece.

The Greek people must make it clear that they want a Greece

———*United:* Where the forces for national division and political disruption will be neutralized and where the major democratic forces will work together for the *National Renaissance* of Greece.

———*Strong:* To pursue consciously the goal of becoming a modern Mediterranean and European nation to be taken seriously by others.

———*Proud:* To be projected onto the world scene not solely because of its illustrious heritage, but also because of its ability to contribute to the modern world. Greece must not be identified exclusively with ruins and statues. It must also be esteemed for the creative achievements of its people today.

———*Independent:* With full power to determine its own future.

We must pursue the realization of our national objectives with determination and with full regard for our long-term interests. We must not squander our national resources, as the Right has so wantonly done. A long-term national program will be required which will determine the fate of Greece. It must concern itself with feasible goals regarding population, industrial and agricultural production, diversification of the economy, infrastructure, urban planning, and so on. We must plan for the time when Athens will have doubled in size. Depending on the policy decisions made now, we will have either an Athens scarred with slums, or an Athens which will be a modern Mediterranean metropolis— an industrial, commercial, and intellectual center.

We must build for the future. Plans and forecasts must be made for the next two decades. 1986 is not very remote for the greater part of the Greek people. We can determine the technical factors for the future development of Greece, and politically we must undertake those policies needed for their implementation. It is only in this way that we will be able to improve our relative position with regard to the more advanced industrial countries of the West. And we must educate the youth of Greece to undertake those tasks that lie beyond the horizon. All this can be accomplished with a progressive and democratically oriented nationalism, and not with the reactionary self-serving policies of the present so-called "nationalist" Right.

II

George Papandreou and the Center Union have set the basis for a Greek foreign policy. The Center Union has proclaimed that it accepts the framework of our existing alliances. But along with the ascent of the Center Union to power, there came a fresh new approach to Greek foreign policy. The sellout of the Right, and the scandalous handling of the Cyprus issue by ERE, was replaced by the realistic and independent foreign policy of the Center Union. Within the framework of our alliance, there arose the proud voice of our much betrayed nation. The great "OXI" ["NO"] of George Papandreou to the proposal for a Greek-Turkish dialogue in June of 1964; the insistence that the Cyprus issue remain within the United Nations; the decisive support of Cyprus which forestalled the aggressive intentions of the Turks; and the public proclamation of George Papandreou in Salonika that an alliance which allows one ally to threaten another with extermination is not an alliance—these and other actions of the Center Union reclaimed our national honor and marked a new beginning in our foreign policy. At the same time, the resolution of our outstanding problems with Bulgaria and Yugoslavia, and the emphasis which was placed on the development of cultural and economic relations with the East and Africa, were further indications of the new foreign policy line of the Center Union.

After many decades, the people of Greece once more returned to power with the Center Union, and Greece was again able as a truly independent and sovereign nation to determine its own foreign policy. This new foreign-policy approach of the Center Union derived its strength from the people and from the overwhelming mandate given to the Center Union by the Greek people in free elections. It was exercised with restraint and within our treaty commitments, but with an all-important difference—Greece was no longer a satellite. It was a sovereign nation free to develop its own foreign policy in keeping with the long-term interests of Greece.

The solution of Greek foreign-policy problems must be based not only on the international rule of law and within present treaty arrangements, but also in keeping with the national interests of Greece. It must be made clear that:

1. Greece is a peace-loving country. It is a principle of transcendent importance that we try at all times to solve our foreign-policy problems by peaceful means. But if our territorial integrity, our independence, or our freedom is ever threatened, we will protect them with all the means at our disposal and at all costs.

2. Short-term problems of foreign policy should be examined in the light of our long-term goal to transform Greece, ultimately, into a major Mediterranean and European nation. The foreign policy of this country can no longer be determined behind the scenes and in violation of Greece's national interests. Greek foreign policy will become the property of the Greek people, and will not be bargained away by puppet governments subservient to foreign interests.

3. We will apply the realistic principle of European diplomacy: that the goal of foreign policy is to achieve concrete results and not merely to score debating points. Greek foreign policy must serve Greek and not foreign interests. Greece must become master of its own destiny.

4. We must see our alliances, in part, as a tool for the promotion of our national interests. The national interests of Greece must serve as a counterbalance to the faithful execu-

tion of our obligation as allies—and Greece will always execute these obligations faithfully within this limit. We will observe our alliances and execute to the full our obligations. At the same time we claim our rights, as we must. Turkey is a prime example; it never found it difficult to exercise pressure for the promotion of its national interests, and on that account it gained more, not less, respect.

5. We must protect our freedom to decide in case of international crises. We must make it clear to our allies that the existing treaties of alliance bind us only in case of unprovoked attack.

6. We must maintain full freedom in the development of our cultural and economic relations with all countries that really wish to cooperate with us on an equal basis and on peaceful terms.

7. We must have full control of the decisions that concern the basic sectors of our economy. It is contrary to the general welfare and to the economic and social development of Greece that autonomous centers, foreign States, or private firms such as Litton Industries, be free to make independent decisions affecting the Greek economy. And the necessary financing for the development of our economy must not contain binding clauses that limit the path of our development or restrict our freedom to plan for the external and internal sectors.

8. We must also develop a collective notion of our country's defense. In the military sector, this requires the development of defense plans not only in terms of a possible World War, but also for the eventuality of local wars—the threat of which, with the evolution of the Cyprus issue as handled by the servile government of the Right, remains always with us.

9. In the economic sector, we will require a careful preparation for, and evaluation of, the hard competition of the Common Market. A responsible re-examination of the terms of our association will also be required.

10. In the political sector, it is mandatory that Greece gain the respect of other countries and be treated as an equal. The public services must be made independent of foreign embassies and businessmen. State secrets must be protected and not delivered clandestinely to foreign governments and interests. Foreigners must be made to learn that no Greek government will tolerate their intervention in Greece's internal affairs. And finally, an inviolable rule of operation must be that the sole instrument of Greek foreign policy is the *legitimate* government of the Greek people—the government, that is, that comes from the *free* expression of the will of the Greek people. No outside force can have the right to determine, or interfere with, the foreign policy of Greece.

Alliances, of course, arise from a conflict of wills and a collision of national forces. From where will Greece derive its strength so that the goals it sets for itself will be harmonized with its international obligations?

First, by using its alliances as a means for applying pressure. That is precisely what Turkey has done in NATO with regard to the Cyprus issue.

Second, by keeping world public opinion informed on matters of national importance for Greece.

Third, by the degree to which the Greek government reflects accurately the popular will. Only when a government of the people is returned to power, when Greek governments are no longer subservient to the Palace or to foreign influence, only then will Greece be in a position to fight for the true interests of Greece and the Greek people.

Fourth, from the political and economic vigor of the country.

Fifth, from the correct functioning of the instruments of State—particularly the Ministries of Foreign Affairs and National Defense.

The primary task of a government based on popular support will be to clean up the Ministry of Foreign Affairs. It must become a Ministry of *Greek* Foreign Affairs. Ministers and staff who collaborate with foreigners or other extra-governmental authorities (without responsible orders politically covered by the responsible ministers), must be summarily removed, and the restaffing of the Ministry with capable, Greek-thinking employees must be quickly realized. And until the smooth functioning of the foreign office is once more restored, the Foreign Minister will be assisted, in the lower echelons of the foreign office, by "counsels" who will assure the maintenance of a national foreign-policy line and guarantee its full implementation.

Equally important for the promotion of national goals is the *professionalization* of the army. Our prestige on the world scene will be greatly enhanced if our armed forces are made to serve the national interest, as they should—if, that is, the juntas within the army are abolished and thus prevented from interfering in the country's internal political problems. When, as it will, the Center Union returns to power with wide popular support, it will limit the political role of the army and put an end to the intolerable factionalism that existed in the pre-July [1965] government. Military officers who dare to question the national character and purposes of a popularly elected government will have no future and no place in the Greek army. Officers of the Greek army will not be allowed to engage in politics. They will be required to serve the public interest in a professional way and under civilian control with regard to overall policy. As Latin America has so often proved, democracy cannot long survive when civilian control is weak and when the army of a nation feels free to determine, without regard for public sentiment, when a government shall or shall not rule. Corruption and dictatorship are inevitably the end result. The new Greek army will be modernized with regard to equipment and the structure of the armed forces, but it will not be permitted to point its sword at the throat of Greek democracy. Together with the Ministries of Foreign

Affairs and National Defense, the Ministries of Coordination, Education, Commerce, and Labor must be reorganized
if they are to deal effectively with the critical and pressing
problems of a reborn Greece.

The Center Union, genuinely expressing the people's will,
has been summoned to a new role. It is no longer simply
the party of democracy. It is now the basic force for national
change. It is, in a word, the party of *progress*. With the
youth of Greece at the vanguard and under the inspired
leadership of George Papandreou, we will march toward a
brighter future and we will transform vision into reality.

On March 1, 1967, Andreas G. Papandreou, gave an address before the Foreign Press Association. In it he gave a brief analysis of American foreign policy as it relates to Greece. He asserted, among other things, that United States foreign policy does not represent the values of American society and that military considerations often determine the attitude of the United States toward a country and its role within it.

Two American Embassy officials, having seen a written copy of the speech during the luncheon, walked out, and later the Embassy released the following official statement:

> *Our representatives judged that it was not permissible, as members of the American Embassy, to remain at the luncheon in view of the broad and general attack which Mr. Andreas Papandreou in his speech undertook against the United States of America.*

The following is an excerpt from Andreas Papandreou's speech.

The cards are stacked in Greece. Ever since it became a free nation, Greece has been under the tutelage of one or more friendly powers. The sponsor nation has always seen fit not only to direct political developments within Greece, but also to shape its foreign policy, more or less independently of vital Greek interests. Since the Greek civil war, the United States has replaced England as a sponsor nation. It poured funds into Greece both for the purpose of guaranteeing the success of the then government forces, and for the purpose of assisting in the reconstruction effort that followed the civil war. This gave it an all-powerful place in Greek political life. In a very real sense it participated in the process of government formation. American diplomats did and still have a very close connection with the Palace, and maintain excellent relations with rightist circles in Greece. This may explain the fact that American officials have almost always argued for the institution of a "strong" King in Greece; in other words, for a constitutional practice which contrasts sharply with the corresponding practice in the crown-democracies of the West.

Of course, it is a mistake to think of American foreign policy in Greece as monolithic. Present in Greece are at least three distinct American agencies—the State Department, the Military Mission, and the CIA. American policy in Greece has displayed the basic characteristics of the cold-war foreign policy which has dominated the world scene since the death of Franklin D. Roosevelt. This policy has been characterized by some insensitivity to the needs and the problems of the allies of the United States, especially so in the case of small nations. Asia and Latin America offer outstanding examples of the tendency of American diplomacy to dominate completely the political development of associated countries. In Europe the pattern is quite different, but maintains the basic characteristics of relative disregard for national sensitivities, and for the independent charting of a nation's own course within the framework of the alliance.

Greece, as a developing nation, a nation barely emerging from a semi-colonial status, is extremely sensitive about its national independence, its freedom to chart its own international political course, its right to pursue freely its own national interests without placing in a quandary its allied relationships. *We do not raise the question concerning the participation of Greece in the NATO alliance.* But at the same time we demand that Greece be recognized as an independent nation which, pursuing its own particular interests, *has chosen* to be a member of the Western Alliance. Greece refuses the status of a poor relative or of a satellite. It insists on its right, while executing its obligations as an ally, to determine its own course. It affirms its right to expand its commercial, economic, and cultural relations with all other nations, independently of the bloc to which they belong. It assigns special importance to developing good relations with its Balkan neighbors, the countries of the Near and Middle East, and the new nations of Africa. It insists on its right to follow closely developments in the European area, where a reduction of tensions, a rapprochement among nations of the East and West, and a new approach to European solidarity is taking place. But above all, Greece insists that its allies cease interfering in its internal political affairs.

Since America itself is the key foreign force on the Greek scene, and since I have lived for almost twenty years as a member of the academic community of America, I should like to express some thoughts which may give a clue to the peculiarities of American foreign policy. It has always been a source of surprise to me how a country which is making democratic progress on the internal front—with persistent difficulties, however, on the race question—could blunder so much in foreign policy as it has in the case of Vietnam, Latin America, and even in its relations with its NATO allies. One has the feeling that somehow it has never felt secure, that it has never been satisfied with a reasonable allied relationship, but has always instead been driven to establish complete dominance in the affairs of allied states.

It has been said quite often that America became a world power so suddenly that it did not have the time to adjust to its new role. But all this is quite superficial. The reason lies far more deeply than this. What makes for the progress of democratic forces in its internal life is the balance of power among organized groups, be they regional or functional. In the end, both parties that govern the country on an alternating basis must pay heed to the needs of the various groups in a deeply pluralistic society. When it comes to foreign policy, this balance is lost. With the exception of involvement in war, the average American displays, in general, little interest in foreign affairs. And then the pressures and counterpressures on the government are limited fundamentally to approximately three groups. First, there is the Pentagon which, with the advent of the cold war, shaped American foreign policy as a tool for the containment of the Soviet bloc. It gave primary emphasis to strategic considerations in all dealings of the United States with other nations. Second, the CIA, as an outgrowth of the Office of Strategic Services which functioned during the Second World War as the key war intelligence unit, expanded beyond all expectations, assumed responsibilities and functions way beyond its initial purposes, and established an independence from the control of the government that made it possible for it virtually to chart a parallel foreign policy for the United States. Last, but not least, there are the American investors abroad and the exporters to the world market who have played an important role as a pressure group in the formation of American foreign policy. Under the circumstances it is not surprising that a military, bureaucratic, intelligence-oriented, and business-dominated foreign policy failed to keep pace with democratic developments at home.

It does not come to us as a surprise to learn that America is going through an internal upheaval. The Negro problem is one cause, but there is probably a deeper cause which underlies the conflict around the Negro problem and the foreign-policy problem. It is that America is not living up to American ideals. And it is felt mostly by the intellectuals and by young people who have come straight from the history books, who have been imbued with democratic principles, who found the War of Independence and the Declaration of Independence a glorious period in their past, who have made a faith out of national independence, national integrity, national self-determination, and the equality of all peoples. For them the American presence in Vietnam is an error of the first degree, and the American involvement in the internal affairs of other nations intolerable. So there exists an internal problem and an external one, both related to the hiatus between ideals and practice.

Surprising though it may seem, the reduction of Greece to

a semi-colonial state and its relegation to the Middle-East desk of the State Department, is a by-product of the conflict which has developed between America's insistence on dominating its Western allies and France's reaction to this insistence by virtually breaking away from NATO. For it is this conflict which has forced America to seek a more solid foundation in its southeastern NATO flank. It is this that has led to its peculiar attempt to link together Greece, Turkey, and Iran. Indeed, it is interesting to note that Johnson's recent budget address indicated that $234 million, or almost half of the total arms aid going to seventy nations around the world, will go to these three countries. It is this that creates the impetus on the part of the United States to force a solution of the Cyprus problem in the context of the NATO alliance. And it is this finally that makes it essential for the United States to demand an allied security in Greece which goes beyond the norms of an alliance with an independent nation such as Greece. The disclosures that are going on now in America concerning the role of the CIA in foreign policy should leave no doubt as to what we mean when we insist that Greece should belong to the Greeks.

The following is a translation from the original text of a speech delivered in Athens to graduates of the School of Economics and Business Administration, the Pantios Graduate School of Political Science, and the Graduate School of Industrial Studies, on February 21, 1967 at the King George Hotel.

ECONOMIC PLANNING AND PRIVATE INITIATIVE

by Andreas G. Papandreou

The topic I have selected to talk about is broad and most ambitious. As a professional economist, I have been concerned both with the process of economic development and with planning. As a man in politics, I have been concerned with transferring some of the skills of the economist to the solution of immediate and pressing social and economic problems in a country which finds itself somewhere between the two extremes—the last and the first on the scale of development.

In a previous lecture I have said that "development" includes all basic political, social, and economic interactions that define and shape life in the twentieth century. Tonight I would like to discuss the concept of development in a more meaningful manner. I would like to propose that development in our day—especially as it relates to the political, social, and economic process—may be defined as follows: *Development is a planned structural change on a national level aimed at achieving a sustained rate of national, social, economic, and cultural growth which would otherwise be unattainable.*

In my view this particular use of the term development serves a number of purposes: (a) it lays emphasis on the fact that the postcolonial development is identified with *national planning* that attempts to bring about structural change, (b) it assumes a strong national character, and (c) it is tied to the movements of national independence. Moreover, the meaning of economic and social development among underdeveloped people is strongly identified with the awakening of national conscience. Indeed, the world's poor nations have been forced to adopt national planning as a tool of development in order to reduce the international inequality of income and wealth, and narrow the existing gap in the standard of living between rich and poor lands.

For these reasons in almost all underdeveloped countries national development plans have become the guiding lines for shaping current economic policies. And in spite of all the technical inadequacies of these plans, the basic characteristic is that they offer a blueprint that outlines the process of social and economic development. It is, therefore, necessary to outline the basic steps in the preparation of an ideal development planning program under optimal conditions. It is also necessary to indicate briefly the nature of the deviations from the ideal model which result from the biases imposed by objective conditions prevailing in the economy.

First, there should be a scanning of alternative paths in order to discover all possible feasible time-paths that an economy may follow. Unfortunately, the limited informational capabilities of any planning agency make such a thorough scanning process practically impossible. Because of these limitations, economists and planners are forced to assume the responsibility of limiting the number of possible alternative time-paths that an economy may follow realistically. The dismal reality of the limited informational capabilities of any planning agency also limits the "field of vision" of the plan that determines the level and composition of the national development program of a country. An example may be cited for better clarification. Isn't it rather peculiar that most development plans have a five-year time target? And how could a planner evaluate social investment in education within this five-year period when the returns from such investment can only be reaped twenty years hence? The five-year limitation of the plan therefore is basically arbitrary. It is a decision that simplifies the task of the scientist as well as the task of the government.

The feasibility of a time-path depends, of course, on the initial conditions prevailing in the country, i.e., national boundaries, national resources, transportation system, educational and technical levels, administrative structure, etc. But the planner's decision on whether or not to consider some particular time-path as being feasible depends directly on the theoretical model he is ready to employ. When empirical data are available, such a model may be used by the planner to forecast a number of alternate development time-paths that may be adopted. Undoubtedly, each time-path requires a variation in the economic policy pursued, if it is to give reasonable results. Alternative hypotheses for development, however, require the accessibility of technical data which are beyond the influence of the State. Because of such limitation in the availability of data, the predictive ability of any model is also limited. As a result, the use of qualitative information in the planning process becomes inevitable.

Second, the political authority should consider the alternate feasible development time-paths offered by the planners and formulate a rule for selecting some optimal time-path. Such a rule is necessarily an expression of the *values* held by the political authority, and therefore it is not scientific. It is purely political. Whether the selection process will be successful depends upon the manner in which the planning agency presents the alternate feasible time-path selections to the political authority. In short, the decision whether a country will adopt a policy of rapid industrial development, or whether it will remain basically an agricultural economy, rests entirely with the political authority. In addition, the selection of measures for the implementation of the economic policy rests also with the political authority and it is of utmost importance. That is, to what extent would the political authority consider it acceptable to undertake institutional changes parallel with the structural changes? The more courageous the political authority is in this realm the wider become the "fields of vision" for the final selection of the time-path for economic development.

The few comments that concern the scientific structure of the plan are being made here in order to dissolve, once and for all, the deliberate or unwillful confusion that has been created by scientific terminology and academic jargon which characterize the various development plans before they are submitted for debate. Of course, the role of the scientist and that of the planner is a fundamental one. But, the prerogative for making the critical and decisive choices rests with the political authorities and constitutes purely a political decision. It is the duty of the political authority and duly constituted government to state clearly to all productive classes and to the people who have vested the government with its powers, the criteria which are being used in taking the critical decisions. The government should not hide its decision-making process behind the cloak of academic respectability, *i.e.*, behind scientific jargon and superficial scientific objectivity. It must always be borne in mind that printing the plan as a document requires its widest circulation among the public. It must also be understood that any development plan is, by and large, a political document. It is indeed a sort of *contrat-sociale*—it is a vector of the prevailing power structure in a society.

For those countries that are seriously concerned with their development, an economic development plan is the *center of gravity* of the political process. It must, therefore, be understood that whoever holds political power will use this power decisively in order to influence the initial formulation of the plan and to tailor the application of the plan in accordance with his own vested interests. It is thus reasonable to expect that pressures will be brought to bear by the various chambers of commerce and industrial organizations, labor unions, farmer cooperatives, local and regional governments, foreign embassies, and international organizations, for the government to adjust the targets and measures of implementing the plan to fit their own vested interests or points of view.

It is natural that a country's development plan generally reflects the established *value system*. And when the political authority oversteps the circumscribed boundaries set by the system, the outcome is, more often than not, that the plan will not succeed. Consequently, when a government wants to implement a plan whose targets are in conflict with the established value system, it will be necessary for the government to undertake difficult, but unavoidable, reforms that will bring about a new balance among the existing political powers, *i.e.*, it will create a new value system, a new mentality if you will.

The long-run target of a democratically elected government should be the formulation of a new balance among the existing political powers that will allow the government to promote the economic development of the country beyond the realm of vested interests, beyond the values of the establishment.

The basic assumption of democratic planning is that all regional productive classes in the country participate actively in the formulation and implementation stages of the plan. And it is very important that all groups participate in the formative stages of the plan. That is, there must be an expression of general and substantive participation of the people in the political authority of the country—democratizing the political process if you will. For as we approach higher levels of political democracy the meaning of the so-called "establishment" becomes progressively less important. For this reason, we must realize that formulation and implementation of a development plan reflects the real development capabilities of the economy which can only be realized when the political authority in the country is truly democratic.

Incidentally, it must be noted here that economic development and development of democratic process in a country are historically inseparable. For a better democratic process and a greater participation of the people in the public decision-making process presumes relatively high per capita income, higher levels of education, a culture that values human self-respect, and modern transportation and communication systems. These objective conditions are the unbroken links of the chain that lead to economic growth and development. Significantly, economic development today requires the formulation of a planning program that reflects not only the people's needs and productive capabilities, but also a program that demands a democratic decision-making process with the active participation of the people.

Private Initiative and Planning

The truly critical aspect of planning, insofar as its success is concerned, has to do with its implementation. In many cases a plan turns out to be a collection of pious hopes which remain unfulfilled because its targets lie beyond the objective capabilities of the economy.

The government's ability to carry out a plan, what I call the *effectiveness* of a plan, depends on two things: First, on the behavior of data which the government cannot control over the life span of the plan, *i.e.,* international prices, wars, etc. The better the forecast concerning data behavior, the more effective the plan will be. Second, on the extent to which *decision making* is centralized. The more centralized is the decision-making process in the economy, the more likely that the plan will be effective.

But we are also concerned with the *efficiency* of the plan.

The efficiency of the plan, in contrast with the effectiveness of the plan, reflects: (a) the degree to which the plan's targets represent real social needs, and (b) the resource cost of achieving those targets. The question of the plan's efficiency suggests another proposition: that the more *decentralized* the decision-making process in the economy, the more efficient is the plan. This last proposition is founded on a basic assumption, namely that the information-processing capabilities of a planning authority are quite limited in relation to the task cut out for it by a centralized authority. That is, extending the information-processing capabilities of a central agency beyond the point where it can carry out a plan efficiently involves a relatively high social cost.

Decentralized decision making in an economy fundamentally means two things: First, information processing takes place in a decentralized fashion. For example, in a market economy it is carried out by the basic pricing system through the behavior of households and the firm. Second, each basic behavior agent behaves according to a *general rule or strategy* which is either self-imposed or imposed by a centralized authority. Significantly, *decentralized decision making is, in principle, compatible with planning.* If the rules or strategies followed by the basic behavioral agents in the decision making are imposed on them by some central authority, we may say that the economy is both *planned* and *decentralized.*

Centralized and decentralized planning, are, of course, simplified ideal-type models which are useful for the analysis of planning problems. However, in reality they do not exist. For there is no case in economic history where the central authority has been able to eliminate the independence or freedom of action of all behavior agents so as to be able to control every single action of these agents.

In reality, a planned economy is based on decision making that is a *mix* of both centralized and decentralized decision making. That is, the decision making of a planned economy is always *dual*. Here, it is useful to avoid irrelevant theoretical discussions that concern the two other poles, *i.e.,* complete centralization, or complete decentralization.

What is more important, in fact, is the degree of mix of centralized and decentralized decision making—a combination which is a function of both magnitudes and targets set in the plan, and the stage of the country's economic development.

The effective use of the concept of dual decision making rests on the assumption that there is an overall plan where the targets (both quantitative and qualitative) and the method of implementation have been carefully selected. On the basis of this assumption the economy is divided into two sectors—let us call them sectors A and B. The performance of sector A is directed by the central authority through: (a) the setting of quantitative targets (tons of steel), (b) the imposition on the components of behavior agents of rules of behavior or strategies, and (c) the degree of mixture of both methods, as the case may be. That is to say, sector A is well represented by the centralized planning model, or the decentralized planning model, or by some mixture of the two.

The performance of sector B, in contrast, is guided by the central authority because it influences the environment of decision making of the units that make up this sector. The environment may be institutional, technological, a market mechanism, etc. It is, therefore, apparent that in reality there are three criteria that enter the dual nature of the decision-making process in a planned economy. First, the division of the economy into sectors A and B. That is, what categories go under sector A and what categories under sector B. Second, in reference to sector A, it is important to determine the extent to which the central authority bases its decision making on quantitative targets, and to what extent on qualitative considerations, or on general rules of behavior imposed on the firms. Third, the degree of determination on the part of the central authority to take the necessary steps that will create the conditions that will guide the decision-making process of the productive units in sector B. On the basis of the above three criteria we can compare the degree of centralization (or decentralization) in decision making. For a number of planned decision-making economies we could further conclude that decision making, as in the case of the Soviet Union, is much more centralized than the comparable process in Yugoslavia, Sweden, Norway, Denmark, and France. Similarly, we can conclude with certainty that the Greek economy today is *totally* unplanned, in spite of the fact that a number of development plans have been prepared by the economists of the Center of Planning and Economic Research.

In Greece there exists governmental interference in the economy of unprecedented magnitude, as well as an unbearable amount of bureaucracy. That is to say, there is a high degree of arbitrariness on the part of the civil servant, a lack of meaningful targets, indifference for any consequences that may result from certain policies, and complete absence of correlation between goals and policy measures which are presumably initiated to facilitate the attainment of these goals. For it is critical, and must therefore be understood, *that government interference and planning are two entirely different concepts.* Planning assumes and requires the interference of the central authority. Such interference, however, is very carefully estimated and guides the aggregate economy toward the targets described in the plan. This type of interference must, of course, be distinguished from what is generally thought of as haphazard government interference—an interference that finally creates more development problems in the country than solutions to specific problems it attempts to solve in a haphazard fashion.

Any serious planning program, any rational decision-making process, must look forward for the complete mobilization of sector B, *i.e.,* the private sector of the economy, whether it be small or large in relation to sector A, *i.e.,* the *public sector.* At this point the question must be raised as to the type of economic activities that will be included in the private sector of the economy. Generally speaking, this will depend on the targets of the plan, the objective capabilities of the economy, and the country's stage of economic development. The wider the gap, *i.e.,* the more ambitious are the targets in relation to the objective capabilities of the economy, the larger must be the public sector and the degree of centralization. In fact, most of the significant development "take-offs" are identified with highly centralized decision making where the role of the private sector is not very significant. For most underdeveloped countries, therefore, economic development and centralized decision making go together. In contrast, for a developed country, like Sweden, future development becomes increasingly decentralized. For a developing country, such as Greece, the equilibrium point of dividing the economy into two sectors, *public* and *private,* can be placed somewhere between the two poles. Perhaps this is the reason why such division creates a number of difficult policy-making problems.

To facilitate economic growth and development in Greece, I believe that the country's infrastructure, transportation and communications, credit, and education and health must belong completely to the public sector. In contrast, agriculture and commerce should be in the private sector. Finally, industry must be both public and private. Heavy industry should probably be public while light industry should be private.

The second question that is of interest is what specifically do we mean by the proposition that industry should be partly public and partly private? Does this mean that the industry must necessarily be *nationalized?* Because there exists considerable confusion as to the meaning of this proposition, I shall undertake a more detailed answer to this question.

Nationalization of industry serves two purposes. The first is to check or control the activities of the economic units that belong to this industry. The second is to transfer the net income or profits of the firms to the public treasury. If the purpose of the government is to control completely the productive units of this sector, or if the country's development plan requires that all profits accruing to this sector be invested in financing the plan, then and only then will nationalization of the industry be necessary. If neither of these two conditions prevails, nationalization of industry is neither necessary nor desirable. At any rate, there are a number of other ways that can be used effectively in placing the industry in the public sector. Using fiscal policy, it is always possible to transfer partly the net income of the industry to the public treasury. However, it is important to differentiate here between the concept of placing an industry in the public sector, and making the firms in the industry public enterprises. Undoubtedly, an industry can be placed in the public sector without making it a public enterprise. One way to achieve this is to draw policy guidelines and rules of behavior that can be imposed on the firm's management.

In the Greek case, it may be necessary to nationalize those industries that are related to the country's infrastructure, *i.e.*, national transportation and communications, credit system, education and health. This does not, of course, mean that such nationalization ought to be complete. A number of exceptions for the development of private educational and hospital units may very well be indispensable for the country's rapid growth and development. Similarly, the economic policy applicable in the case of heavy industries should also be flexible.

Nationalization of the conversion of private enterprises into public enterprises is, of course, a prerogative limited to the central political authority. It must be understood, however, that various local governments, such as provinces, towns, and villages, can generate or operate certain types of municipal enterprises. The capabilities for local development in this direction are indeed considerable. In this context, the meaning of community development as a social process is broader than that of nationalization. That is, community development creates the incentives for the development of producers' cooperatives and the establishment of municipal enterprises, such as local public utilities. For all levels of local government our analysis imposes no specific constraints. Local governments should be in a position to undertake the establishment of municipal enterprises that are directly related to the economic base or the infrastructure of the local economy.

Farmer cooperatives, for example, have an unlimited "field of vision" in undertaking business initiatives. Freed from governmental interference and governed democratically they could begin to display more initiative in establishing enterprises in all three sectors of the economy, *i.e.*, agricultural, commercial and marketing, and light industrial.

Such municipal social cooperation can contribute significantly to economic growth and development. The character of this type of social cooperation is basically decentralized, for the decision-making process of municipal cooperatives belongs to the private sector of the economy.

Both formulation and implementation of a development plan must be based on regional units that have executive authority. They can either be quasi-public or quasi-private. These organizations will be responsible for guiding the development plan, the structure and the level of economic activity in the respective regions of the country. These units should also be vested with the power of establishing regional enterprises that private initiative is not attracted to or is unable to undertake, that is, projects deemed necessary for the development of the region.

The basic reason for choosing small regional organizational units to develop business initiatives is that when *external economies to scale* exist—that is, when there is interdependence in efficiency among the various economic activities—the market mechanism in conjunction with private initiative does not lead to rational economic solutions. In such cases, the "field of vision" for the enterprises must widen so as to be able to use effectively the gains that result from economic interdependence. For those enterprises or industries that fall into the private sector of the economy the government must outline the institutional framework under which the firms will operate. In this manner the government can optimally mobilize private initiative and influence, indirectly, the level and direction of the private sector of the economy so as to facilitate the attainment of the targets outlined in the plan. In contrast, the existing institutional framework inhibits entrepreneurial growth and limits private initiative. In short, the established institutional framework undermines the fulfillment of the targets set in the plan.

Currently, if a businessman wants to survive and succeed he must use influence-peddling intermediaries to carry out his business with minimum bureaucratic interference. Purely legitimate commercial businesses, for example, cannot be transacted unless influence is peddled. Thus, you need such influence to get credit, protect your profits from domestic and foreign competition, prevent labor wages from rising and last, but certainly not least, to evade taxes. The tradition of influence peddling in Greece is, indeed, pitiful. The moral character of the people has been affected, and a high degree of immorality has permeated both private and public life. The magnitude of immorality becomes more apparent when it is realized that the influence peddled by the politicians is identified with the few oligopolies and industrial complexes in the country. As a result, politicians assume certain obligations toward these groups which conflict with their duty to protect the public interest. This kind of behavior also prevails among Greek civil servants. The outcome of this influence-peddling system is that the powerful entrepreneurs and businessmen are treated individually with special favors.

To break free from the vicious circle of influence peddling and favoritism it is necessary to introduce, in double-quick time, a considerable amount of objectivity in the bureaucratic process. That is, we must simplify and reduce bureaucratic red tape, and make public the process of dealing with governmental agencies. Moreover, the citizen and businessman must be informed of his lawful rights as well as his obligations. In general, it is necessary to adopt business incentives in the private sector that will eliminate the peddling of influence and the personal character attached to favoritism.

The current regime of rationing credit and granting tax incentives must also be abandoned. In turn, the allocation of credit and the granting of tax incentives must be placed within the framework outlined in the plan so as to facilitate the attainment of the plan's targets. In addition to these reforms, it is necessary to simplify the tax system in order to reduce the extent to which entrepreneurs are intimidated by the tax collector. Beyond these reforms, however, Greece's tax system must be restructured so as to permit the introduction of additional tax reforms that will promote economic growth and development, will contribute to a more equitable distribution of income, and will permit a fairer participation of the less well-off people in national consumption.

The credit system in Greece must undergo grass-roots reforms. Above all, it is imperative that objective criteria be established for allocating credit. These criteria must not only be rational and fair to all businesses, but they should also promote economic development. In short, the banking system must abandon the mentality of "money-changer" that has made the cost of credit unjustifiably expensive.

The central government, together with the regional and

local authorities, has the obligation to expand the country's industrial base. Otherwise, it will be impossible for the private sector of the economy to fulfill successfully its own share and responsibilities. One way to start is to establish, as soon as possible, a public organization with sole responsibility for the preparation of feasibility studies concerning all sectors of industrial activities in Greece in order to help firms and banks to reach more rational economic decisions.

Finally the government must make a serious effort to protect and promote small industries and handicraft enterprises. Over and above the attempt to make credit more readily available to these enterprises it is necessary to establish a service that will provide firms with consulting services on market information, administration, and research.

Another unique characteristic of the influence-peddling establishment is the large number of monopolies and oligopolies that exist in Greece. Undoubtedly, monopolies result in the misallocation of resources and, therefore, inhibit economic growth in a developing country. At the same time, monopolies earn abnormal profits and prevent a fairer or more equitable distribution of income. Often monopolies are justified by their supporters on purely economic grounds. It is, for example, argued that technological requirements and the size of the market justify the existence of monopolies. It can be argued, however, that opening the national frontiers to foreign competition and to a large and expanding market may be the answer to this argument. Such action alone may not be the solution to the problem. For a country such as Greece the lowering of protective tariffs and the increase of international competition must go hand in hand with the industrialization of the country and the lowering of average unit costs. In case this kind of development is not realized, the Greek economy will end up subservient to foreign capital. We must therefore search elsewhere for the solution to our problem.

For those monopolies which depend entirely on favoritism, advertisement, and aggressive activities, there can be only one solution, namely the "busting of the trust." Breaking up these monopolies will result in greater competition and efficiency among firms, higher quality products, lower unit costs, and lower prices. In case, however, there is a need for the establishment of giant-size units—needs that may be dictated by technological and market size requirements—the solution to the problem is not the breakup of the monopolies, but rather their control. But it must be emphasized, once again, that both control and guiding behavioral rules must be geared toward the fulfillment of the plan's targets. Such policies will also take care of the problem of abnormal profits. Fiscal policy can be used at any time to transfer these profits to the public treasury. In case neither controls nor fiscal policy nor a combination of these two measures is sufficient to do the job, the only alternative left is to place the enterprise under the public sector.

Foreign Investment and Planning

Any kind of national development planning program is strongly related to the role of foreign investment and foreign enterprise. Greece, I have stated elsewhere, needs a foreign capital inflow of $200–250 million per year for a period of ten years in order to attain an annual growth rate of 8 percent. This is the order of magnitude of foreign investment that international experience suggests will be needed by a country at a stage of economic development comparable to Greece's. Assuming that this kind of capital is used to fulfill the targets of a plan which is scientifically drawn up, it will be possible ten years hence to bring about a viable structure of the Greek economy and to put the economy on a sustainable growth path.

To achieve rapid growth, however, it is necessary to utilize existing resources in the most efficient and productive manner. Borrowing abroad to pay for increased consumption of luxury goods today not only inhibits current economic growth and development, but it also creates obstacles to growth because of the existing balance-of-payments constraints. Consequently, it is imperative that efforts be made to reduce or even eliminate conspicuous consumption and luxury imports so as to channel scarce resources to areas that are more productive. Thus, a more efficient use of existing resources will help reduce our foreign-capital requirements for a sustained 8 percent growth rate.

There is, however, another question that must be answered which is basic to the type of development we decide to pursue. Under what conditions and under what terms ought we to accept foreign investment in our country? Foreign investment is, of course, welcome in Greece as long as it serves mutual interests. And this general rule has not been kept thus far. In most cases foreign capital was treated preferentially and was granted monopoly rights for the exploitation of the domestic market and the country's natural resources. And on many occasions foreign investments were *prevented* from entering areas where domestic monopolies have been operating. The reason is, of course, obvious. *Vested interests will not permit unwanted competition coming from abroad.*

It is, therefore, necessary to stop granting monopoly preferences in order to attract business investments from abroad. At any rate, foreign investment contributes to the country's economic growth and rapid industrialization as long as it increases domestic competition. Monopolies, in contrast, reduce the competitive market conditions and inhibit economic growth. Moreover, powerful monopolies undermine the democratic institutions in the country. It is easy to realize, for example, that in Greece's case there are a few monopoly industrial complexes which are not only completely controlled by foreign capital, but are also supported actively by their respective governments. In addition, these monopolies use their gigantic economic powers to corrupt the country's public administration, to wield undue influence in the governmental decision-making process for the protection of their vested interests, and in the final analysis, to topple any government that attempts to follow a national economic policy that is bound to abolish monopoly preferences or eliminate privileges granted unjustifiably to influence-peddling foreigners.

It is reasonable to ask now what will happen to the Greek economy if the inflow of foreign business capital is seriously curtailed as a result of adopting a new foreign economic policy. I have already said, and I am saying it again, foreign capital is welcome in Greece so long as: (a) foreign investors are willing to invest in Greece competing with the domestic investors under similar competitive conditions, and (b) foreign investments contribute to Greece's industrialization. Another way of accomplishing exactly the same goals as those of foreign direct investment is to substitute partly foreign business investment with borrowing in the international market. Direct borrowing is, more often than not, much less burdensome than the preferential terms usually granted to foreign capital. In this manner we could use the borrowed funds to finance, in whole or in part, the establishment of Greek industrial enterprises. Such a solution has distinct advantages. First, it precludes foreigners from controlling a significant portion of the Greek economy, and second, the cost of borrowing in the international capital markets is lower in the long run.

The prevailing rate of interest in the international money market, for example, ranges between 6 and 7 percent. In contrast, the monetary burden for servicing foreign business investments, on many occasions, is three times higher. The cost differential between direct borrowing and servicing direct investments—which is in excess of 15 percentage points—will be sufficient to finance the cost of training businessmen, managers and administrative executives, and technical personnel. In the meantime, Greece can hire the services of foreign experts to organize the technical and managerial parts of the newly created enterprises. In this manner Greece can attain: (a) a greater supply of foreign capital in the international money markets at substantially lower cost, (b) greater benefits from the use of modern techniques and modern organizational experience, (c) more rapid transformation of modern technical and organizational methods in the domestic economy that will permit the country to catch up with the operations of the foreign firms, and (d) a strong national character among the Greek enterprises.

Finally, I would like to add that the views I hold on this subject rest upon the basic premise that economic development in Greece can only be realized when the Greek people control their own economic and political decisions, or better yet, when the duly elected government in Greece represents truly the will of the people. Economic subjugation, in contrast, inhibits growth and development and it conflicts with the goals of national economic and social development. In conclusion, it may be said that, in spite of the well-known statelessness of all capital, it is necessary that there should be an equilibrated balance between borrowing in the international capital markets and the acquisition of capital goods through bilateral clearing agreements. If this can be achieved, Greece will not depend entirely on the supply of capital of any single country.

Appendix II

Diplomatic Exchange Between the Danish and Greek Governments

Text of telegram sent to all NATO members by the Danish government on May 5, 1967.

Developments lately in Greece have made a profound impression in Denmark. The Danish Prime Minister and Minister for Foreign Affairs, Mr. Krag, has on several occasions expressed publicly the deep concern felt by the Danish Government and the Danish people over the abrogation of democracy and of the constitutional rights of liberty which has taken place in a country to which we have several links. The Danish Government hopes that present conditions in Greece will be of short duration and that the multitude of people who have been imprisoned—or deported—on political grounds will be set free at the earliest. On the whole we hope that Greece will at the earliest time return to free and democratic conditions. The Danish Government believes that it is of the utmost importance that no doubt could be cast over the will of the North Atlantic Alliance to safeguard its democratic ideals.

NOTE VERBALE

The Royal Embassy of Greece present their compliments to the Ministry of Foreign Affairs and have the honor to inform them that they have been specially instructed by the Greek Government to draw the attention of the Danish Government upon the following:

The Greek Government considers recent manifestations in Denmark and most particularly after the last political developments in Greece, as intolerable interferences in purely internal Greek questions and are therefore obliged to address to the Danish Government the strongest protest.

Statements by Danish officials questioning the right of the Greeks to settle their own internal problems, the Danish insistence upon trying to raise before such an evidently incompetent jury as NATO a discussion offending Greece, the openly hostile manifestations of part of the Danish public against the King and the Government of Greece, denote a voluntarily planned campaign by which a direct intervention in internal affairs is attempted, and Greece is slanderously attacked by false and perfidious accusations, fabricated in the workshops of international communism.

The Danish Government are gravely mistaken if they think that their attitude helps democratic forces in Greece. In reality they are merely encouraging Greek communists in their subversive activities.

If the Danish Government are so much concerned over internal Greek affairs they should have been better informed about the situation prevailing in the country and should know that the new Greek Government does not seek to abolish democracy but to fight against communism, which is, as everybody knows, the permanent strangling of freedom.

They should also know that nobody is persecuted in Greece for his opinions, unless he has committed crimes or has tried to help, by underground activities against the security of the state, at enforcing a communist dictatorship in Greece.

It is to be regretted that allied governments in NATO should be so unaware of recent political history in Greece or of the delicate and vulnerable position of a country, which has faced continuously during the last twenty-five years a deadly communist threat, imposing special measures for the safeguarding of freedom and democracy.

The Greek Government are at a loss to understand the reason of the deep concern shown by the Danish Government as regards the acts of Greek communists. This is not smaller than the interest expressed by communist countries.

Nevertheless they refuse to give credit to the view that the clamorous and unwarrantable Danish reaction regarding the Greek Government might be dictated by internal political considerations. Such considerations for party reasons at the expense of the internal difficulties of an allied country would of course be contrary to the generous traditions of the Danish people and for this reason the Greek Government discard a similar eventuality.

Moreover it was accepted until now that only totalitarian states interfered directly in the internal affairs of foreign countries and a dangerous precedent will be created if such tactics were to be followed also by democratic governments. Because these tactics should not only be condemned from a point of view of political ethics and international law, but are also extremely harmful when applied by one member of an alliance against the other; frictions thus created fatally result in weakening of ties and decrease of defensive capabilities.

The Greek people bitterly resent the intolerable attitude of the Danish Government and their efforts to misrepresent a patriotic movement whose aims are to renew on sound bases and consolidate a truly democratic regime.

The Greek Armed Forces who unanimously intervened to avert a civil war are mostly made of men having fought against fascists as well as totalitarian communists; men who have risked their lives and have shed their blood to defend the ideals of the Free World. They are deeply offended by slanderous attacks alleging that they wish to abolish freedom in Greece.

The Greek people and their Armed Forces who have so often stood up against tyranny, are not prepared to receive directives or guidance as regards the way in which they should fulfill their duties toward their fatherland, in view of the fact that they have suffered far greater sacrifices to defend their liberties and free institutions than those who today appear as their censors.

If it is true that the Danish Government's interferences in Greek internal affairs are conditioned by good will, Denmark should in fairness take also into consideration the repeated and long-since publicized decisions of the new Greek Government headed by the Attorney General of the Supreme Court of Justice to restore the country to normal parliamentary life as soon as conditions will permit.

The present National Government of Greece in any case have no intention of abandoning their line of patriotic political orientation and are firmly determined to pursue their historical task as they are in a better position to know the aspirations and interests of the Greek people.

They feel obliged to protest most strongly against the hostile Danish manifestations, coming particularly from an allied country with which Greece wishes to maintain the closest friendly ties, and they request the immediate cessation of Danish interferences in Greek internal affairs.

Copenhagen, 16 May 1967.

[Seal: Ambassade
de Grèce,
Copenhague]

To the
Ministry of Foreign Affairs,
Christiansborg Palace,
Copenhagen.

P.J.I. Ref.No. 124.D.1.
NOTE VERBALE

The Ministry of Foreign Affairs has the honor to refer to the Note of May 16, 1967, from the Royal Greek Embassy and, in reply, to inform the Embassy as follows:

The Danish Government must reject the protest of the Greek Government.

The objective of the NATO alliance is to protect the freedom, democracy and internal rule of law of the Member States.

The violations of the fundamental principles of democracy that have recently taken place in Greece may raise doubts about NATO's will to safeguard its basic principles.

The Danish Government reiterates the hope that the present state of affairs in Greece will be of short duration and that the country will very soon revert to free and democratic conditions.

Copenhagen, May 23, 1967

To
The Royal Greek Embassy
Copenhagen.

The following letter, published in the New York Times *(May 21, 1967), is included in this Appendix for the questions it raises concerning NATO. The writers are professors in various universities in Italy.*

FATE OF GREECE

To the Editor:

As colleagues of Andreas Papandreou we are understandably anxious about his fate. As his hosts last August for a series of lectures on mathematical economics, we grew to respect him both as a scientist and as a man. But aside from this special case we, along with many of our fellow citizens, are deeply concerned over the broader tragedy which has befallen Greece. The Italian government and Parliament have expressed this concern in no uncertain terms.

One aspect of recent events in Greece is particularly disturbing because it points to a possible threat to our own country as well. We feel this aspect deserves close scrutiny by the American people.

How is it possible for an army which is a part of NATO (as is our own) to be used by a partisan faction of officers to suppress the very freedom it was supposed to defend, without as much as losing its good standing within the structure of NATO? Even if we can rule out any more direct role by NATO, is this not already a form of complicity?

We have always believed that NATO was designed to defend us from tyranny, but episodes such as this—and Greece was only the most recent and most shocking incident of a series—cannot fail to erode our trust in NATO and thereby in its most powerful member: the United States of America.

What we need are concrete proofs that our faith has not

been misplaced. The United States must beware of dissipating that accumulation of goodwill which reached its peak in the final year of the Kennedy administration.

Bruno De Finetti
Federico Caffe
Siro Lombardini
Luigi Passinetti
Antonio Pedone
Luigi Spaventa

Rome, May 12, 1967

Appendix III

Resistance Manifestoes of the Greek Underground

FIERY RESISTANCE MANIFESTO

All Greek Patriots Arise As One Against The Rapers Of Our Freedom

Mikis Theodorakis, Member of Parliament in the United Democratic Left party (EDA), president of Democratic Lambrakis Youth movement and leading figure of *Laiki* (People's) Music Movement (Composer of the music for films such as *Zorba the Greek* and *Electra*), has issued this fiery resistance Manifesto. It is the voice of embattled Greece heralding the new anti-fascist resistance. It is the voice of our indomitable people, the voice of the courageous Greek Youth, the voice of the generation of "114."

MANIFESTO OF MIKIS THEODORAKIS

The King, conspiring officers, and perjured judges, co-operating with the imperialists, dissolved Greek democracy. This treasonous act is a result of panic and will lead directly to the inevitable resolution of our internal political crisis. It will lead directly to the uprooting of the throne and its protectors and its vassals from our land.

With their execrable act the pitiful puppets of foreign powers have placed themselves outside of the Greek nation. The Greek people have condemned them. Their end, which is nearing, is the final blow that all free people deal to tyrants.

Our country is a captive country. Arrests have reached tens of thousands, hundreds of thousands are persecuted, no one yet knows the exact number of victims. Among the imprisoned, who have been inhumanly tortured, are the outstanding leaders of the Left, the EK, and even the Right. The rapers of our people's freedom are preparing new concentration camps and have set up death courts.

Fascism has struck Europe again after thirty years; it struck at the cradle of civilization, at the heart of democracy, at the bright and proud acropolis of humanism.

We appeal to all the world's democrats and particularly to those of Europe to stand decisively at the side of the embattled Greek people. We Greek patriots, for our part, are organizing the patriotic, democratic resistance, with optimism and faith in the indomitable strength of our people. Our country's history is great and glorious. We have, tens of times, confronted ironclad enemies, and have been victorious. We realize that the new historic struggle is very difficult and hard as it is decisive and beautiful because it will lead us to a brilliant victory to freedom, to freedom in a non-crown—a real—democracy; to national independence, to the patriotic unity of our people, and to a national renaissance.

Greek workers, peasants, public servants, professionals, technicians, intellectuals, patriotic officers, navy and air force men, the proud youth, men and women, young and old, all Greek patriots arise as one against the rapers of their freedom. They put aside their political differences uniting under a common standard that reads: *Freedom, Democracy, Greece*. They join to do battle in one national, patriotic, anti-dictatorial front. For us there exists now but one common ideal, one common purpose: How shall we take Greece out from under the shameful tyranny, at any cost? In our hearts flares a burning hatred for the tyrants, the liquidators of the Constitution, the rapers of democracy, the enemies of freedom, the traitors of the nation, who believed that with force they could bring our free people to their knees. Let them be sure that soon they will be trembling before the anger of the heroic Greek people. And then there will not be found a nook or cranny of Greek soil to hide them. In the land where democracy was born, tyrants die.

Down with the monarcho-fascist dictatorship! Out with the foreign locusts!

Down with perfidious Kollias! Long live democracy! Long live the Greek people!
Long live Greece!

Athens, April 23, 1967

Mikis Theodorakis

Postscript: Urgent appeal that this message reach its destination. Let it be copied by hand, by typewriter, by mimeograph, be printed and distributed from friend to friend, from house to house, from city to city. Let it reach its destination outside of Greece; and be distributed in Greek and other languages to foreign newspapers, foreign commercial representatives, travel agencies, foreign diplomats, and foreign embassies.

OPEN LETTER FROM THE GREEK PATRIOTIC FRONT TO THE FREE PEOPLES OF THE WORLD

Democrats of all countries,

Above the wall of the enormous concentration camp that Greece has now become, the whole of the Greek people send you their fraternal salutations and express their deep gratitude for the solidarity which from the very beginning was evident in the entire world through popular, student, and union movements and, in the case of Scandinavian countries, governmental actions.

The upswell of world public opinion, the demonstrations which took place in most of the capitals and the main cities of Europe against the outrageous violation of the undeniable rights and the most elementary liberties of man perpetrated by the CIA and King Constantine of Greece, succeeded momentarily in slowing down the repression, the pattern of which is only too familiar, by those who have usurped the name of the "Greek government."

In May 1967, General Patakos, Minister of the Interior of Greece declared: "We are not murderers." Twenty-two years before, Marshal Goering, Minister of the Air Force during the Third Reich, himself declared at Nuremberg: "Never have I ordered the murder of any person; never have I ordered cruelty as long as I had had the power of preventing it." What Hermann Goering's declarations were worth is well known. The murder of the lawyer N. Mandilaris "by the crew," so they say, "and the captain of the freighter which transported him clandestinely" was made public reluctantly and gradually in order for the Junta to pretend ignorance and even surprise of ("the body of a man with an unknown identity has been washed ashore . . ."), informs us on the one hand of the value of Patakos' declarations, and on the other causes us to worry about the fate of political prisoners, the number of which increases daily by the hundreds. Thousands of families have not been able to find the names of their arrested relatives on the published lists.

———*Where are these men?*

———Is the Island of Youra only a "façade" to hide the existence of secret concentration camps, from where the "bodies of unknown men" will begin to float in our oceans?

To answer these questions, it is sufficient to underline the fact that, besides a complete lack of control, the Junta has illegally rescinded Article 18 of the Constitution, the very article which stipulates the prohibition of torture and the death penalty for political crimes; this has been done with the obvious intention of covering its acts with a pretense of legality.

However, world public opinion has already judged them, and the government of free Greece will judge them for what they are: criminals of the law.

Yet, meanwhile, the lives of the democratic elite of Greece, of political men, of thinkers, of poets who are not only ours but also yours, are threatened.

The only means of efficient control is the coordinated and decisive action of a free people who want to stay free.

We, the Greek Patriotic Front, in the name of the persecuted Greek people, call upon all free men, all the truly democratic governments, to strengthen and coordinate their efforts to save the lives and force the immediate liberation of Greek political prisoners.

Athens, May 29, 1967
The Greek Patriotic Front

[Translated from the original French by Françoise Genty]

Patriots, democrats, friends of the Greek people.

Spread all over the world, by all possible means, the news of our people's struggle against fascism and dictatorship.

United, let us overthrow tyranny.

United, let us raise the sun over Greece again.

NEWS BULLETIN OF THE PATRIOTIC FRONT. ATHENS, MAY 1967. No. 2

DEMOCRATIC RESISTANCE

In spite of the suddenness of the attack, the massive arrests, and the cynical reign of terror which the fascist dictators have let loose over the whole of Greece, the Democratic Resistance of the Greek people made itself felt from the very beginning of the coup d'état. In Athens, Piraeus, and Salonika, proclamations and tracts were immediately put into circulation calling upon the people to unite in the resistance against tyranny. All patriots who escaped the Nazi-inspired blockades of the military met with the warm and active cooperation of the people and immediately organized themselves in groups for the Democratic Resistance. Three days after the coup d'état, printed proclamations were circulating widely, bearing slogans, directions and news. On April 23, a written and taped declaration by Mikis Theodorakis, composer and deputy to the National Assembly, circulated widely throughout Greece. In this declaration Mikis Theodorakis said: "The King, the conspiring officers, and the perjurious members of the judiciary have, in co-operation with the Americans and merchants of arms, abolished democracy in Greece. The sorry instruments of foreign interests have thus placed themselves outside legality and the Greek nation. They have already been condemned by all Greeks. Their end—which is not far away—will be the end free peoples reserve to tyrants. We call upon democrats throughout the world, and more especially Europe, to stand decisively by the side of the Greek people and their struggle. We, Greek patriots, are organizing the Democratic Resistance against tyranny with absolute faith and hope in the unvanquishable powers of our people."

All Greeks, in a common movement, are putting political differences aside and are uniting beneath the common flag, bearing, as its motto: "Liberty, Democracy, Greece." For us there exists but one ideal: "to deliver Greece from the shame of tyranny. In the land which gave birth to democracy, the fate of tyrants is death."

Hundreds of clandestine meetings have been and are being held throughout the country, with the defense of the political leaders' lives and the liberation of all political prisoners as their aim and slogan. The menace to Andreas Papandreou's life; the kidnaping toward an unknown destination of Ioannis Passalidis, the aged president of EDA, and of Ilias Iliou, the leader of the Left, who is gravely ill; the brutal handling and the humiliations that Kanellopoulos, Papligouras, Rallis, and other leaders of the Right have been and are being subject to; as well as the information pertaining to the projected assassination of Manolis Glezos and other leaders—have shaken the entire nation and have multiplied the efforts of every patriot toward the rebuilding and unification of all patriotic forces, with no political distinction.

Patriotic solidarity, expressing itself through the people's eagerness to help those fighting for democracy, has surpassed all expectations. Patriots are being hidden from the fascist rage. Printed material is being circulated with enthusiasm. On Holy Thursday, the Resistance Organization of Athens put into circulation thousands of tracts bearing the slogan: DOWN WITH THE CRUCIFIERS OF DEMOCRACY. On Easter Sunday, all the age-long, customary meetings took on a marked resistance character. Post office censorship, in some instances, went as far as to prohibit the transmission of the usual Easter greeting "Happy Resurrection," because of the connotations it had acquired. Ever since Easter Monday, walls in Athens, Piraeus, and other cities in Greece are filled with Resistance slogans. The paid instruments of dictatorship, infuriated, are reinforcing their blockade system, hoping to arrest patriots and stifle patriotic conscience in our land. Simple housewives are forced to scrape the slogans off the walls, but they, heroic mothers of Resistance fighters, have nothing but scorn for the executioners of democracy. The militarists, faced with the mounting wave of popular opposition, are losing their *sang-froid*. The bandit Patakos has declared that all patriots surprised in the act of diffusing tracts or writing slogans on walls will be shot on sight, but the heroic youths of Greece have always despised such threats.

FORMATION OF THE PATRIOTIC FRONT

The news of the formation of the Patriotic Front has been hailed with enthusiasm. Patriots are continuing the forming of the organization. It is characteristic that everybody has, in these moments, completely put aside the political differences which formerly separated him from his comrades in today's common struggle. The youth of all political parties is fighting a brotherly fight in the formation of the Democratic Resistance. The unity of action of young people in the universities, the factories, and the various quarters of Athens and the other towns is such as has never been achieved before. The creation of the Patriotic Front will help strengthen the faith and will of the Greek people, increase the movement of Democratic Resistance and promote international solidarity, the expression of which by free peoples all over the world is being watched with gratitude and emotion by the people of Greece.

In its efforts to pursue exactly these aims, the Athens Organization has distributed written proclamations in the center of town, as well as in the following neighborhoods:

Kokinia, Kaissariani, Ilioupolis, Brakhami, Daphne, Hymmetus, Gyzi.

PASSIVE RESISTANCE

Another form of struggle is the passive resistance against dictatorship. The forces of the Patriotic Front have called upon the people to boycott all the State mechanisms as well as the State-controlled means of information and propaganda. The slogans, "No collaboration with the fascist regime," "The militarist tyrants are nationally illegal. The right to govern and decide is not theirs," "Boycott the Press and Radio of Tyranny," and "Keep yourselves informed," are beginning to bring results. The people of Greece are following the instructions of the Patriotic Front. The dictatorial press is dying of inanition. For example: The morning newspaper *Ta Nea,* which before the coup had a circulation of 180,000 copies per day, has now come down to 5,000 and its circulation is still decreasing. Inside all Greek homes, the fascist radio stations have been condemned to silence, while the Greek people keep well informed through the stations which, opposed to the fascist regime, show their solidarity with the struggle of all patriotic Greeks.

RESISTANCE BY THE INTELLECTUALS

Dictatorship has put a muzzle over the liberty of thought and expression. All Greek intellectuals and artists are desisting from any kind of active creative presence within the framework of the fascist regime. Their work and presence are slowly shaping themselves according to the framework of the Democratic Resistance of the Greek people. Following the great historical tradition of all Greek artists and writers, from Solomos down to Sikelianos, they are becoming the guides and shapers of patriotic ideals. They are proving themselves to be the worthy intellectual leaders of a courageous democratic people. The firm position that Irene Papas took against the regime has made a big impression on our people. As "Ici Paris," the Greek program of the French radio transmitted, the great Greek actress, actually in Cannes, declared that the instigators of the military putsch, as well as their instruments, are nothing but Nazis and that the entirety of the Greek people is in radical opposition with them. Irene Papas added that she intends to stay abroad and fight with all her means until democracy'is reestablished. Another Greek who recently left in order to become the messenger of the Greek people's struggle aboard, the writer Kostas Kotzias, has called on all intellectuals, artists, scientists, on all the governments and the peoples of Europe: "The blow which fascism has dealt Greece is a blow on all of Europe," stressed the patriot writer. "Remember where compromises with the fascists led humanity in the past. The counteroffensive must be decisive. Greece is calling on you for help."

The Patriotic Front is, in its turn, calling upon all Greek artists, writers, scientists actually abroad to follow the example of Kostas Kotzias and Irene Papas in denouncing the fascist regime, and to demand the immediate liberation of the thousands of prisoners the Junta have taken, among whom are the poets Kostas Varnalis, Vassilis Rotas, Yannis Ritsos, the writers Elli Alexiou and Leon Koukoulas, the painter Vasso Katraki, Professor Antonis Kitsikis, as well as hundreds of lawyers, doctors, engineers, architects, and people from every walk of life.

THE PROJECTED POPULAR ANTI-FASCIST PROTEST ON MAY 28

On Sunday, May 28, the day on which the elections, solemnly guaranteed by the King in person and through which the people's will for democracy would have triumphed, would have been held, the Patriotic Front has decided to engage the first major popular battle against the fascist dictatorship. The people throughout Greece have been called upon, by every means possible, to abstain from any kind of public and social activity, from sunrise until sunset, and to remain in their homes in a silent protest against the strangling of the expression of their will.

The Patriotic Front

Patriots, democrats, friends of the Greek people, spread the news of the fight of our people against fascism throughout the entire world and by all means.

Go forward to make the dictatorship fall, go forward to make the sun shine over Greece.

BULLETIN OF INFORMATION CONCERNING THE PATRIOTIC FRONT. ATHENS. JUNE 1967 No. 3

MURDER OF N. MANDILARIS

The Patriotic Front has made the following declaration: "We denounce to the people of Greece and to world public opinion the new crime of the dictators, of the Palace, and of the CIA: the murder of Nikiforos Mandilaris, the lawyer, politician, and fighter for democracy."

The odious murderers in vain try to deny their guilt by placing the responsibility for the murder on the captain and the crew of the freighter "Rita B." We warn these murderers and their accomplices: the Greek people will know how to inflict on them the punishment that they deserve, and this sooner than they imagine. We call upon the Greek people and world public opinion, independently of all political convictions: By means of a general mobilization, let us stop the murderers' hands, strengthen our fight for saving the lives and the liberation of the leaders and the fighters for democracy.

Let us never forget Nikiforos Mandilaris and the other patriots who have fallen while resisting the dictatorship.

Through its democratic resistance, through its organization and its patriotic union, the Greek people will come out victorious. Dictators, vulgar murderers, will be swept away. Democracy will triumph in the country where it was born! Athens 5/25/67   The Patriotic Front

DECLARATION OF THE EXECUTIVE COMMITTEE OF EDA AND OF THE ORGANIZATION OF LAMBRAKIS DEMOCRATIC YOUTHS.

On April 30 a declaration of the executive committee of EDA was spread by the thousands of copies answering the Junta's decision to dissolve the democratic party of the United Left. In this declaration we say that no order of dissolution coming from dictators who respect neither the law nor the popular will could have an influence on the legality and the legitimacy of the existence of EDA, and consequently could not have any influence on its determination to fight with all the patriotic and democratic forces in order to overthrow the fascist tyranny and establish democracy and the independence of our country.

The Central Committee of the "Organization of the Lambrakis Democratic Youth" spread a similar declaration.

STOCKHOLM ANSWERS THE JUNTA'S ENVOYS

Two Greek newspapermen, P. Troumbounis and D. Chronopoulos, have agreed to become the spokesmen for the militarist Junta abroad. Both of them have a fascist mentality, and believed that the law of the jungle and of the tanks would still protect them outside the Greek frontiers from the hatred of the peoples of Europe for dictators' servants. They have just received a severe lesson in Sweden, a country with a long democratic tradition, where they have been denounced by the population. Let these fascist dictators and their handymen be convinced: they will always be the lepers of Europe. The Greek Patriotic Front congratulates the Greek patriots of Sweden and thanks the people of this northern democratic country. It calls upon all the other Greek patriots abroad, all the people, to follow Stockholm's example: "Patriots, condemn the criminal Junta's agents, denounce and send away from your countries any man who would dare present himself in the home of the criminal dictators and of the Nazis of April 21."

FORTY DAYS OF DICTATORSHIP

In the patriotic resistants' general opinion, the following points can be underlined as a conclusion to be drawn from the first forty days of dictatorship:

1) The whole of the fascist government's actions, and the continuous persecutions directed against all the Greek people, have confirmed the anti-popular, anti-national, and Hitlerian character of the regime.

2) The general attitude of King Constantine and the CIA with regard to the fascist regime, and the support they give to its work, have confirmed their active complicity with the organization of the coup.

3) The recent events in the Middle East clearly demonstrate that the fascist coup in Greece, conceived and made through the CIA, has been a prelude to a more general plan with the ultimate aim of creating regimes with fascist dictatorships in all these countries, regardless of the legitimate aspirations of their peoples and their national independence. The installation of a Nazi regime in Greece, the tensions created in the Middle East by the CIA, the shameful use of Cyprus as a lead base for their surprise attack, are all proof of a concerted political drive to resume the cold war.

4) The first initiative taken by the fascist dictators in the economic sector has been the signing of the "Litton Agreement." The signing of this agreement had previously been rejected by the Greek Parliament on the grounds that it subordinated the development of the peripheral regions of

the country as a whole to a foreign monopoly, without any possibility of government control, which is nothing but going back to traditional style of colonial exploitation. This, looked at in relation with the new activities of other monopolies, demonstrates that the fascist dictators' mission includes, among others, the complete surrender of the natural wealth and of the Greek work force to the American monopolies.

5) The patriotic resistance of the Greek people appeared earlier than had been anticipated. In particular, the creation of the Patriotic Front synthesized the major aspirations of the Patriotic Resistance. Patriots from all parties and all political persuasions are collaborating within Greece in order to face up to the necessity of liberating the country from the yoke of dictatorship.

6) The gap between the Junta government and the Greek people is getting larger. No worthwhile person has up to now undertaken to collaborate with the regime. It is the first time in European history that a military coup d'état set up a dictatorship without a minimum of popular support. It is under this condition of isolation from public opinion, Greek as well as international, that internal conflicts have begun to appear at the center of the team in command.

7) The Greek people gratefully take note of the mass protest of the world and especially European public opinion against the dictatorship, and it is convinced that this solidarity will develop and strengthen Patriotic Resistance in Greece.

CALL UPON THE PATRIOTIC FRONT

In front of the wave of terrorism that the fascist regime has unfurled in Greece, in view of the continuation of the arrests and of the threat which weighs upon the lives of political prisoners, the Patriotic Front has decided to multiply protests and demonstrations during the month of June, to use all possible ways of fighting—inside Greece as well as abroad—toward the end of avoiding the mass extermination of the arrested patriots and of achieving their liberation through the pressure of popular indignation both in Greece and abroad.

In a declaration toward this end, addressed to the Greek people, the Patriotic Front emphasizes that:

1) The prisoners' names published in the newspapers are but a small fraction of the number of arrested people which, on one hand, confirms the existence of secret concentration camps and, on the other hand, provokes the greatest worries about the fate of non-listed prisoners, since no checking can be made.

2) The plan for mass executions having been stopped for the moment in response to the rising protest of world public opinion, the threat of death still hangs upon the heads not only of political and union leaders, but also of all the arrested opponents to fascism and of any Greek man capable of opposing the regime in action. Consequently, the Greek people are called upon to form committees of patriotic solidarity in order to help prisoners and their families, and above all to resist the planned extermination of their democratic avant-garde by all means possible via popular action. In the same way, the Patriotic Front calls upon all democrats from all countries and especially Europeans to support it in its fight to save the life of the Greek patriots and to assure their freedom.

[Translated from the original French by Françoise Genty]

Appendix IV

The Main Text of the Aspida Report October 1966

The following English translation of the Aspida Report was circulated in Athens. It is virtually a literal translation, riddled with errors, using Greek sentence structure and grammatical form, and makes, therefore, for very difficult reading in English. It has been decided, however, to resist the temptation to edit the Report with regard either to length or style, and to reprint it exactly as it was circulated. The reader is left to his own devices to flavor the substance of the charges and the "evidence" presented in their support. The Report was written by a Greek army colonel who had been appointed to conduct the investigation.

October 1966

THE EDICT "ASPIDA" FOR POLITICAL PERSONS

PARTICIPATION OF THE POLITICAL LEADERSHIP OF THE CENTER UNION IN THE ORGANIZATION OF "DEMOCRATIC" OFFICERS "ASPIDA"

From the interrogation is ascertained, and particularly so from the deposition of retired Major-General Panayotis Koureleas, the involvement of the then Minister, Andreas Papandreou, in matters of the Armed Forces, because, whilst in the month of April 1964 (Koureleas) Brigadier General in active service then, through the mediation of Mrs. Skiadaressis, and within one hour's time, met the aforementioned minister in his office in the Old Palace, to whom, having followed him in his car and during the ride to his house in Neo Psychico, he expounds in general his views on military matters, with the certainty that thus he would be facilitated in an audience with the competent minister of National Defense. On the contrary, after having stated (the Brigadier General Pan. Koureleas, that is) his views consisting of an avoidance of politics in the Army, and the affirmation that the officers, despite running rumours, do not belong to the then camp of the opposition, (ERE), but are devoted to their duty, and that it would be nationally risky to immediately replace the head of the Gen. Army Staff so much the worse by a retired officer, who had long left the army, right or wrongly, (Lieutenant General Vlachos appointed as Director of the G.D.E.A.—General Directorate of National Defense)—the said minister Andreas Papandreou recommends to the witness to write down these views and bring them to him on the next day, without putting any signature on that document, to which the Brigadier General reacted, adding that he will put a very "legible" signature and that he assumes the responsibility of his actions.

Although on the next day the above views, written and signed, were handed to the above Minister, by the witness Koureleas, (the Minister even left the meeting of the Ministers' Council in order to get them) since that time, during repeated meetings of the above in both the office of the Minister, 58, Soudias and Acadimias for a purely personal matter, no discussions were whatsoever held on the above military question.

The witness Panay. Koureleas, on the grounds of the conditions of his meeting with the said Minister and their discussion on military matters in his car about 10 o'clock in the evening, his non introduction by the above Minister to the Minister of National Defense, the recommendation "not to put his signature" under his written views, the fact that since then a "deadly silence" fell on them, the phrase proferred with indignation by Mrs. Skiadaressis "the Greek people does not understand, it needs communism or dictatorship" when Andreas Papandreou left the Government, formed the impression that the views of the above minister did not coincide with those of the witness. Similarly, from the combined depositions of Michael Dessipris, lawyer Ghofas, his wife and P. Kanellopoulos, it is ascertained that deputy Andreas Papandreou, keeps on 58, Soudias street, a private office, outside the door however the plate up to Summer 1965 indicated "ANT. STRATIS" in which he sees, during the critical period of time, army and airforce officers in uniform, which is besides confirmed by the aforementioned witness, and that about the beginning of February 1965 there was observed a great flow of visiting officers, with two of which, belonging to the Airforce, the one with golden laces around the armpits, the witness Ghofas met in the elevator, and two others were noticed by her mother-in-law and the housemaid, on that same day, and they wore caps with a red ribbon.

But Andreas Papandreou himself, interrogated when he was a Minister on August 7, 1965, states that twice he saw in his office Captain Bouloukos, the first time when he left from his Cyprus assignment—consequently towards the end of the first fortnight of February 1965—when he begged that a permanent "free" ticket from Athens to Nicosia and vice versa be granted to him, and the second time during Bouloukos leave—consequently during the first fortnight of March 1965, when he moved from Cyprus after a signal of the then Minister of National Defense Papaconstandinou—which visit had a double purpose, that is on one hand for Bouloukos to express his grief for not having been granted the requested permanent ticket, and on the other, in order that he expresses conclusions on the situation in Cyprus and particularly the restlessness concerning the relations between President Makarios and General Grivas. The question arises by itself: Wherefrom does a captain derive the right to visit a deputy and "claim" the granting to him of a "free transportation card" so much the more for abroad? And how does a captain dare express his bitterness for the non granting to him of the aforementioned card to the same deputy? And under what capacity the captain, assigned to a unit of the KYP (Central Information Service) gives a report on the situation in Cyprus to a mere deputy, and the latter allows this lower officer to express conclusions on such a serious issue as the Cyprus—it is known to the interrogators that Bouloukos did not execute a responsible task in Cyprus—and to comment on the relations between the Leader of a State and a commander-in-Chief in cyprus, and even to express his anxiety? The conduct of both is very much contrary to the orthodox handling of nationally important problems. The answer, however, to these questions is given by the accused Bouloukos, when he claims in Cyprus that he is personally connected with deputy Andreas Papandreou, because, according to the usual course of things, only when a captain is particularly connected with a deputy does he dare to act as, according to this deputy's deposition, Bouloukos did, otherwise he would be severely censured and dismissed. Of course, the assertion is pointed that the involvement of the name of deputy Andreas Papandreou by Bouloukos, at the time he attempted to initiate officers in the organization ASPIDA, was arbitrary and misleading made so as to add prestige to his action, and this assertion is not a priori negligible. What assertion, however, is to be made for the involvement of this deputy's name, after this organization has been disclosed by said accused? To the probable answer that Bouloukos tries to expose this deputy, one will on good grounds counter-answer that if this were true, Bouloukos would not claim to Kounenos (see his deposition) that his lawyers are appointed by the Party, (that is the Center Union) nor would the confessed by friendly towards deputy Andreas Papandreou press (see newspaper ANENDOTOS of December 3, 1965, newspaper VIMA of . . .) would assume the protection of Bouloukos. Evidently, therefore, the assertion will be made that Bouloukos never mentioned the name of Andreas Papandreou but this the witnesses report of themselves, of their own will, or in execution of orders received from third parties, unknown forces, for political exploitation, that is the annihilation of a political opponent and the defamation of the Center Union. If however there were ground to this assertion, how does it concur, one may ask, that Bouloukos knows and has really visited deputy Andreas Papandreou, and this event is known to these witnesses?

The witnesses, however, who depose that Bouloukos spoke to them on the involvement of Andreas Papandreou in the case under investigation, differ in ability, place and time, by no means is there considered likely a connection between them, and such an assertion is checked as altogether unacceptable.

On the contrary, the interrogation has yielded incidents that promote in an non-permissible way this deputy among the officers, although as testified by witness Farmakis, this is checked as unjustifiable, since he does not maintain from the past in Greece connections with officers, particularly so in view of his political convictions at that time, as this is attested by the attached photostatic copy of note deposited by police captain Nic. Papanastasiou, nor did he during the period he was in office head a military ministry so that there may be really justifiable the knowledge of his abilities and the presentation of his name. Hence, however, there come clear indications of participation by him in the organization under investigation, ASPIDA. Thus:

The Head of the military defense forces of Cyprus, general Grivas-Dighenis, in his report of May 10, 1965 to the minister of National Defense, considers the visit to Cyprus of deputy Andreas Papandreou as the cause of disturbance of discipline among the Greek officers and that impermissible blames were formulated against some of them that they should be recalled as belonging to ERE, that the above general Grivas reported to the then Premier George Papandreou on January 26, 1965 in the presence of National Defense Ministers Garoufalias and Sossidis, and that he got from him the reply "it is poor Andras again".

The Cyprus subdivision of KYP (General Sotopoulos) transmits through the telex of the service to the Director of KYP the following no. 802/November 20, 1964 signal of "direct delivery" as though the KYP were the political office of deputy Andreas Papandreou: "Besides the other preparations for today's great popular welcome of Mr. Andreas Papandreou the coordination committee which was set up to organize his welcome widely circulated the following leaf-lets . . ."

The Cyprus subdivision of KYP (General Sotopoulos), sends through the telex of the service, impermissibly and illegally the two signals of May 2, 1965, the one to "Mr. Andreas Papandreou Minister of Coordination submit warmest congratulations for appointment at Ministry of Coordination. Your re-entry in the Government caused great satisfaction to the Cypriot people and received very satisfactory comments everywhere". The second to: Pavlos Vardinoyanis Minister to the Prime Minister 7, Loukianou street, 3rd floor, Athens.

I submit warmest congratulations.

"To be placed in a good envelope and sent to the homes of each one by a good (presentable) soldier".

By its above actions, the KYP deviates from its national mission, appearing as a "publicity agency" of deputy Andreas Papandreou on the charge of the Public Administration.

The accused Bouloukos discloses to Damelakos that the organization ASPIDA is under the auspices of Andreas Papandreou and of his father (Damelakos's plea, Bouloukos has in fact visited twice deputy Andreas Papandreou).

The accused Kopenos tells to captains Chloros and Nonas that Andreas Papandreou is the only person capable of governing in Greece and the officers should organize around him. He considered him competent for promotions of officers (depositions of Chloros, Nonas, Avramakos).

The accused Bouloukos, represents in Cyprus to the accused Makridis, the witnesses captains Theofilogianakos and Roris, as they testify, Andreas Papandreou as the only person well versed in the problems of the economy and of Cyprus, and for this reason the officers must organize around him.

The accused Damvounelis telephones from Cyprus to Bouloukos, when the organization ASPIDA had been disclosed, whether he informed in this respect Andreas Papandreou and what the latter's action. Damvounelis accepts that the telephone call was made in order that he be informed the course of the ASPIDA interrogation, but does not accept the other portion of the call (deposition of Kyratzis).

The accused lieutenant colonel Tsamasiotis, represents to captain Sofikitis Mich., according to the latter's deposition, in the presence also of the accused Chondrokoukis, Andreas Papandreou as involved in the military organization.

The accused Bouloukos confesses, in June 1965 to retired Major General of the gendarmerie Marakas Const., that Andreas Papandreou is the Leader of the Organization ASPIDA (deposition of Marakas).

The accused Bouloukos confesses before his arrest in the house of retired officer Pavlos Melas and in the presence of politician Farmakis, that leader of the organization ASPIDA is Andreas Papandreou (deposition of Melas, Farmakis).

The accused captain Papagheorgopoulos P., had undertaken the mission of taking protection measures within the aircraft and in Cyprus for deputy Andreas Papandreou, (depositions of Ioanna Michalopoulou, G. Madouri).

The accused Damvounelis presents himself to the unreletated to the Armed Forces Minister Alternate of Coordination Andreas Papandreou, compliaining for his recall from Cyprus, and not to the hierarchy of the Gen. Army Staff.

The accused captain P. Papagheorgopoulos sends his well-known letter, as it is given here above, to the then Minister Andreas Papandreou, through his lawyer, from which it clearly results that the Minister participated in the actions on June 30 for which the said captain and his fellow-accused were under pending trial, that is in the organization ASPIDA. The original of this letter was torn to pieces by the father of the above deputy, Premier at that time George Papandreou, and the pieces were handed, to be glued together, to the Director of the KYP at that time, accused colonel Anagnostopoulos, the interrogation thus being deprived since that time, of an important piece of evidence through the purposeful action of the most responsible State Instrument.

Andreas Papandreou is represented by the accused Panoutsos, in a discussion in the Gen. Army Staff with his colleagues, as the leader of the organization ASPIDA, given that he (Panoutsos) declares: "The leader Andreas Papandreou said that we will take two months prison and will be settled in jobs", (deposition of Nonas).

Bouloukos and Costopoulos reveal to accused Kaloghenis, that Andreas Papandreou has under his protection the organization ASPIDA and will reinforce it with cars, wireless, and money.

Major D/B Sdralis, of the group Lefakis-Paralikas, asks from Kanakis information on the existence, in the American bases, of stores of nuclear missiles, to be transmitted to the Minister at that time Andreas Papandreou for chanelling to the foreign press for a campaign against the allies Americans and the NATO.

Deputy Andreas Papandreou is informed, outside all military deontology and without a relevant order, by the Commander of the Greek Forces in Cyprus, major-general Georghiadis, his chief of staff colonel Mourghela G., and lieutenant-colonel Opropulos (and not the Head of the Second Staff Office), according to them on military matters. Andreas Papandreou, interrogated, deposed that with no military officer did he ever engage in private discussion.

Andreas Papandreou is reported as having offered a service to an unknown captain, for the transfer of his teacher wife to Athens, through the Gen. Secretary of the Ministry of Education Papanoutsos, requesting immediately after this captain to become a member of the organization ASPIDA (deposition of Chloros, from an account given by captain Yannakopoulos, who denied however, but not altogether, his discussion with Ghloros).

Civilian Koulourianos, special adviser to the Ministry of

Coordination, of the close environment of Andreas Papandreou, visits regularly, by night, Papaterpos and Anagnostopoulos in KYP, and also the KYP subdivision in Nicosia. His assertion that he was making studies of an economic nature in Cyprus is untrue, because the Ministry of Coordination affirms that never Koulourianos had a service assignment in Cyprus. During the interrogations carried in Cyprus, Koulourianos is closely following same, he even travelled with the interrogator to Cyprus (July 8, 1965) on the day after Andreas Papandreou had been interrogated in Athens. He travelled to Nicosia prior to the arrival there of deputy Andreas Papandreou, he prepared his welcome, obviously having come back together with the members of his escort, as in the Aliens Center his return to Greece from Cyprus has not been recorded.

Civilian Katsifaras, ex-private secretary of deputy Andreas Papandreou and actually a member of the staff of the ETVA (National Bank of Industrial Development), associates in the pastry shops of Victoria Square and Aghios Panteleimon, with airforce officers and although he asserts they were his friends in the past, does not remember their names. Of these, Mytas, Soumboyorgos, and Papagheorgiou provocatively talk politics in favor of the Papandreous, and are reported seriously to participate in the organization ASPIDA, being saluted by a raised right arm and the word "ALPHA".

Andreas Papandreou maintains a special bond with the Airforce officers squadron leaders Erotokritakis G., and Papadhonikolakis I., who visit him at his political offices. They openly express their friendly feelings for him and his policy in the home of the father in law of Papadhonikolakis in Volos, who is President of the movement of the 115 labor Unions, where there dined together after July 15, 1965, A. Papandreou, the Center Union deputy Koniotakis and Papadhonikolakis. The above two squadron leaders have in a proven manner interfered with unjustifiable and not by the provisions of the Royal Decrees adopted extraordinary security measures in the area of responsibility of the III P.N. on July 3, 1965 having neutralized loyal officers during the absence of the commander of the base, and having occupied this base by officers openly favoring the Center Union. These happened during the tense political crisis, obviously for the neutralization of the reaction of the loyal officers of the aisle against whatever coup favoring the views of Papandreou on account of his conflict with H.M. the King.

Although, from the aforementioned letter of the accused Papagheorgopoulos, the involvement of Andreas Papandreou in the case of ASPIDA is obvious, the latter not only continued to remain as Minister, but furthermore his father, the Prime Minister, insists on personally heading the Ministry of National Defense.

Andreas Papandreou is reported as directing the operation for the trapping of ERE leader P. Kanellopoulos so that there be achieved the arrest, in the very act of his relative and ERE politician Livanos, when he was handed top secret KYP documents by G. Madhouris (case of tapping of P. Kanellopoulos's telephone—deposition of G. Madhouris) agent of Papaterpos-Anagnostopoulos-Katsimetros-P. Papagheorgopoulos).

Soon after the return of Andreas Papandreou from Cyprus (November 1964), colonel Papaterpos went right away to the Island, and upon his return he handed to the then Minister of National Defense Garoufalias a list of names of officers of the Staff of General Grivas to be recalled, on the request of Cypriot minister Gheorgantzi, attestedly considered as unfriendly towards the policy of the Papandreous. Since then, that is after the visit of Andreas Papandreou in Cyprus, the discipline among officers is shaken, as general Grivas reports to the Minister of National Defense.

As it results from a publication in the newspaper "Gazette" of Antwerp, under the title "the Old man and Greek sea" and under the title "I have been careless", republished translated in the local press (newspaper "Imera" of January 12, 1966), the Belgian journalist Dycaert Wilhem sustains that in his interview with deputy Andreas Papandreou, the latter confessed to him fully his involvement in the Organization ASPIDA. The text of this interview appears as follows: the journalist Dykaert maintains that on October 8, 1965 and about noon, following an arrangement from the day before, he was received at the office of Andreas Papandreou on 58, Souidias street, and during the discussion he had with him, he analysed to him the various economic, political, and social problems of Greece, his father's policy in their respect, and when, as it was matural, the deputy was asked with regard to the armed forces he supported the view that the organization ASPIDA is an organization of democratic officers, of young age, for their defense against IDEA, which dominates the army. The journalist astonished by this definition and having gathered information on the case of ASPIDA related to the deputy a "short story" using the third person.

That the prime minister Papandreou, in his wish to impose his designs for the democratization of the Army provoked the scandal of ASPIDA through the interference of general Grivas.

That the ASPIDA was a union of Neo-Turks aiming at establishing a Nasser-type regime in Greece and in taking out the country from the NATO. Andreas Papandreou is involved in this organization, whom the conspirators would in time bring to power.

That Garoufalias (Minister of National Defense) close friend of King Constantine and since that time of George Papandreou, having been opposed to this design was expelled from the Center Union, and George Papandreou demanded to head the Ministry of National Defense. The King, did not refuse but he claimed that the Ministry be headed not by George Papandreou, but any of his political friends till the

ASPIDA case be cleared up. The Prime Minister considered this as a lack of confidence and resigned on July 15 in the midst of an atmosphere of manifestations and a press campaign against the Court.

When in 1943, for the first time, and in April 1944 subsequently, there broke up in the Greek Army a communist rebellion, and when in joint agreement between the then Premier in the Middle East George Papandreou and the Minister of National Defense Kanellopoulos (now ERE leader), the IDEA was established consisting of loyal officers, as a counterbalance to the existing communist organization. This (the IDEA) got an official character and played an important role in the struggle against communist rebels, when in 1961 the PERICLES plan was executed, it was by many attributed to IDEA. Then the ASPIDA was set up, an organization of lower rank officers of small importance, behaving rather childishly, the members swore to assist each other, to struggle for democratic rights, and to maintain in the army a really national character, exempt from any influence of the Right, royalist or foreign. The chart of the Organization in a secret place in Athens.

Now Bouloukos makes his appearance, a subject not at all interesting, a plotting officer, he is in prison. Which master does he serve? When he was arrested together with some ten other officers, Andreas Papandreou declared under oath to a military interrogating committee, that he ignored everything concerning ASPIDA, testifying that he saw Bouloukos twice in his office, that he had come to ask for an air ticket to Cyprus, because he had there a girl friend, and the second time when he refused to give him the ticket.

That Bouloukos, in the beginning of the year 1965, succeeded in obtaining an audience with his Minister and that to a question of Andreas Papandreou "am I this Minister" he Ducaert answered "in fact".

That Bouloukos spoke to Andreas Papandreou on the establishment of an organization of free officers to stop the existing influence of the Right in the army and that they are willing to assist his task.

That they were a few hundred and that the Organization will expand on a big scale. Major X, one of the founders of IDEA, now retired, ready to assume the direction of ASPIDA and render it the counter-balance of IDEA and that you must come into contact with major X and that the Minister was persuaded.

That Bouloukos said to major X that Papandreou wants you to undertake the direction of the democratic organization of the army ASPIDA and that eventually he will come to see you and that the major accepted provided the Minister would come to meet him.

That Bouloukos wanted to go to Cyprus to support this cause, but did not receive a free ticket.

The secret service told to the Minister that Bouloukos was not worthy of trust and that he tried to get rid of him, but in the meantime his name had been used for recruitin members for ASPIDA.

That Bouloukos went to Cyprus and informed General Grivas, his guardian angel, that he feigned sympathy and that when he heard that behind this plan was Andreas Papandreou, he wrote a report, that led to the arrest of Bouloukos and the explosion of the scandal.

Dycaert further asserts that after his narrative was finished, Andreas Papandreou after a short pause and to his great surprise declared to him "your theory is correct. However you do not place events at their exact date; this happened before". Dycaert retorted, because he too knew what the Minister had just declared, asks "the conclusion that is to be derived will be that the minister in question was careless" and the reply of Andreas Papandreou was "yes, in fact". To a question by Dyceart how does Andreas Papandreou explain the fact that Bouloukos mentioned the above to general Grivas, whose political beliefs he knew, the above deputy answered: "Bou-loukos was also a personal friend of Grivas and things were never good between my father and the general". Dycaert wonders in his article, how Andreas Papandreou "committed the foolishness to accept his carelessness, approving our theory, which in any point said much on this or very little. Can it be because from this representation of events be ap-peared as victim . . . At any rate he accepted at the same time that he had let himself be carried away in the case of ASPIDA, a fact which he had before always denied in the most positive manner."

As soon as the interview under judgment is published in the local press, a declaration is also given for publication on January 12, 1966 by deputy Andreas Papandreou, by which he declares that he ignores the newspaper "Gaz-ette" of Antwerp and that he never gave an interview to it, adding that on the next day he would lodge a complaint against the newspaper and the journalist, which he in fact did. The question of the interview was the object of investiga-tion of the present interrogation, as referring to the case of ASPIDA, and from the depositions received by the Belgian journalist Dycaert Wilhelm, the Director of the United Press Agency in Athens Filemon Dopoulos, journalist Chrestos Eliou, and retired journalist Demetrius Travlos, the private secretary of deputy Andreas Papandreou in his office of 58 Suidias street Helen-Ermans Nachnikian, in conjunction with the deposition of this latter witness forwarded by the 8th Interrogator of Athens, as well as with that of Andreas Papandreou forwarded by the Interrogator, it results that the newspaper "Gazette" of Antwerp, politically belonging to the Center of the political camps in Belgium, is considered a serious newspaper, and also the above Dycaert Wilhelm is considered a serious journalist.

It is also evidenced that Deputy P. Vardinoyannis was used for the meeting between Andreas Papandreou and said

Belgian journalist, and that also a telephone arrangement was made between the above press agency and the office of Andreas Papandreou so that it is considered bery probable that since the foreign journalist in fact went to the above office of Andreas Papandreou at the arranged hour in order to obtain an interview as it is customary, the interview must have been obtained, and preference, among other visitors of the above deputy, has been given to the foreign journalist for reasons of deontology. The text of the interview is now the object of investigation by the Common Penal Justice, where the case under judgment is pending.

It is evidenced that the Organization of "Democratic Officers" ADPIDA, is real and existing, and this, as besides mentioned detailedly in Chapter 12, is being confessed indirectly, but however explicitly, by accused P. Papagheorgopoulos, both in his seized diary and in his letter given to his lawyer Andreas Papagheorgopoulos for Andreas Papandreou. In this letter, as aforestated, the accused captain transmits also a request, which at the same time is a threat, to the above then Minister Andreas Papandreou, from which it is inferred that since "it is not in" this Minister's "interest" that the officers held in prison together with Papagheorgopoulos and for the same reason as he, "talk", it is unquestionable that Andreas Papandreou is related with the charge brought against Papagheorgopoulos, Bouloukos, Damelakos, Theodossiou and Kepenos, who from June 30, 1965 are held in prison pending trial for their participation in the organization ASPIDA. What is the content of this charge results also from the aforementioned diary, but particularly from the printed oath of ASPIDA that bears the handwriting of Bouloukos. Mathematically, therefore, is one brought to the conclusion that also Andreas Papandreou knows the content of the oath although when asked, during his interrogation, he replies by subterfuge, depositing that "just now did I read the full text of the oath. First I confess that I do not fully understand it, second in the measure that I understand it, I see that it is far from the principles that I profess both as an individual and as a member of the Center Union". It is characteristic, however, that after the Papandreous got informed of the text of the above mentioned letter, the accused in fact "did not speak, although Papagheorgopoulos kept them with his teeth", since even he himself, during his plea, refused the authorship of his handwritten diary, although the handwriting is obviously his which can be established very easily by the simple comparison of this diary's handwriting to any whatever proven text written by him, as his pleading report submitted to the interrogation on July 5, 1965. These being accepted incontestably, the following conclusions are drawn by reasonable judgment:

That the persistent effort of the then Premier George Papandreou to personally head the Ministry of National Defense, was the consequence of knowledge of the letter of the accused captain, and on this account the assertion of the then Premier George Papandreou, which is being presented as an excuse for his resignation, that is that his persistence to head the above Ministry aimed at defending his personal honor and the honor of democracy, is checked as still-born and at the same time as hypocritical and ungrounded, since the above two protected legitimate goods, the one composite, of the individual and public man, the other of only the public man, he, the then Premier, had brutally hit, destroying impermissibly one piece of evidence of such importance for the granting of justice, describing thus the relative clauses of the Penal Code, even if this same action creates for him, as relative of deputy Andreas Papandreou, a personal reason for exemption from punishment, (art. 232 Penal Code), however this does not hush the moral law.

That the conditions of submission of the resignation of the Government by the then Premier G. Papandreou, verbally, his remaining however in power till the next day when he

would submit a written resignation—which witnesses Garoufalias and Athanassiadis-Novas condemn as alien to the political history of Greece, and also as guileful—indicate the
existence of a plan, whose objective was to exercize pressure
on the Supreme Ruler to maintain in power G. Papandreou
through popular manifestations, demonstrations and disturbances. Subsequent, however, to the swearing in of the Government of Athanassiadis-Novas, the continuation over a long
time of mob manifestations, gives a clear indication that it
aimed also at the creation of political insecurity and insta-
bility, so that the hope may be kept alive in the accused
officers for involvement in the case under investigation, that
their camp maintains its integral power, is dynamic, and
claims power, when it will rehabilitate them to the full, and
consequently they should remain loyal and not create fissures
in the "wall of silence and negation" that went up right from
the beginning (see newspaper "Anendotos" of May 23, 1966
"Vima" of August 6, 1966 and of December 5, 1965).

The view clearly supported by P. Garoufalias and G.
Athanassiadis-Novas that, during the verbal submission of
the Papandreou Government's resignation by the Premier
himself, on July 15, 1965 to the King, there existed a plan
of mob demonstrations and other disturbances, as this besides
is being confirmed from the depositions of general P. Nikolopoulos and of his wife Mina Nikolopoulos, it is also
frankly confessed in the report sent to the American journalist
Drew Pearson on July 8, 1965 by Margaret wife of Andreas
Papandreou, in which she knew with mathematical exactness,
much before July 15, 1965, that there would follow "a
series of strikes, disturbances and marches". This portion of
the report, as well as other in this report which is given here-
below translated, and which was published in the local press
on July 28, 1965 (see newspaper "Eleftheria" no. 6402 issue
of July 28, 1965) are an evidence that only the signature is
of the wife of the deputy Andreas Papandreou, as this is

testified by Petros Garoufalias and George Athanassiadis-Novas, whilst the author of the text of the abovementioned report is obviously, unquestionably, her husband (the hands are the hands of Esaw, and the voice that of Jacob).

From this report and other incidents reinforcing the above mentioned, that in fact the then Prime Minister G. Papandreou placed in the ministry of National Defense Garoufalias not because the latter was "pleasurably accepted by the King", but because he aimed, through this spectacular gesture—in essence an artifice—to proceed through the above Minister, his friend, to the necessary changes in the Army, so as to give to it "a more democratic character". This, in conjunction with what is also being mentioned in the report, that the then Premier G. Papandreou offered to the King as a bait the assignment of General Gennimatas, faithful to the King, as Head of the Gen. Army Staff, who however under constant pressure and the claim of democratic elements for his removal, would be forced to resign, make up data—admitted obviously by Andreas Papandreou, because such information could not possibly have been gathered by any person discussing with Margaret Papandreou, nor did they see the light of publicity in the press, since, on the other, they were the inward thought of G. Papandreou, that he from the beginning aimed at the factionalization of the army, and for this reason and in order to achieve this he used the conflict between the will and the declared will in his relations with the King. Certain erroneous events, included in the report, that the organization ASPIDA had been organized during the times of Karamanlis, that the Prime Minister sent to Garoufalias a list of officers acceptable to him, in order that they participate in the Court Martial (whilist they were not members of a Court of Justice but interrogators) and other such, obviously were purposely inserted so as to create the doubt that this report had probably been written by Margaret Papandreou.

And in fact, as it results from 45 reports of the Sub-Directorate of the Athens General Security, communicated to the interrogation by the no. 3803/24.12.65 document of the Ministry of Public Order, from July 15, 1965 till September 17, 1965 when the S. Stephanopoulos Government was sworn in, there were effected more than 45 meetings and demonstrations together with disturbances, on the initiative of deputies of the Center Union and of EDA, with the participation mainly of the Lambrakis youth, builders, students, and others, in which the prevailing slogans were, among other, "the Court should be shut up in a pen—Plebiscite—King conform—Constantine the way you go you will eat up your head—out of the country the German woman—out the Gestapo woman—the King leader of the Right—kitchen the Golden Court—The court, land lots—King take your mother and go the people does not want you—plebiscite Papandreou. The involvement of Andreas Papandreou, outside the participation in these manifestations by the deputies of the Center Union, clearly results from his special connection with the Vice-President of the National Students Union of Greece (E.F.E.E.), student Ioannis Manos, on the initiative of whom were realized most of the meetings, superficially only of students, but in essence of followers of the Lambrakis Youth, and the builders, with main speaker and representative always the above mentioned student, who also has the responsibility of the formulation of the slogans, and the participation of deputies of the Center Union and EDA, and which connection is clearly derived from the note sent by said student I. Manos, through journalist Al. Regas, to above deputy, when this student was in prison in the Averoff gaol, on account of above events, the note having been deposited to the interrogation by this witness, who verbally transmitted its text reading as follows:

"For A.P.

Many greetings—situation indescribable—wretched—request: Spare no efforts for release, to every direction. Pressure on Government and high rank magistrates—Continuous visits by Deputies—A.P. Big positive step President's visit. Relative rumor alarmed and surprised. My nerves are highstrung, believe and struggle to endure. Everything will be allright. Yannis".

The view concerning the particular connection between A. Papandreou and Manos is strengthened by the ensuing visit of G. Papandreou to the prison (see I. Manos deposition), as the request formulated in the note, from which is deducted the influence of A. Papandreou over his father, but also from Manos's suggestion that the students arrested for above disturbances be visited by Deputies of A. Papandreou, whom he begs to make efforts for his release.

Source 3001 by its informative bulletin of December 31, 1964 to the KYP, transmitted to the interrogation by no. F. 702975/19.4.66 KYP document, reports that EDA executives and members feel a strong restlessness and demand a new positive political center-left pattern to solve the question of "democratization" and to this end it is supported that all the excellent personalities of the democratic camp must rally under Deputies A. Papandreou and E. Tsirimokos and form the new pattern, and that according to concurring information the name of Andreas Papandreou is attractive in the democratic camp and enjoys great prestige with high ranking EDA officials . . . "And whilst accused Papaterpos agreed up to the submission of this bulletin with the authenticity of the information of source 3001, as soon as he was informed of the contents of this bulletin and of another of January 20, 1965 by the same "source" he summoned the editor in contact with that source, witness Yannakopoulos Vas. and maintained that this source forges its information and that same appear in "Avghi" after or four days. In reply, Yannakopoulos mentioned that this "source" has a fifteen-year past with the KYP and a guaranteed authenticity, and the fact that KYP gets information prior to their publication in the official EDA newspaper "Avhi" by 4 days, gives the measure of the value of this "source". It was thus that this source was fired.

Interrogated witness police captain N. Papanastassiou submitted a photocopy of a note, withdrawn from the file of communist Megariotis of Menelaos, who in 1939 was reported to be Secretary of the Central Committee of the organization of the members of the Fourth International, from which it results that in the house of Andreas George Papandreou, member of this organization, there were seized a mimeograph machine and a typewriter, by which were printed the "Proletarian" and various other prints and proclamations, and that all the arrested, except Megariotis, made full confessions of their activities and subsequently submitted declarations of repentance and of disavowal of their Communist princeples and on this account they were set free by the Ministry of Public Security. The witness submitted this document because, as he deposits, from the letter published in the newspapers written by captain Papagheorgopoulos, accused for ASPIDA, there are indications that deputy Andreas Papandreou was involved in this illegal organization, which according to his information, in his ability as competent officer of the Gen. Security, was suggested, set up and supported by communists, in order that it may serve as a bridge for the future socialistic transformation of the country, since through the activity of the cadres of the illegal organization ASPIDA, there would crumble down all the National supports of resistence. The support granted by the Communist Press to this organization and the accused officers for participation therein, is typical.

Related to the activity of Deputy A. Papandreou, data are granted by the deposition of witness lawyer Petros Kroussas, who was his special political friend up to July 10, 1965. From it, it results that Deputy A. Papandreou and within the Party of the Center Union was being publicized by men of his environment, and particularly by Andonis Papadhakis, general Director of the Center Union organization. He further mentions the names of fellow-citizens of A. Papandreou, whom he utilized in his political tours and later had employed in ETVA (cases of his private secretary Katsifaras, lawyer Koutsoyorgas, Kyrkos, etc.) or in other services, as the brother of accused colonel Anagnostopoulos, whom he appointed President or General Director of OGA and who even in a recent meeting with him after the downfall of G. Papandreou government, told him that "his brother is unjustly imprisoned, that all is a plot and machination and that Democracy is in peril".

Similarly, same witness deposits that A. Papandreou was friendly receiving in his office persons who served in ELAS, such as captain Mavros (deputy Lazaridis) and Nikos Papaioannou, politician from Agrinion, whilst on the contrary the witness who had a private conversation with him shortly before Andréas Papandreou's appointment as Alternate Minister of Coordination, in his office 58, Souidias street, the entrance door of which bore an inscription with the name "A. STRATIS" and declared to him that "he went to Sweden a socialist and came back an anti-socialist" he dismissed him for ever from his office, obviously in disagreement with his views. In the political offices of Andreas Papandreou, the witness had seen a "high ranking airforce officer" and very often had seen police captain Dodos. He too confirms the view, as above exposed, and accepted by the interrogation, that the assertion presented by the accused that accused Bouloukos is a man of Grivas and of the Intelligence Service and that the ASPIDA case is a machination for the annihilation of Andreas Papandreou, is checked as untrue and malicious, launched by the environment of above deputy, with the particular logic and argument, according to which if Bouloukos is, as they untruly spread the rumor, a friend of Grivas, how can there be justified the interpellation of Center Union deputy Alevras, who is absolutely trusted by A. Papandreou with whom he cooperates, by which he protests that the officers arrested for ASPIDA, including Bouloukos, are subject to an illegitimate treatment and mental pressure, as a consequence thus Bouloukos being placed under the shelter and protection of Alevras, that is of A. Papandreou.

The witness finally having evidenced the noisy welcome reserved on July 10, 1965 in the Ellinikon Airport to A. Papandreou, contrasting to the cool reception of Premier at that time G. Papandreou leaving for Corfu, perceived that purposefully and systematically A. Papandreou was pushed up in the Party's leadership, which now became personalized and no longer democratic, and for this reason he severed his relations with it, even turning back the "free entrance card to all Public Services" granted to him, considering now Andreas Papandreou as having pledged "an engagement with EDA" to bring him rapidly in power through a sort of a coup like that of 1909, like another Eleftherios Venizelos.

Similarly, from above stated real incidents, the indications are granted of participation in the political leadership guiding the organization of democratic officers ASPIDA, of ex-ministers Papaconstandinou Michael, Vardinoyannis Pavlos, and Stylianos Houtas, which indications will make the object of an investigation by Common Penal Courts, as competent in this respect.

Thus:

Michael Papaconstandinou, deputy minister of National Defense at that time, is reported as effecting the transfers of Officers on the basis of lists of names prepared by the KYP, which service he visited (during suspicious night meetings held by Papaterpos etc.), and transmitted to the Ministry to the Prime Minister (Lefakis group) and finally in cooperation with Bouloukos and his aid, accused captain Georghiou Marinos.

Appointed to important posts were the accused captain

Theodossiou to the Infantry Directorate Gen. Army Staff, and accused captain G. Costopoulos to the 1st Staff Bureau, General Army Staff, on the suggestion of Bouloukos and orders of the then Deputy Minister of National Defense.

Following action by him, there was assigned to the KYP by signal, his personal friend accused captain P. Papagheorgopoulos, although, as it results from his file, his appointment to the KYP was unacceptable, to which defense witness major Vallidis Evangh. admits as well.

He insistently ordered, in the presence of brigadier-generals Koumanakos and An. Ballas, in July 1964, lieut.-colonel of Artillery An. Pallas to take the post of sub-commander of the School of Artillery. Pallas in his deposition to the Committee of Administrative Research (E.D.E.) of general Simos insists that IDEA exists, explaining that he maintains this because he suffered several transfers—and that ASPIDA does not exist but the noise was raised purposefully to cover up the action of IDEA—this assertion being fully belied from the totality of data of the legal proceedings, and being on the same line as the assertions presented by the accused.

He collaborated with civilian Lefakis, whose participation is known, from what precedes, as regards the whole case under investigation (transfers of "rightist" officers from Athens and their replacement with "democratic" officers, the case of wireless sets, from the deposition of Kanakis, and other).

He attempted to remove the chief of staff of the Third Body of the Army, brigadier General Nap. Palaiologopoulos as not inspiring confidence to the political camp in power at that time (this brigadier general had facilitated greatly the discovery of the group Hondrokoukis which had a suspect activity in Salonika etc.).

He appointed to the KYP subdivision in Salonika Major Harissis Anagnostopoulos, suspected for participation in the case under investigation.

He held under his protection colonel G. Mourgelas and

lieut.-colonel Opropoulos, also with a suspect activity in Cyprus.

He cancelled from the list of names of High ranking officers to be transferred to Cyprus, the names of Colonel K. Mitrelis, of lieut-colonels Michalakis, Galanis, and D. Karalis, having replaced same by others who had served in the EAM-ELAS, such as colonel G. Niketas, lieut.-colonels Stergiopoulos, Roussos, and Polychronis Alexopoulos.

He profusely granted freedoms to accused Bouloukos and his brother, private Dionyssios Bouloukos, in the expression of the sub-direction of the Athens General Security, "a dangerous communist able to commit whatever anti-national action". He ordered in the beginning of March 1965, by signal and without competence, the granting of a leave to accused Bouloukos commissioned to the Cyprus KYP, this signal having disappeared from his office. Through his action, private Bouloukos was constantly in Athens and not in his Unit (28 Body of Artillery) in a manner unacceptable and irritating, and the same having been proclaimed a deserter, there was subsequently transmitted a signal from his office, to the effect that the absence of this private was justified, he having granted him a relative leave of absence but he had by error failed to communicate this to his Unit. In the trial by appeal of private Bouloukos in the Revisional Court, he attended and was examined as a witness, confirming the above incident, and on this account the accused was found not guilty. In his office, or in the office of his aid, every Wednesday, meetings were held of certain officers under squadron commander Chicopoulos, who as it results from the written proceedings, had a suspicious correspondence with accused Damvounellis.

In the deposition of journalist Regas Alexandrou on the evaluation of which can be seen in Chapter 9, he is reported as actively participating with his wife, and the present Deputy Minister to the Prime Minister Takis Georghiou in the appointment, as Deputy Director of KYP of accused Papaterpos, with the approval of then Premier G. Papandreou "for the rescue of democracy".

The then Minister Pavlos Vardinoyanis is particularly connected with Andreas Papandreou, a Minister too as well, and visits him regularly in his office 58, Souidias, and at his wedding Margaret, wife of Andreas Papandreou acted as bestwoman (see deposition of Lawyer Kroussas).

The appointment of personnel in the KYP is shaped out with the intervention of the above two Ministers, of which Vardinoyaris participates in the special night sessions held by Papaterpos, Anagnostopoulos, Damvounelis, Stegakis, Lefakis and others for the preparation of lists of names on the basis of political beliefs of officers and civilian employees, for the effect of transfers, firings, assignments, and hirings, so that KYP may be organised according to their views. He is particularly connected with Damvounelis and retired major Ioannis Daskalakis serving in the KYP, and still more with retired major Emm. Stegakis, for which two employees there are indications of participation in the ASPIDA. Damvounelis visits him regularly in his house and in Parliament, prior to his appointment in the KYP and after he has been recalled from that service. He similarly appoints to the KYP Ioannis Papademetropoulos, of his absolute confidence, apparently as an electrician in fact as an observer of the political leadership of the Organization ASPIDA, since he somehow managed the KYP, taking part in the meetings of Papaterpos-Anagnostopoulos etc., on very serious matters, outside the national mission of the KYP. He is reported to have acted for the contact, through the United Press Agency, of Belgian journalist Wilhelm Dykaert with deputy A. Papandreou. It is typical that after his appointment as Deputy Minister to the Prime Minister he too, same as A. Papandreou, received a congratulatory telegram by the Cyprus KYP subdivision, transmitted through its service telex.

In his political office is employed Christina wife of air force lieutenant Patrikiadis, born Vavourakis and reported as liaison with the Personnel Department of the Gen. Army Staff, as well as with the office of A. Papandreou.

He maintained a connection with accused Bouloukos, who in the house in Cyprus of accused Stavropoulos praised him greatly, and knew that he would head a specific ministry, which he did.

Papaterpos had as a liaison with Minister Vardinoyannis an employee called Anghelis, who declared in the KYP that there are persons that cleverly guide Papandreou's representative Papateipos, for the purge of the service from the reactionaries now that we have a merit system.

The witness, ex-Director of the KYP major-general S. Doukas, depositi for ex-minister P. Vardinoyannis, appeals to professional secrecy as stipulated in art. 212 para 1 letter d' of Common Penal Law with regard to questions of National Security connected with above mentioned deputy. The interrogation having had recourse to the legitimate procedure in order to raise the prohibition stipulated by above article, the Prime Minister, who obviously heads the KYP according to the law, wherein the relative data on above case must be kept, through his no. PDAK—1/17-8-1966 confidential document, informs that the release from this prohibition of professional secrecy of this witness S. Doukas is not considered necessary, because the ouestion with which his deposition deals refers to a period of time past the time of the case under judgment.

Ex-Minister Stylianos Houtas is being visited in his house by accused Paralikas, obviously on no service reasons, not also on the reason presented by the accused, of the competence of the Ministry of National Works, headed by said Minister, this reason having been fully refuted in Chapter 7. Suspicions concerning one at least of these visits, arise from the fact that the accused Paralikas on his way to the house of Houtas was followed by Kanakis and Pantzalis of the group Lefakis-Paralika, and on his way back within the car, contrary to the mood he had when he was on his way to the house of Houtas when he was pessimistic, was more optimistic declaring to the two above persons that the case of ASPIDA will have a favorable conclusion with the report of General Simos. And the wife of accused Paralikas in a tape-recorded conversation she had with Kanakis expresses the view that the visits of her husband to Houtas created an unfavorable climate against him.

It is remarkable that ex-Minister Houtas expresses to the then President of Parliament Athanassiadis-Novas views similar to those the accused Paralikas had expressed to this same President of Parliament, according to which the IDEA and the "Right" were acting for the overthrow through a coup of the Government of G. Papandreou, which view the then Premier G. Papandreou accepted as true.

The accoused Mahas particularly connected with accused Paralikas, appears in the written proceedings as taking orders by the then Minister Houtas, and lieut.-colonel Anagnostou deposits that this accused confided to him that during one of his visits to Houtas, in the beginning of 1966, whilst in the past he had dissuaded him from submitting his resignation from the army, he revealed to him that there is a plan for the seizure of the Palace and the thorough extermination of the "Right" by popular forces, to which will be rallied thousands of K/S (?).

Same above ex-Minister Houtas, as deposited by ex-Minister of National Defense P. Garoufalias, on the night of 14 to 15 July 1965 supported in the house at Kastri of then Premier G. Papandreou, that the Government of said Premier should remain in power, even if "blood were to be shed", with the mobilization of democratic citizens, as well as a section of the army of the Attica basin sympathetic to that government. This view as supported by Houtas is indirectly put explicitly confirmed by then Premier-Athanassiadis-Novas, who deposits as above stated, that on the morning of July 15, said ex-Minister Houtas announces to him that "everything is ready, radio proclamations to the people, etc"., by which means there would be created once more a national division. The knowledge by minister Houtas that the Papandreou Government predominated among the military units of the Attica basin, constitutes an indication of the existence of a military Organization to support that Government.

CONCLUSION

From the whole interrogation and in an objective estimate of the evidence material collected, one is necessarily brought to the conclusion that the illegitimate organization of "democratic" officers under the name of "ASPIDA", whose establishment as of the end of summer or the beggining of the Fall 1964, and its existence still is evidenced by the interrogation, is directed by members of the political leadership of the Center Union, with indications of participation in which existing, to a greater or lesser degree, for ex-Ministers Papandreou, Michael Papaconstandinou, Pavlos Vardinoyannis, and Stylianos Houtas, and from adequate indications being deducted that the leader of the above illegitimate organization is Andreas Papandreou and that during that crucial period the premier (his father) G. Papandreou had knowledge of these events, for which reason he, forgetful of the very special obligations deriving from his above ability of Prime Minister and depository as a consequence of the National values, the validity of the institutions and the laws, he tore to pieces, immediately after having read it, on July 2, 1965, the hand-written letter that reached him, by Captain Pan. Papagheorgopoulos accused for participation in this illegal organization, and addressed to his lawyer Andreas Papagheorgopoulos, containing clear indications of the participation of his son Andreas Papandreou in this same illegal organization, and from that action on he undoubtedly has knowledge of all these events, rendering thus accusable, for reason of hypocrisy all his subsequent decisions and actions. Thus:

While with his no. 1014 of July 3, 1965 written mandate to the President and Royal Commissioner of the Revisional Court, he summons them, with no adequate reasons, to take all necessary measures, in order that the interrogation on the case of ASPIDA be effected according to all the formalities and the guarantees provided by the law for the ascertainment of the truth, on the contrary he himself, on the previous day July 2, 1965, had already covered up this truth by arbitrarily withholding the above letter, and depriving justice of a very substantial piece of evidence, having he first raised obstacles for the interrogation's task to investigate the crime and thoroughly disclose the conspiracy, which was directed directly against the security of the Armed Forces and the form of the regime.

While verbally, through the director of the Political Office of H.M. the King, and in written to him by his letter of July 9, 1965, insistently he requests his appointment to the ministry of National Defense, sending attached for signing the relative Royal Decree, thus insisting on the acceptance of his request, for the sake of, as he ungroundedly asserts in his second letter sent to the King on July 15, 1965, defending his personal honor and the honor of Democracy, on the contrary the true aim of his above insistence is obvious, that is once more to cover up the truth, the prestige of both his personal honor and the honor of democracy having been lost at the same time with his arbitrary destruction of the above described important piece of evidence, that is the letter.

While on July 15, 1965 he submits to H.M. the King verbally, as is customary, the resignation of the Government he heads, maintaining the above assertions, and on the contrary suggesting no solution to the King, he declares to him in a manner unusual for Greece's political history, that he reserves himself to submit the written resignation of his government on the next day, obviously in order to exploit the dead interval, in order that in the meantime, as evidenced by the interrogation, through the planned popular manifestations, demonstrations and disturbances and the utilization of those military units and officers of the Armed Forces sympathizing with him, and since he would continue to remain prime minister, succeed in keeping himself in power, acting in this way once more in order to cover up the truth on the case under interrogation. This last view is reinforced by the report prepared and sent to America by Margaret Papandreou on a date prior to July 15, 1965, by which the national sensitiveness of Greeks is unacceptably wounded, and in which strange enough are preposterously anticipated the above popular uprisings, but also from the demonstrations and disturbances effected between July 15 and 19 September, 1965 in various spots of greater Athens, always with the cooperation of Center Union and EDA deputies, and most of which superficially by the National Students Association of Greece (E.F.E.E.) but in essence by the followers of the organization "Gr. Lambrakis" and the builders, and even Vice-President of EFEE student Ioannis Manos, from the letter of which to Andreas Papandreou, submitted as above stated by witness Alex. Regas, it clearly results that these were realized under the guidance of Andreas Papandreou and by approval of G. Papandreou, who latter even visited Manos, according to his wish and request, and his fellow-prisoners in Averoff prison, and in which above mentioned meetings the basic slogans were the removal of King Constandine, with simultaneous threats against him ("King you will eat your head"), and the reinstatement in power of Papandreou as the "people's leader".

As a reason justifying the destruction of abovementioned letter and the silencing of the crimes under judgement, may be presented, in the most objective and indulgent judgement, the blood relationship existing between the premier G. Papandreou and his son deputy Andreas Papandreou against whom there exist indications of participation in the illegal organization, from which relationship there derives for above ex-premier a personal reason for exemption from punishment as stipulated in paragraph 2, article 232 of the Penal Code, however on all those matters that are the object of investigation by the common Penal Justice, this Justice will pronounce itself, a copy of the edict to be published, to be transmitted to the competent district attorney, since there does not exist in this regard the possibility of applying the provision of article 97 para 2 of the Constitution in force, the question being necessarily investigated by us as related absolutely with the establishment of the illegal organization, its leadership and the aims it pursues.

In the evaluation of the above events, there should not be overlooked the moral unworthiness of the action of the then premier George Papandreou (the positive action of the destruction of the letter and the omission to make a denunciation for the discovery of the plot), when so much the more the legal good sacrificed in this respect is of the greatest value compared to the good preserved cf. Chorafas, Penal Procedures General Principles pub. eighth page 385 "there is a punishable action, but there is not a punishable culprit").

CHAPTER 14th

Responsibilities of political leadership:

From same interrogation it results that, when Minister K. Mitsotakis, Deputy K. Stefanakis, and Director of newspaper "Eleftheria" P. Kokkas, all with law degrees, got knowledge of the contents of the letter, by lawyer Andreas Papagheorgopoulos, of accused for ASPIDA captain P. Papagheorgopoulos, they did not proceed to the action imposed to them by the Law, depriving thus for a long time the interrogation of a very important piece of evidence, which the conspiratory character of the case would evidently maintain secret from the side of the accused.

And of course one could counter-maintain that of the above, Minister K. Mitsotakis hastened in time to announce this to the most competent Administrative Authority (see Toussis, Penal Procedures, page 478), that is the then Premier, nevertheless this was not done in order to cover the letter and the spirit of the Law (art. 232 Penal Code) but obviously for the taking of measures ensuring the maintenance of the Party unity and the staying in power of G. Papandreou government, as explicitly deposited in his deposition given to District Attorney Tarasouleas under oath by lawyer Andreas Papagheorgopoulos, because if he (K. Mitsotakis) was acting otherwise within the Law, he should together with the others who got knowledge of the letter, after the resignation of above Government and the severence of their political responsibilities, since G. Papandreou, to whom there had been denounced the crime of conspiracy resulting from the letter of accused captain, had passed it under silence, they should hasten to fulfill the obligations imposed to them by Law (art. 232 Penal Code), and having omitted to do so over a long period of time, they will be judged on this in a competent manner, by the Common Penal Justice, although K. Mitsotakis and P. Kokkas, summoned by the interrogation, confirmed the events hereby related and explained, and the unquieting moral issue that rises for them from an untimely denunciation.

On this same case Minister K. Stefanakis, summoned to testify, claims the right of professional secrecy, art. 212 para. 1, line b, period b, of Common Penal Justice, because he had originally been appointed lawyer of accused, for the case under investigation, cavalry captain Evangelos Koufalitakis, which is proven true, from the written authorization that exists in the respective file of said accused officer. This view,

however, is checked, by law and substance, as being ungrounded, given that as explicitly deposited by lawyer Andreas Papagheorgopoulos in his examination by Attorney
Tarassouleas, said Minister K. Stefanakis got knowledge of
the contents of the letter of accused captain P. Papagheorgopoulos not as a result of the exercize of his profession of lawyer, that would made him act as a fellow-prisoner of Papagheorgopoulos, but in a conference of Minister K. Mitsotakis,
the director of newspaper "Eleftheria" P. Kokkas, and the
Minister in question K. Stefanakis, to all of which Andreas
Papagheorgopoulos displayed the letter in question, so that
in their ability of leading officials of the Center Union, and
one of them being a Minister of the then Government, they
estimate the eventual risks for the political party then in
power, for the Government, and for themselves as politicians,
from the disclosure of the contents of this letter, for which
reason concern should be displayed for the accused officers
of the case under investigation.

Therefore, the persons present in that conference and the
reason for which the letter was displayed to them do not
favor the view stated by Minister K. Stefanakis in his deposition.

On the contrary, if concerning his person there concurred
one of the two cases of article 212 para. 1, line b of Common
Penal Justice, from the combination of the provisions of articles 232 and 371 para Penal Code, there would result an
obligation for him to denounce the prepared or under execution crime of extreme treason, as this could easily be characterized by the witness, since there had appeared in the press
the genuine oath of the organization ASPIDA and consequently in comparison of the legal benefits, derived from articles 212 of Common Penal Justice and 371 of Penal Code,
together with the legal benefit of article 232 of the Penal
Code, there should be preferred the superior benefit, that
is that protected by art. 232 of the Pen. Code (see Pen. Code

special section, volume E, page 208–210, no. 29/51 opinion of Deputy Attorney General of the Supreme Court Kollias in P. Chr. 1951 page 256, Karanikas Penal Law B p. 384 prot. no. 234/59 in Varvaretos Penal Code Second edition, page 463).

In consequence of these, since said Minister K. Stefanakis upon getting knowledge of the contents of the letter, was not acting as lawyer, but as a political person, there obviously existed for him the obligation of article 232 of the Penal Code. All these of course will make the object of investigation of Common Penal Courts, and are hereby mentioned on account of the contents of the deposition of the witness as related all of them to the action under investigation. The above being accepted for witness K. Stefanakis, are also valid for lawyer Andreas Papagheorgopoulos, who irrespective of the fact, established by the interrogation, of his having violated his professional secrecy, since he announced the contents of the letter of his client to third parties, should, examined by the present regular interrogation, deposit on the substance, obliged by the provision of article 232 of the Penal Code, since all the more, the action under investigation constitutes offenses of high treason.

The interrogation investigated also, as above in Chapter 9 stated, two written notes brought to it from the Army Prison S.V.O.P., the one written by the brother of accused (and isolated at that time) cavalry Captain Koligris, and the other written by this latter, and addressed to the special staffer of the Ministry to the Prime Minister Michael Lefakis, in which are also mentioned the names of Minister K. Mitsotakis and the Director of newspaper "Eleftheria" P. Kokkas. The accused Koligris, interrogated, during his supplementary plea, on the contents of his written note, does not answer clearly, nor does he give sufficient explanation on the meaning of his threats against Michael Lefakis and the above mentioned persons, and this bears witness that something suspect is concealed in this note, when so much the more there are mentions of promises given to him by Lefakis, whose evidence however is not at all to be trusted, and would be of no value for the present interrogation, since by an explicit legal provision, he would be protected in non-depositing events from which there would derive his culpability in a punishable action (art. 223 § 4 Com. Pen. Law in connection with 434 S.K.K.(?)). Thus, in the absence of any other event supporting the contents of the note under judgement—for Lefakis of course there exist the events stated in Chapter 7—particularly on account of the indications contained therein, that Koligris has knowledge of incidents that may expose the persons mentioned therein, this will make the object of investigation of the Common Penal Courts, a copy of the Edict under publication to be transmitted to the competent Attorney, according to art. 305 period b of S.P.K. (?), for the exercise of appropriate penal persecution against the civilians, for whom in the present written proceedings result indications of participation in the conspiracy under judgement, for high treason or passing under silence this crime (232 Pen. Code).

PARTICIPATION OF CIVILIANS

Given that from the beginning of the interrogation there result indications of participation in the illegal conspiratory organization under judgement against
  1. Lefakis or Lefas Michael,
  2. Sfaghakis Emmanuel, major in active service,
  3. Daskalakis Ioannis, major in active service,
  4. Aikaterini Economou, ex-press employee,
  5. Papademetropoulos Ioannis, ex-press electrician,
  6. Mitsianis Apostolos, ex-press employee,
  7. Anghelis, ex-press employee,

8. Kostaras, police captain,
9. Bertsos, journalist, ex-special counsel in the Ministry to the Prime Minister,
10. Sotopoulos, ex-director of KYP subdivision in Cyprus,
11. Koulourianos, ex-counsel at the Ministry of Coordination,
12. Katsifaras, ex-private secretary of deputy Andreas Papandreou,

who come under common courts of justice, a copy of the edict under publication must be transmitted to the competent Attorney for the exercise of penal persecution against these and any other participant.

THE OFFICERS

According to the edict, the officers are charged with two actions: First, association for rebellion and second conspiracy for the execution of an act of high treason.

The first charge is formulated according to article 63 of military Penal Code, which stipulates that "in a state of rebellion are considered the officers who, associated in a group of three or more, serving under arms, refuse to a first summons to obey to the orders of their commanders, they get arms without permission, summoned by their commanders they refuse to deliver same, they make acts of violence against persons or things or disturb in general public tranquility and peace, and when summoned by their seniors they refuse to return to order." Also according to Article 63 of military Penal Code association for rebellion or group disobedience is effected "when three or more military officers have agreed and decided jointly to proceed to a rebellion or group disobedience . . ."

The second charge is based on articles 134 and 135 of the Penal Code, according to which punishment is inflicted on the preparatory action of conspiracy for the execution of an act of high treason and in the present instance the change of the regime of the State.

Specifically, there are referred for trial by the permanent court martial as "heads" colonels Papaterpos Alexandros, Hondrokoukis Demetrius, and Anagnostopoulos Panayotis, has having "taken leading action" in the establishment of illegal organization "Aspida" and in the success of its aims. There are also referred as "instigators" colonel Tsamasiotis Spyridon, lieut-colonels Katsimetros Taxiarchis and Paralikas Demetrius, Captains Bouloukos Aristodemos, Theodossiou Ioannis, Katsaris Thomas, Kepenos Athanassios, Papagheorgopoulos Panayotis, Papayannopoulos Demetrius, Panoutsos Ioannis, Vlachos Anarghyros, Koufalitakis Evanghelos, Gheorgiou Marinos, Kostopoulos Georghios, Machas Panayotis, Kalligris Pandelis, Economou Demetrius, Tombras Theofanis, Theodorou Chrestos, Marketis Georghios, Kladoghenis Georghios, lieutenant Stavropoulos Theodoros, air-force lieutenant Charalambopoulos Georghios, and gendarmerie adjutant Delidhakis Ioannis. These instigators are specifically accused of having prepared the success of the aims of the illegal organization, conferring with others, etc.

Particularly with regard to lieut.-colonel Paralikas, the edict mentions in page 467 that he developed a strong action for the success of the aim of the organization, namely by assigning to Kanakis Ch. the mission of murdering the personal Secretary of King Constantine.

The edict accepts that the accused, together with others not yet exactly identified, established an illegal conspiratory organization of officers under the name of "Aspida" or were initiated to it and consequently had knowledge of the aims and pursuits of the organization, as these are stated in the printed oath of its members. From the analysis of the text of this oath, the writer of the introductory report deducts that the accused, when the agreed plan would be put into application, would take arms arbitrarily, would refuse to return same when summoned by their unit commanders, as provided by regulations, and that they participating in public gatherings of people with united forces, would commit unjust attacks, ill-treatments or homicides against persons of contrary views, or would destroy other people's property, or break illegally into houses, residences or other immovable property, or in general would disturb public peace.

The writer of the introductory report finds in the text of the oath the elements forming the foundation and preparation of the second charge, that is the conspiracy for the execution of an act of high treason, that is the change of the form of the existing legitimate regime. According to the writer of the introductory report, from the printed oath it results clearly that there exists a specific plan for the attack of the legitimate power, since as the only responsible for such power is considered by the accused in case of action, the leader of "Aspida", with a specific objective, essence, and nature of the attack, that is a plan for the violent abolition of the prevailing constitutional regime of crowned democracy, and the establishment and maintenance by all forces and means, even forcefully, of a regime of their own inspiration and terminology under the name of "democratic regime," in the concept of the merit system by refusing to whatever form the existence of outside respectability. The basic aim of the organization, according to the writer of the introductory report, is the forceful change of the form of the regime, that is the expulsion of the king.

The accusations are also based on material yielded by the interrogation. Specifically, the writer of the introductory report mentions that the anti-royalist spirit prevailing in the KYP during the crucial period of time, being expressed with insults, threats and other shameful characterizations against the person of the King and of the royal family by officers and civilian employees, the threatening declarations that the enemy is the Right and not Communism and that consequently it should be thoroughly annihilated, the unacceptable and anti-constitutional trailing of political and military personalities, the organization of a network for the interception of telephone calls, the transfers of certain officers to certain key positions in the armed forces and on the basis of lists of names, so that the persons assigned be of the absolute trust of the organization, conferences held in the KYP to reinforce the policy of then premier G. Papandreou, who disagreed with the King, and therefore directed against this latter. These according to the writer of the introductory report are elements for the foundation of both crimes under judgement.

As an incriminating element is there also mentioned the manifest and impermissible, for permanent officers of the armed forces, propaganda in favor of the policy of the Papandreous and the hero-worship to Andreas Papandreou, as well as their participation in the popular manifestations of "Lambrakis" followers and other manifestations by common action of EDA and Center Union deputies after August 15, 1965, and the regular association of some of them with the private secretary of deputy Andreas Papandreou civilian Katsifaras, who is considered a liaison.

The Council accepted as correct the proposal of the Royal Commissioner and refers to an audience the 23 officers, having admitted that sufficient indications have resulted to support the charge of association for conspiracy for the execution of an act of high treason. The Council orders the extension of imprisonment pending trial of the accused officers. It exempts captains Makridis Theodoros and Damilakos Gheorghios, for whom there have not resulted sufficient incriminating indications.

The Council orders a separate interrogation for airforce lieutenant Mytas Chrestos, for airforce petty officers Papagheorghiou Achilleas and Zoumboghiorgos Nikolaos, and a captain of unknown identity and other not-named suspects.

Among the three "heads" the committing Edict seems to assign the heaviest responsibilities to colonel Papaterpos. Because it accuses him for leading action in the "establishment" of the illegal organization etc., whilst colonel Hondrokoukis is accused for leading action in "supporting" this organization, and Colonel Anagnostopoulos for leading action in "the success of the organization's aims" etc.

Captain Bouloukos is more specifically accused—among instigators—for leading action in the establishment of the organization and the success of its aims, as mandatory of its leadership, responsible for the increase in the number of its members, and also responsible for the expansion of the organization in Cyprus. All other instigators are accused for preparing the success of the aims of the organization through the initiation of new members and various other actions.

As to the second charge of conspiracy for the execution of an act of high treason, the edict does not discriminate and does not particularly divide responsibilities among the accused. They are all of them indiscriminately referred to trial, on the sole element that they established and participated in a secret and illegal organization, which, among other things, aims at abolishing the prevailing constitutional regime of crowned Democracy.

NO